CW00558366

Dictionary of Translation Studies

Mark Shuttleworth

&

Moira Cowie

St JEROME
PUBLISHING

Manchester, UK

First published 1997 by

St. Jerome Publishing
2 Maple Road West, Brooklands
Manchester, M23 9HH, United Kingdom
Telephone +44 161 973 9856
Fax +44 161 905 3498
stjerome@compuserve.com
http://www.mcc.ac.uk/stjerome

ISBN 1-900650-03-7

Reprinted 1999
© Mark Shuttleworth & Moira Cowie 1997

All Rights reserved, including those of translation into foreign languages.
No part of this publication may be reproduced, stored in a retrieval system
or transmitted in any form or by any means, electronic, mechanical,
photocopying, recording or otherwise without either the prior written
permission of the Publisher or a licence permitting restricted copying
issued by the Copyright Licensing Agency (CLA), 90 Tottenham Court
Road, London, W1P 9HE. In North America, registered users may contact
the Copyright Clearance Center (CCC): 222 Rosewood Drive, Danvers
MA 01923, USA.

Printed and bound in Great Britain by
St. Edmundsbury Press Ltd, Bury St Edmunds, Suffolk

Cover design by Steve Fieldhouse, Oldham, UK (+44 161 620 2263)

British Library Cataloguing in Publication Data
A catalogue record of this book is available from the British Library

Library of Congress Catalguing in Publication Data
I. Shuttleworth, Mark   II. Cowie, Moira
Dictionary of translation studies / Mark Shuttleworth & Moira Cowie
Includes bibliographical references
1. Translating and interpreting
2. Dictionaries
P306.2.S65   1997
418/.02/03 21   98-209732
ISBN 1-900650-03-7 (pbk)

Introduction

Translation Studies – A discipline and its terminology

The 1990s are an exciting time for Translation Studies. Worldwide, the study of translation-based topics is assuming an increasingly high profile. International conferences are being organized, PhDs are being written, and new MA programmes are being set up all the time; in Great Britain alone, for example, at the time of writing postgraduate programmes in various aspects of Translation Studies are being offered by at least ten universities. Similarly, new textbooks and monographs are being produced at such a rate that it is becoming increasingly difficult to keep abreast of all the developments in thinking about translation. Furthermore, the whole endeavour has been characterized by a sheer determination to move forward in what can be meaningfully, usefully and – perhaps most importantly – non-trivially said about the practices of translation and the characteristics of translations. There is a positive feeling in the air that, while our grasp of certain matters connected with translation remains somewhat hazy, we are gradually increasing our knowledge and understanding of this intriguing yet highly complex subject.

However, Translation Studies as a discipline is in many ways still in a state of flux. Translation can be seen as a point of intersection between many different academic subjects; it is an area in which many other disciplines have legitimately expressed an interest, and conversely one which has provided its own experts with insights which can profitably be shared elsewhere. There is for example a considerable exchange of knowledge, insights and methodologies between Translation Studies and fields as diverse as literary studies, philosophy, anthropology and linguistics; indeed, such is the level of intellectual cross-fertilization that some writers have suggested that the field should be known as an *interdiscipline* (see Snell-Hornby 1991, 1994). Similarly, there are a number of equally legitimate reasons which scholars have had for pursuing an interest in Translation

Studies. For example, some are motivated by highly practical concerns, such as the need to provide future translators or interpreters with training which is of the highest possible quality, the desire to raise the professional profile of translators and interpreters, or the wish to develop increasingly powerful machine translation systems; others, on the other hand, simply seek to provide ever more accurate and comprehensive explanations for certain phenomena in the world about us, without being primarily concerned with the possible practical applications which may accrue. Thus goals and objectives can vary considerably within the discipline. Of course, Translation Studies has been enriched by dint of possessing such a multi-faceted nature. However, at the same time this very nature has meant that there is still considerable lack of agreement on the irreducible minimum of concepts which should form the foundation on which to build; added to this is the fact that Translation Studies is a relatively new discipline which is in many ways still "finding its feet". The result of such a situation has often been that different branches of the discipline have at times experimented with widely differing methodologies, some of which have been imported wholesale from other areas of academic study, and not all of which, unfortunately, have been entirely germane to the study of translation. This is perhaps particularly true of certain approaches adopted from various branches of linguistics.

The impact that this situation has had on the evolving terminology of Translation Studies has of course been considerable. Along with their methodologies, whole terminologies designed as the descriptive apparatus for completely different areas have been taken over by the discipline. A particular instance of this is the way in which a number of writers interested in investigating translation from a linguistic angle have in the past adopted terms coined in linguistics, often optimistically assuming that these terms and the notions which lie behind them are equally valuable in the investigation of translation. However, there have of course been many occasions where terms have been borrowed and successfully adapted to their new environment; in this way the terminology of Translation Studies has been enriched by imports from disciplines as varied as linguistics, literary theory and even mathematics and biology. Finally – and probably most significantly from the point of view of the long-term health of the discipline as a whole – there has also been a huge amount of "native" terminology, or in other words terms which have been coined in order to describe concepts and phenomena specifically relevant to the study of translation.

This last category of terms – which is the area on which the *Dictionary* is almost exclusively focused – can be said to derive from a number of sources. First of all, many terms have been coined using what one might call "standard terminological morphemes". For example, a number of terms contain that highly productive suffix *-eme* (for example *architranseme* and *repertoreme*). Similarly, other terms have been formulated by using recognizable roots to create a semantically transparent compound (such as *minimax*, *polysystem* and *translatology*). However, such coinings are probably in a minority, as most of the terms in the *Dictionary* are quite simply "normal" English words which are being used in a new, technical sense. Indeed, the English language (among others) has been rifled for ideas which might cast new light on some aspect of translation. *Abusive translation, compensation, identity, loyalty, mapping, overt translation, protest, target language, thick translation, third code, unbounded translation* and *voids* are all examples of such terms. In this connection words containing the prefixes *re-* (e.g. *recodification, recomposition, re-creation, reformulation, restatement* and *rewriting*) and *trans-* (e.g. *transcendence, transfer, transfusion, transmission, transmutation* and *transplantation*) have (quite understandably, given the nature of translation) found a particularly widespread application.

In each case, the meaning (or one of the meanings) of the word in question is figuratively extended so as to encompass the translational phenomenon to which it refers. Moreover, some of these uses (such as *mapping, target language* and *transfusion*) are clearly metaphorical in that they invite comparison between (some aspect of) translation and some other real-world phenomenon. Clearly, as Nida points out when talking about *models* of the translation process, our choice of *terms* must above all be dictated by "their practical usefulness and their explanatory power" (1969:489). Of course, most terms – including those listed above–succeed in reflecting important aspects of translation. However, there is surely a sense in which the terms which we choose to coin will influence the way in which we view translation. Many words could be used as translation terms but for some reason are not. Indeed it would be possible to argue that a large proportion of the words in any standard English dictionary are at least potentially applicable to translation; however, it is purely a matter of speculation whether Translation Studies would have been channelled in a significantly different direction had another, parallel set of terms been selected. We must therefore conclude – as Nida does in the case of models – that, while terms are "essential aids to comprehension", they must not be allowed to "dictate the nature of what they are supposed to explicate" (1969:488).

However, if the terminology affects the way thinking develops, its precise shape can also in some ways be said to provide a kind of profile of the way the discipline of Translation Studies as a whole has been evolving. Thus, for example, a considerable number of terms have arisen to describe types of translation which represent various stages between the extremes of *literal* and *free* translation (e.g. *interlinear translation*, *word-for-word translation*, *metaphrase*, *idiomatic translation* and *imitation*), while a large number of (generally speaking more recent) terms bear witness to the remarkable parallel evolution of the idea of distinguishing translation according to the extent to which the function of the original can or needs to be reproduced in the translation (e.g. *covert translation*, *secondary translation*, *observational receiver* and *documentary translation*). In this way, many of the issues which have occupied centre stage in the discipline over the last few decades are reflected in the sheer number of synonymous or related terms which refer to them. Detractors might wish to argue that this situation represents a conceptual log-jam in which a small number of concepts are endlessly reworded and relabelled without anything being brought into sharper focus. On the other hand, it could also be taken as evidence that people working in different parts of the world – and often in different languages and traditions – have frequently shared concerns and preoccupations which have been remarkably similar. While those who hold such a view would argue that translation is infuriatingly difficult to pin down with a single theory, always keeping one step ahead of one's attempts to categorize it in some way, they might also hope to see the terminology undergo a process of crystallization as various clearly defined approaches and commonly accepted insights gradually emerge.

Aims of the *Dictionary*

It is against this background that the *Dictionary* has been written. For this reason one of its aims is – within the limitations of a reference work of such dimensions – to provide an overview of some of the issues, insights and debates in Translation Studies, inasmuch as these are reflected in the discipline's terminology. What this means in practical terms is investigated below.

Firstly, as stated in the previous section non-Translation Studies terms have been kept to a minimum in order to be able to devote as much space as possible to terminology specific to the study of translation. This means that while such terms are sometimes given a brief gloss in the discussion of a translation term, they rarely themselves form the subject of a separate entry.

Secondly, as a kind of "snapshot" of the discipline, the *Dictionary* tends to concentrate on work produced within the last three or four decades. This is not to say that nothing has been included which originates from before this period; however, most of the earlier works which have been consulted (such as those by Dryden, Schleiermacher and Walter Benjamin) are generally considered to be classics.

Thirdly, in order to give the *Dictionary* a broader overview it has been decided to include some important non-English terms. These have mostly been taken from works by the major scholars writing in French or German. However, it should be pointed out that the *Dictionary* is not intended as a multilingual glossary. It is thus not the work to consult if you are wanting to know the German for *pseudotranslation*, for example; similarly, very few entries are included with the main purpose of explaining interlingual differences in usage. The principle reason for discussing foreign terms is simply to provide monolingual readers of English with access to some of the important approaches which have been developed in these languages by making available in English some of the terms which they have generated.

The fourth point concerns the need to provide a reasonable breadth of perspective on terms, rather than just one point of view. Translation Studies contains many different and often conflicting perceptions, insights and beliefs, and reflecting this, the *Dictionary* does not exclusively follow one single approach. It is therefore possible to find statements in different entries which, taken out of context, seem to contradict each other. For example, terms such as *exegetical fidelity* reflect the conviction of most Bible translators that their source text has a single, correct meaning which has to be retrieved and conveyed, while in the entries on *information offer* or *metatext*, for example, one finds the opposite view that the meaning of a text is determined not only by the author's original intentions, but also to a large extent by the language in which it is written, the context in which it is meant to be read and indeed the personality, interests and beliefs of the reader (or, of course, translator). A further, natural consequence of trying to provide a balanced overview is that no particular attempt has been made to reconcile differing attitudes to the validity and applicability of such translation strategies as *adaptation* or *literal translation*. However, it is of course impossible to rid oneself of all bias, although the attempt has been made, for example, to avoid using certain terms and stylistic effects (such as *target-oriented*, *traditional*, *pre-scientific* and *prescriptive*, or unnecessary inverted commas) in such a way that they might appear to be conferring either strong approval or strong disapproval on what they are being applied to.

The *Dictionary* is thus designed to follow a basically uncritical, "hands-off" approach. In line with this, it seeks to document the accumulation of knowledge and insights which has occurred over the last few decades, rather than introducing large numbers of new terminological distinctions. The one main exception to this is that on occasion attempts have been made to suggest ways of distinguishing between various terms which refer to a similar phenomenon (such as *third code*, *third language* and *translationese*), or in areas where some confusion seems to exist (such as the terminology used to describe different types of *corpora*). However, there will no doubt be those who argue with the emphases that the *Dictionary* contains or consider that a particular group of terms should not have been given the prominence accorded it. In response to such potential criticism, it should be pointed out that a work of this type inevitably represents a *selection*, and that one can only hope that the criteria used are not too personal, partisan or slanted in any other way.

While the *Dictionary* offers an overview of the discipline in the ways described above, it is essential to remember that it is a dictionary of terms, not topics. Consequently the *Dictionary* has tended to draw mainly from sources which are rich in terminology, regardless of how well established they are considered to be. Reading the *Dictionary* the user might thus get the impression that certain very important figures in the discipline (such as George Steiner and Georges Mounin) are not properly represented. It should be stressed that this is not due to any lack of appreciation for the major contributions which these writers have made to the discipline; it is simply a result of the fact that their contributions, important as they are, are not terminology-rich. Similarly, many important topics (such as *literary translation*, the *translation of names* or the *impossibility of translation*) have not been included as entries in their own right, although many of the issues which they involve are raised in the discussion of specific terms. Readers can properly expect all prominent authors and major themes to be better represented in encyclopaedias, which essentially deal with topics and not with terms (see for example *An Encyclopaedia of Translation: Chinese-English- English-Chinese*, published by the Chinese University of Hong Kong, *The Routledge Encyclopedia of Translation Studies* (in press) and the de Gruyter encyclopaedia, which is due to appear sometime after the year 2000).

Some theoretical problems

The problems involved in writing a dictionary of this type are considerable. Many of them do not need to be aired in public; however, in order for the user to obtain a fuller understanding of the nature of translation-specific terminology, it will be necessary to discuss two particularly problematic areas.

Firstly, as stated above, there is the question of selection. It is clear that no reference work can hope to be completely exhaustive; in the case of the present *Dictionary*, there were certainly a large number of terms which were considered for inclusion, but were eventually rejected, at least as separate entries. Thus for example, many minor terms have either been omitted entirely, or explained briefly in the context of a more important term (so that *junction* is explained under *texteme*, and *cultural filter* under *covert translation*). Furthermore, there would quite simply not have been room to accommodate all the "normal" English (let alone French or German) words which are constantly being press-ganged into service in Translation Studies. Many words of this type are used in ways which are clear and transparent, and often also informal and *ad hoc*; consequently, no separate entry has been considered necessary for such items as *cover-to-cover translation*, *content-based translation*, *naturalization*, or *reader-oriented translation*, as well as for many of the *re-* and *trans-* words listed above.

Of course, selection problems do not cease once the basic headword list has been settled. Probably more significant than decisions about including or excluding a particular term are the problems involved in determining the shape of each article. Which sources should be used? Whose pronouncements on a given term should be considered most definitive? Issues like these need to be confronted for each entry if the *Dictionary* is going to combine its unavoidable brevity with a high level of informativeness.

The second problematic area concerns what is sometimes termed *fuzziness*, or in other words the tendency of natural phenomena to resist classification in rigid, clear-cut categories. It is sometimes thought that the fuzziness of meaning does not extend to terminology; however, while this may be the case with terms specially coined with a precise function in mind, there are nonetheless several important ways in which the drawing of cut-and-dried distinctions is problematic.

Firstly – and probably least problematically – is the fact that most pairs or groups of terms which are seemingly intended to contrast with each other in reality usually represent different tendencies, or different positions on a cline, rather than being polar opposites. This means that notions such as *overt* and *covert translation* or *rules*, *norms* and *conventions* are quite clearly overlapping concepts, at least to some extent.

Secondly, it must be emphasized that the terminology of Translation Studies does not break down into uniform, discrete units. This means for a start that a particular item (such as *adequacy* or *competence*) will sometimes be used in a special technical sense, but sometimes in a way which is to a greater or lesser extent more in accordance with its "normal", everyday meaning. However, there are in addition further dimensions along which the limits of different terms can be difficult to determine. Usage of a particular term will vary among writers. For example, some writers treat *word-for-word translation* as distinct from *literal translation*, while others consider it as a special type of this latter category; similarly, there is considerable variation in the use of the various terms denoting different types of *corpora*. In the case of some of the more central terms it thus becomes difficult to decide whether writers who opt for different terms reflect subtle distinctions in meaning, or simply the fact that the terms are largely interchangeable (a problem which arises with *faithfulness* and *fidelity*, for example). Probably more serious than this is the Pandora's box of deciding when and how major terms should be broken down into more than one separate meaning. On the basis of what criteria does one decide if a term really is being used differently in a variety of contexts, rather than the usages found in different authors simply being examples of *parole*, i.e. permissible variations within the limits of a single definition? (In this respect *back-translation* and *linguistic translation* are both problematic entries, since for both of these a whole range of sub-meanings could be distinguished, although in the event the *Dictionary* does not in fact subdivide the former and crystallizes out only three separate meanings for the latter.) Furthermore, what does one do when an author includes a standard term in a typology alongside a number of his or her own coinings (as Lefevere does with *literal translation,* for example)? Is one to split the entry or deal with both usages within one unified entry? Once again, it is only possible to judge each case on its own particular merits, and the decisions one reaches will of course always contain a subjective element.

The third important way in which fuzziness manifests itself is in the treatment of foreign terms. There is some debate within the discipline about whether the terms used in different languages to denote major concepts can in fact be assumed to be completely symmetrical (see for example Snell-Hornby 1988/1995:15-19 for a discussion of English *equivalence* and German *Äquivalenz*). Thus the decision has to be taken whether to treat "similar" terms from different languages as separate entries with distinctive definitions, or whether the obvious "family resemblances" which exist between them should be taken as sufficient grounds for handling them as single entities. The *Dictionary*'s general favouring of the latter policy can be justified not only in the light of the above comments on permissible variation, but also simply because most of the more important work on translation is read, absorbed and developed by scholars writing in various languages, thus creating a reasonable level of interpenetration and interdependence between the ideas, concepts and terms produced in different languages.

How to use the *Dictionary*

The *Dictionary* is intended to be used as a reference tool by students, teachers and researchers working in the field of Translation Studies. It aims for a high level of transparency, flexibility and accessibility, and with this purpose in mind each article follows the same basic format and uses the same general conventions. These are described briefly in the following paragraphs.

Broadly speaking, each term is presented and defined within the context in which it first occurred. Major entries also generally include a discussion of a number of different viewpoints on the term as well as comments on how usage and application might have developed since it was first coined or used. In the interests of consistency and accessibility nearly all foreign terms are cited in English translation (e.g. *loyalty* and *coherence* rather than *Loyalität* and *Kohärenz*), even if this has on occasion meant coining a new term (e.g. *verifiability*); conversely, if a headword is supplied with a translation in another language this usually indicates that the term originates from – or is at least widely used within – that particular language.

In addition to the information it contains, each entry includes two important features which should be utilized if maximum use is to be made of the *Dictionary*. These are the extensive cross-referencing to other entries and the suggestions for further reading.

While every entry is intended to be as free-standing and intelligible as possible in its own right, it is hoped that in the case of major theories and approaches enough articles have been included in the *Dictionary* to enable the user to acquire a systematic knowledge of a given theme through an intelligent use of the suggested cross-references. Any headwords which could profitably be read in conjunction with a particular entry are indicated in SMALL CAPITALS, either in the body of the entry or in the "see also" section at the end. While the "see also" section is fairly self-explanatory, the following brief points need to be made about cross-references which occur in the body of an entry:

- To avoid littering the text with large amounts of extra formatting, a headword is generally given in small capitals only the first time it is mentioned in any particular entry.

- When a major article is broken up into sub-entries, the first is usually the most general one. When cross-referencing to such entries, in the interests of readability the number 1 is frequently omitted; thus a cross-reference to *literal translation*, for example, implies that the reader should consult *literal translation 1*.

- In some of its cross-references the *Dictionary* may use just a keyword (e.g. *descriptive* and *literal* for *Descriptive Translation Studies* and *literal translation*) or a variety of grammatical forms which may differ slightly from the actual headword (e.g. *dynamically equivalent, map* and *rewriters* for *dynamic equivalence, mapping* and *rewriting*). The purpose of this is to make cross-referencing as flexible and as unobtrusive as possible. (This also explains why the *Dictionary* prefers the term *faithfulness* to the virtually synonymous but perhaps slightly commoner *fidelity*: quite simply, the former has a cognate adjective ("faithful"), while the latter does not.

- An item is not cross-referenced if it is felt that in that particular context it is not being used in its technical sense. Similarly, very basic terms such as *source language, translation* and so forth are not generally cited in small capitals unless there is a good reason for doing so (for example *source text* in the entry on *target text*).

Suggestions for further reading are given at the end of nearly every entry. These are listed alphabetically, rather than in some kind of order of importance; in the case of foreign terms, at least one English reference is given wherever possible. It should be noted that the works chosen for inclusion in this section are not necessarily those which are cited in the course of the entry, some of which might contain just a single relevant sound-bite; they have been selected simply because they are important sources for information on the term under discussion. Sometimes the further reading section includes works which do not mention the term as such, but clearly address the same subject, e.g. Lehmuskallio et al. (1991) in *degree of differentiation*.

Abbreviations

The following very standard abbreviations are used throughout the *Dictionary*:

SL Source Language
ST Source Text
TL Target Language
TT Target Text

Any other abbreviations used are glossed in the article in which they occur.

Note on quotations

All quotations from non-English sources, unless otherwise stated, have been translated specially for the *Dictionary*.

Acknowledgements

Finally, writing a work of this kind inevitably – and rightly – involves the participation, help and encouragement of many people. I am lucky to be surrounded by colleagues at the University of Leeds who have on every occasion shown themselves more than willing to offer assistance in various ways. In this connection I should in particular like to thank Professor Michael Holman for his constant encouragement, and also for his unflagging willingness to lend me books. My sincere thanks go to the staff of the inter-library loans section of the Brotherton Library, and in particular to Pat Shute and Carol Coggill, for the patient and helpful way in which they tracked down innumerable works for me. I should also like to acknowledge with gratitude the advice of Tony Fox, Peter Fuller, Peter Millican and Ian Moxon, all of whom helped to resolve various queries which arose.

I am very much indebted to Mona Baker for much encouragement, innumerable pieces of advice and the loan of many books, articles and other material.

I should also like to thank Moira Cowie for her contribution to the writing of the *Dictionary*.

I am very grateful to Yelena Belyaeva of Voronezh State University and Peter Fawcett of Bradford University for initial guidance on Russian and German writers respectively. Peter Fawcett and Juan Sager read the entire manuscript and offered much valuable advice on possible ways of improving it, and Kirsten Malmkjær offered on more than one occasion some very useful comments on the difficult area of the Quinean terms.

I should finally like to express my gratitude to my wife Tanya and my mother, brother and all my friends for being so patient with my prolonged unsociability.

It goes without saying that none of the people whose advice I have followed bears any responsibility for any mistakes or deficiencies which the *Dictionary* may contain.

Mark Shuttleworth
Leeds, November 1996

Absolute Translation (French *Traduction Absolue*) According to Gouadec (1989, 1990), one of seven types of translation which can be used by professional translators to respond to the various translation requirements which can arise during the course of their work. In absolute translation the whole of ST is transferred into TL, with no alteration to the content or the form of the original document. Clearly, there are constraints on this type of translation, as if the "quantity of information" and "quality of communication" (1990:335, translated) are to be retained in this way, there can be no technical or linguistic variation from the original text, and all terminology must be exactly as in ST (1989:28). See also ABSTRACT TRANSLATION, DIAGRAMMATIC TRANSLATION, KEYWORD TRANSLATION, RECONSTRUCTIONS (TRANSLATION WITH), SELECTIVE TRANSLATION and SIGHT TRANSLATION. Further reading: Gouadec 1989, 1990; Sager 1994.

Abstract Translation (French *Traduction Synoptique*) One of seven strategies proposed by Gouadec (1990) to fulfil the various translation needs which arise in a professional environment. In abstract translation a condensed translation of all the information in ST is made in order to give the client "rapid access to specific types of information" (1990:335, translated). This may be done in various ways. Firstly, the generic themes of the text may be translated; secondly, a description may be given of the generic content and the objectives of the text and its sub-units; thirdly, an abridged translation of all the useful content of the text may be supplied (1990:335). See also ABSOLUTE TRANSLATION, DIAGRAMMATIC TRANSLATION, KEYWORD TRANSLATION, RECONSTRUCTIONS (TRANSLATION WITH), SELECTIVE TRANSLATION and SIGHT TRANSLATION. Further reading: Gouadec 1990; Sager 1994.

Abusive Translation A term used by Lewis (1985) to refer to a radical alternative approach to literary translation. Conceived on the basis of Derrida's (1978) comment that "a 'good' translation must always commit abuses" (quoted in Lewis 1985:39), abusive translation is based on a view of translation as "a form of representation that necessarily entails interpretation" (Lewis 1985:39) and also as a process which produces gain as well as loss (1985:40). Lewis stresses the importance of avoiding "weak, servile translation" (1985:40), or in other words translation in which the translator compromises by "[giving] primacy to message, context, or concept over language texture" (1985:41). He argues that the translator should instead opt for "whatever might upset or force or abuse language and thought, might seek after the unthought or unthinkable in the unsaid or unsayable" (1985:41); what he means by this might include the idea of attempting to use types of discourse and modes of expression which are not in any way typical of TL. He therefore defines abusive translation as "strong, forceful translation that values experimentation, tampers with usage, seeks to match the polyvalencies or plurivocities or expressive stresses of the original by producing its own" (1985:41). In this way the adoption of abusive translation gives rise to a new concept of FAITHFULNESS (1985:42), as the translator compensates for the inevitable loss incurred in translation by directing the abusive move towards "clusters of textual energy" (1985:43) in order to "renew the energy and signifying behavior" of the original (1985:42). However, Lewis also states that "the translator's aim is to rearticulate analogically the abuse that occurs in the original text ... [and] also to displace, remobilize, and extend this abuse in another milieu" (1985:43); abusive translation therefore constitutes a complex compromise between reproducing the abuse found in the original, and adapting or extending ST for the purpose of compensating for any loss caused by the act of translation (1985:45). See also FOREIGNIZING TRANSLATION and RESISTANCY. Further reading: Lewis 1985.

Acceptability A term used by Toury (1980, 1995) to denote one of two tendencies which can be observed in translated texts. Toury's approach to literary translation rejects any notion of there being one "proper" way to translate, and aims rather to describe the translational NORMS which operate in the output of a single translator or which typify the translational practices prevalent in a particular literature at a given time. In Toury's model, translation is seen as involving "an encounter, if not a confrontation, between two sets of norms" (1980:55), one of which is drawn from ST or SL and the other from TL. Any translated text occupies a position between the two poles of ADEQUACY 2 – or adherence to the norms (both linguistic and textual) of the source SYSTEM – and *acceptability* or adherence to those of the target system. Which of these poles is favoured by a given translation is determined by the value of the INITIAL NORM, although almost all TTs represent a compromise between the two tendencies. Translations which lean towards acceptability can thus be thought of as fulfilling the requirement of "reading as *an* original" written in TL rather than that of "reading as *the* original" (1980:75), and consequently generally have a more natural "feel". See also DESCRIPTIVE TRANSLATION STUDIES and TARGET TEXT-ORIENTED TRANSLATION STUDIES. Further reading: Puurtinen 1989; Toury 1980, 1995.

Accuracy A term used in translation evaluation to refer to the extent to which a translation matches its original. While it usually refers to preservation of the information content of ST in TT, with an accurate translation being generally LITERAL rather than FREE, its actual meaning in the context of a given translation must depend on the type of EQUIVALENCE found in the translation; thus – to take an extreme example – accuracy in the Zukofskys' translation of Catullus would be primarily a question of copying the sound patterns of the original as closely as possible (see PHONEMIC TRANSLATION). Put in more general terms this means that, as Venuti argues, the "canons of accuracy are culturally specific and historically variable" (1995:37). The establishment of accuracy for a given translation is of course a painstaking procedure which in practice has to be carried out "unit by unit at the level of the phrase, clause, sentence, paragraph and the whole text" (Sager 1994:148). Because of its PRESCRIPTIVE nature, departures from strict accuracy are frequently perceived as shortcomings; however, in reality such deviations – especially in the translation of literary texts – are often inevitable, as the translator will need to introduce SHIFTS in order to reproduce the original "in its totality, as an organic whole" (Popovič 1970:80). See also FAITHFULNESS and NATURALNESS. Further reading: Chukovsky 1966, 1984.

Action, Translatorial See TRANSLATORIAL ACTION.

Adaptation 1 A term traditionally used to refer to any TT in which a particularly FREE translation strategy has been adopted. The term usually implies that considerable changes have been made in order to make the text more suitable for a specific audience (e.g. children) or for the particular purpose behind the translation. However, the phenomenon has frequently been approached from a PRESCRIPTIVE point of view, and many comments have been pejorative. For example, Nida & Taber equate adaptation with CULTURAL TRANSLATION 2 (1969/1982:134); thus for them – who are writing about Bible translation – an adaptation cannot be considered FAITHFUL. In a similar vein, but

perhaps more extreme, Radó characterizes adaptation as a type of
PSEUDOTRANSLATION 2, or in other words not as "real" translation at
all (1979:192). Indeed, SOURCE TEXT-ORIENTED comments of this
nature abound. However, other writers take a more flexible view of
the subject. Nord, for example, views adaptation as a relative quantity reflecting a translation's SKOPOS; according to her, any one
translation will be characterized by the relative proportion (or per-
centage) of adaptation which it contains (1991a:29-30). Approaching
the subject from a different angle, Bassnett, writing about literary
translation, observes that much time and ink has been wasted "attempting to differentiate between *translations, versions, adaptations*
and the establishment of a hierarchy of 'correctness' between these
categories" (1980/1991:78-79). She argues that the reason for this is
that the text has been perceived as "an object that should only produce a single invariant reading", so that "any 'deviation' on the part
of the reader/translator will be judged as a transgression" (1980/
1991:79). Like Bassnett, Toury also views the phenomenon from a
non-normative perspective; he thus sees prescriptive comments like
those cited above as examples of "a priori, and hence non-cultural
and ahistorical" distinctions which can be imposed on translation
(Toury 1995:31). Another DESCRIPTIVE approach, this time concerned
with how literary SYSTEMS develop, sees adaptations simply as
one of a number of different types of REWRITING. See also IMITA-
TION 1 & 2 and VERSION 1 & 2.

2 (French ***Adaptation***) A term used by Vinay & Darbelnet (1958,
1958/1995) to refer to one of seven translation procedures. Adaptation is described as a type of OBLIQUE translation, which means that it
does not rely on the existence of structural and conceptual parallels
between SL and TL (1958:46-47, 1958/1995:31). According to Vinay
& Darbelnet, adaptation is a strategy which should be used when the
situation referred to in ST does not exist in the target culture, or does
not have the same relevance or connotations as it does in the source
context. As such it is a kind of "situational equivalence" (1958/
1995:39; see EQUIVALENCE 2) as it works by replacing ST elements
by TL items which in some way serve the same function and are thus
"equivalent". For example, a reference to *cricket* as a popular sport
in England could be replaced in a French translation by a reference to
the *Tour de France* (1958:53, 1958/1995:39). Vinay & Darbelnet
argue that adaptation represents "the extreme limit of translation"
(1958:52, 1958/1995:39), in that it involves a considerable amount
of rewording. They also point out that an avoidance of adaptation can

result in a text which is perfectly correct, yet retains the unmistakable feel of a translation (1958:53, 1958/1995:39). See also BORROWING, CALQUE, LITERAL TRANSLATION, MODULATION 1 and TRANSPOSITION. Further reading: Vinay & Darbelnet 1958, 1958/1995.

Adequacy 1 A term used by some commentators on translation to discuss the nature of the relationship between ST and TT. However, even where it does occur there is little agreement over the proper application of the term, as it is used sometimes synonymously with, sometimes instead of, and sometimes in contrast with the related term EQUIVALENCE. Various definitions for adequacy have been suggested by various writers; in most of these the term has an evaluative, even normative character (in contrast to ADEQUACY 2 below). However, where the two terms are used side by side, adequacy generally refers to a looser, less absolute ST-TT relationship than equivalence. Thus Reiss & Vermeer, for example, use adequacy within their SKOPOS THEORY model when referring to a translation which has a different communicative function from ST; in this context it therefore denotes "the relationship between ST and TT with due regard to a purpose (or *skopos*) which is being followed in the translation process" (1984:139, translated). Shveitser, who writes in a tradition which views equivalence as an absolute criterion, defines adequacy in terms of the translator's response to the communicative situation: "adequacy proceeds from the assumption that a decision taken by the translator frequently has the nature of a compromise, that translation demands sacrifices, and that in the translation process the translator frequently has to resign himself to certain losses for the sake of conveying the main, essential aspects of ST (i.e. its predominant functions)" (1988:96, translated). Thus a translation can be adequate even if it is equivalent with ST only in one functional dimension; however, it is necessary that "any deviation from equivalence should be dictated by objective necessity, not by the will of the translator" (1988:96, translated). See also CORRESPONDENCE. Further reading: Reiss & Vermeer 1984; Shveitser 1988, 1993; Turk 1990.

2 According to Toury (1980, 1995), one of the two poles of the continuum which relates to the NORMS used in the translation process. A translation is termed *adequate* if the translator seeks throughout to follow source rather than target linguistic and literary norms. In other words, a translator who is translating adequately will perform only those translational SHIFTS which are truly obligatory, thus producing a TT which where possible retains ST features unchanged. Such a

translational procedure may of course produce a TT which in some respects is incompatible with target linguistic or literary norms. The reason for this is that "... the translation is not being made into TL at all, but into a model-language, which is at best some part of TL and at worst an artificial, as such non-existing language, and that TT is not introduced into the target literary polysystem but imposed on it" (Toury 1980:56; see POLYSYSTEM THEORY). However, such an imposition can have positive as well as negative consequences, as not only violations but also innovations may be introduced into the target linguistic and literary SYSTEM. Clearly, most TTs are a compromise between adequacy and the opposite pole of ACCEPTABILITY, in some matters following ST norms and in others conforming to those of the target system. Toury (1980) also suggests using a maximally adequate translation, which he terms "the Adequate Translation" and which contains only obligatory shifts, as an "invariant of the comparison" (or TERTIUM COMPARATIONIS; 1980:49); the purpose of this is to reveal what kind of optional shifts have occurred in a translation, and consequently, the type of translational strategies which the translator has been using. However, Toury (1995) rejects this notion as being an unnecessary factor in the process of translation analysis. See also INITIAL NORM, TARGET TEXT-ORIENTED TRANSLATION STUDIES, THIRD CODE and TRANSLATIONESE. Further reading: Hermans 1995; Toury 1980, 1995.

Adjustment According to Nida, a set of techniques used in Bible translation which are designed to "produce correct equivalents" in TL (1964:226) and thus help a translation achieve DYNAMIC EQUIVA- LENCE. More specifically, Nida defines the purposes of these techniques as follows: "(1) permit adjustment of the form of the message to the requirements of the structure of the receptor language; (2) produce semantically equivalent structures; (3) provide equivalent stylistic appropriateness; and (4) carry an equivalent communication load" (1964:226). Although such aims will frequently entail minor changes in form, Nida emphasizes that the translator's task is to reproduce, not to improve. Radical changes may be necessary in certain circum- stances, however, if the use of a close FORMAL EQUIVALENT gives a translation which is meaningless or causes TT to convey a wrong meaning (1964:226). Techniques used in adjustment include addition or subtraction of material, alteration, inclusion of footnotes (explain- ing LITERAL translations which are preserved in the text) and modification of the language to fit the experience of the target audience. It should be pointed out that the notion of adjustment was replaced in Nida & Taber (1969/1982) by TRANSFER and RESTRUCTURING. See also COMMUNICATION LOAD. Further reading: Nida 1964.

Aesthetic-Poetic Translation According to Casagrande (1954), one of four types of translation. Casagrande's classification relates to the possible purposes which may lie behind the act of translation; aesthetic-poetic translation thus refers to the translation of poetic texts, where it is necessary to retain the expressive and stylistic features of the author's work to as large an extent as possible. Casagrande states that, while the content is clearly important, "express consideration is given to the literary or aesthetic form of the message in both languages" (1954:335). This type of translation thus places heavy demands on the translator, since elements of poetic or aesthetic expression such as rhyme, metre or metaphor are "precisely those aspects of language which are most resistant to translation" as they "partake of the unique qualities of the individual language" (1954:336). See also ETHNO-GRAPHIC TRANSLATION, LINGUISTIC TRANSLATION 2 and PRAGMATIC TRANSLATION 2. Further reading: Casagrande 1954.

Agent A term used by Sager to refer to the person who is "in an intermediary position between a translator and an end user of a translation" (1994:321). According to Sager, any translation process will involve a number of participants. These include text producers, mediators who modify the text (for example abstractors, editors, revisors and translators; see 1994:111), communication agents, who commission and send the text, and recipients, or end users, although it is possible that one person may perform more than one of these functions (but may not, of course, be both producer and recipient). The agent of a translation may be a publisher who commissions a translation, or any other person who assigns a job to a translator. He or she is independent of both writer and reader and decides whether or not a document is to be translated. According to Sager, the agent "is at the beginning and the end of the speech act of translation; the previous speech act of writing the document, and the subsequent speech act of a reader receiving the document are both temporally, spatially and causally quite independent" (1994:140). Further reading: Sager 1994.

A.I.I.C. (Association Internationale des Interprètes de Conférence)
An organization founded in November 1953 to protect the interests of
conference interpreters. The A.I.I.C. numbers among its aims the
assessment and maintaining of levels of linguistic competence among
its members, the development of professional and ethical codes of
practice, the monitoring of working conditions and agreements with
international organizations, and the improvement of standards of training. The two main organs of the association are the Assembly and the
Council, while a number of Commissions and Committees monitor
such issues as interpreter qualifications and grading, and the setting
of International Standards for interpreting booths. The A.I.I.C. furthermore conducts negotiations with various international bodies (such
as the United Nations, the European Union and NATO) on matters
relating to working conditions, rates of pay, and suchlike. See also
CONFERENCE INTERPRETING, F.I.T. and INTERPRETING. Further reading: Osers 1983.

Analogical Form According to Holmes (1988d), one of four
approaches which a translator may use when translating verse form.
An analogical form is defined as a TL verse form which fulfils a
similar function to that of the SL form in the source culture. Holmes
gives the example of a translator choosing to translate an SL epic into
a TL verse form which, although different from that used in ST, is the
one traditionally associated with epics in TL. As Holmes points out,
the effect of using an analogical form is to "naturalize" an ST by
making it conform to traditionally accepted target norms; such a
technique is typical of introspective, self-sufficient cultures and ages
(1988d:27). Along with MIMETIC FORM, Holmes classifies analogical
form as one of two types of FORM-DERIVATIVE FORM. See also
CONTENT-DERIVATIVE FORM, EXTRANEOUS FORM, MAPPING and
METAPOEM. Further reading: Holmes 1988d.

Analysis A term used by Nida & Taber (1969/1982) to describe the
first of the three stages of the translation process (see also TRANSFER 2
and RESTRUCTURING). The model which Nida & Taber describe is
intended first and foremost to provide Bible translators with guidelines
on how to approach the task of rendering the ancient STs effectively
into modern TLs whose structure may differ radically from the
languages in which the originals were written. Using elements of
Chomsky's transformational grammar as their starting-point (see for

example Chomsky 1965), they define translation as a process in which "the translator first analyses the message of the SOURCE language into its simplest and structurally clearest forms, transfers it at this level, and then restructures it to the level in the RECEPTOR language which is most appropriate for the audience which he intends to reach" (Nida 1969:484, emphasis original). The act of translation is thus likened to that of travelling downstream to cross a river at an easier place (Nida 1969:484). Analysis, the first stage in this process, is defined as "the set of procedures, including back transformation and componential analysis, which aim at discovering the kernels underlying the source text and the clearest understanding of the meaning, in preparation for the transfer" (Nida & Taber 1969/1982:197, emphasis removed). The term *kernel* is used in a broadly Chomskyan sense to denote "the basic structural elements" (Nida & Taber 1969/1982:39) which can be said to underlie the syntactically more elaborate "surface structure" of any language. The rationale for Nida & Taber's model thus lies in the fact that languages "agree far more on the level of the kernels than on the level of the more elaborate structures" (Nida & Taber 1969/1982:39). According to Nida, kernels consist of combinations of items from four structural categories – "objects, events (including actions), abstracts (as features of objects, events, and other abstracts), and relationals" (1969:485) – while the kernels in any language are "the minimal number of structures from which the rest can be most efficiently and relevantly derived" (Nida 1964:66). Kernel sentences are derived from the actual sentences of an ST by means of *back-transformation*, a kind of paraphrase in which surface structures are replaced by structures of the types listed above; if translating from English, this would among other things entail transforming "event nouns" into verbal expressions (Nida 1969:485). In this way back-transformation analyzes the grammatical relationships of ST. At the same time, the referential meaning of the individual items of the original message undergoes *componential analysis*, by means of which the meanings of words are broken down on the basis of "shared and contrastive features" (Nida 1964:82); finally, stylistics and connotative meaning are also analyzed and noted. Further reading: Gentzler 1993; Nida 1969; Nida & Taber 1969/1982.

Appeal-focused Texts (German *Appellbetonte Texte*) See OPERA-TIVE TEXTS.

Applied Translation Studies The area of investigation within TRANSLATION STUDIES contrasted by Holmes (1988e) with THEORETI-CAL and DESCRIPTIVE TRANSLATION STUDIES (the two of which together make up the field of PURE TRANSLATION STUDIES). In Holmes' scheme, Applied Translation Studies is further divided into four subsections. The first of these is translator training, and is probably the main area of concern. The second is the production of translation aids such as lexicographical and terminological reference works, and grammars which are tailor-made to suit the needs of translators (to which list one might now want to add the various aids associated with MACHINE-AIDED TRANSLATION). The third area is the establishment of translation policy, where the task of the translation scholar is "to render informed advice to others in defining the place and role of translators, translating, and translations in society at large" (1988e:77-78). Finally there is the activity of translation criticism, the level of which is frequently "very low, and in many countries still quite uninfluenced by developments within the field of translation studies" (1988e:78). Other people have also written about the applied "sub-discipline" and have suggested further areas which it should include; Wilss for example characterizes the applied SCIENCE OF TRANSLATION as essentially language-pair-bound (Wilss 1982:80), and lists error analysis, translation criticism, translation teaching and the study of translation difficulties as the four main areas of interest (1982:159; see also PROSPECTIVE and RETROSPECTIVE TRANSLATION). As pointed out by Toury, such applied "extensions" tend by their very nature to be PRESCRIPTIVE, as they are intended to "set norms in a more or less conscious way" (1995:19). Further reading: Holmes 1988e; Toury 1995; Wilss 1977, 1982.

Archaism (or **Archaicism**) A term which refers to the use of obso-lescent language in a translation (or alternatively, a single instance of such usage). While a simple tendency to avoid modern idiom is a very widespread translation practice, a more deliberate archaizing strat-egy is sometimes employed to translate an ST which dates from an earlier historical period; its purpose is to attempt to create the il-lusion that the translation, like its original, is not a product of modern culture. Sometimes a translator attempts to produce a TT in language actually contemporary with the original (e.g. a new translation of Shakespeare formulated in late sixteenth century Hungarian), but perhaps more frequently only aims to create a text which seems to stem from a less remote historical period; however, in extreme cases translations have been produced which are written in such obscure language that they are only accessible to a few. When producing an archaizing translation, the danger is that the translator will be unable to maintain his or her use of older language with complete consistency and will thus produce a hybrid text, the language of which does not properly reflect older usage (Steiner 1975/1992:360). However, according to Steiner, even when the translator manages to archaize consistently, a more fundamental problem arises, which is that the old-fashioned language used in the translation cannot be separated from the connotations or alternative meanings which it has subsequently acquired, and which will inevitably be uppermost in the mind of the modern reader (1975/1992:352). In spite of such drawbacks, Steiner suggests that the strategy of archaism serves at least one important function, which is to give the impression that a translation is firmly rooted in the target culture, as if it were (and always had been) a native part of that tradition (1975/1992:365). As an example of such a translation Steiner cites the King James Bible, which he argues owed its original success partly to the seventeenth-century translators' policy of using language which was two or three generations out of date (1975/1992:366-67). See also INTERTEMPORAL TRANSLATION. Further reading: Bassnett 1980/1991; Diller 1992; Holmes 1988h; Steiner 1975/1992; Zimmer 1981.

Architranseme (or **ATR**) A term coined by van Leuven-Zwart (1989, 1990) to designate a theoretical concept used in the close linguistic comparison of literary texts and their translations. To facilitate such a comparison, van Leuven-Zwart suggests dividing both ST and TT up into phrase-length units which she terms TRANSEMES; she then introduces the architranseme as a kind of theoretical common denominator which is used as the basis for comparing ST and TT transemes. The common features reflected in an architranseme are expressed in terms of the content words shared by the ST and TT transemes, or by paraphrases, so that the architranseme of "His wife saw him" would be "wife + to see", while that of "He bent down" would be "to curve the body from a standing position" (see van Leuven-Zwart 1989:157-58). On the basis of the aspects of *conjunction* (similarity) and *disjunction* (dissimilarity) which are observed between the ST and/or TT transeme and the architranseme it is possible to posit one of three types of microstructural SHIFT: MODULATION 2, MODIFICATION or MUTATION. If clear trends emerge from the comparison of a large number of transemes and archi-transemes, then light is shed on the translator's opinions, interpretation and translational policy, and concrete insight is gained into the ways in which ST and TT differ. See also GENERALIZATION, INTEGRAL TRANSLATION, SPECIFICATION and TERTIUM COMPARATIONIS. Further reading: van Leuven-Zwart 1989, 1990.

Area-restricted Theories of Translation Defined by Holmes as PARTIAL THEORIES OF TRANSLATION which are restricted with regard to the languages and/or cultures which are being considered (1988e:74). Such theories may be pair-restricted (e.g. translation between German and English), group-restricted (e.g. translation within the cultures of Western Europe) or group-pair restricted (e.g. translation between Slavonic and Germanic languages). Research undertaken in *language*-restricted areas shares many insights with the fields of comparative linguistics and stylistics, while there has up to now been little work done on any detailed *culture*-restricted theories. Area-restricted theories of translation sometimes claim a greater generality, but in fact are usually only relevant to certain (generally Western) cultures (1988e:75). See also MEDIUM-RESTRICTED, PROBLEM-RESTRICTED, RANK-RESTRICTED, TEXT-TYPE RESTRICTED and TIME-RESTRICTED THEORIES OF TRANSLATION. Further reading: Holmes 1988e.

ATR See ARCHITRANSEME.

Audio-medial Texts (German *Audio-mediale Texte*) See MULTI-MEDIAL TEXTS.

Auftrag See COMMISSION.

Automatic Translation See MACHINE TRANSLATION.

Autonomy Spectrum A concept introduced by Rose (1981) to provide a framework for categorizing translations. Described by Leighton as "one of the important breakthroughs" of modern translation study (1991:62), the autonomy spectrum is distinguished from previous attempts at translation classification by the fact that it forms a continuous scale, rather than a simple binary contrast (such as the age-old LITERAL versus FREE dichotomy) or a choice between a limited number of discrete categories. The autonomy spectrum is a continuum, the two poles of which are "source text autonomy" and "target audience needs" (Rose 1981:33). A translation's position on the autonomy spectrum in this way reflects the translator's relation to the source material and the translation's relation to its intended audience; at one end, "the complete textual autonomy of the source text is observed" (1981:33), while at the other, "complete adaptation" to target conventions and expectations occurs (1981:34). Since the autonomy spectrum is defined in relatively general terms it can be used to categorize translations according to type, function or process. Further reading: Rose 1981.

Autotranslation (or **Self Translation**) Defined by Popovič as "the translation of an original work into another language by the author himself" ([1976]:19). However, while Popovič argues that the autotranslation "cannot be regarded as a variant of the original text but as a true translation" ([1976]:19), Koller distinguishes between autotranslation and "true" translation by saying that the issue of FAITHFULNESS is different in the case of autotranslation, as the author-translator will feel justified in introducing changes into the text (1979/1992:197) where an "ordinary" translator might hesitate to do so. Little work has been done on autotranslation; however, it is possible that closer study could yield some interesting insights into the nature of bilingualism and the relationship between language, thought and personality. It should be pointed out that while the standard terms for this phenomenon are *autotranslation* and *self translation*, Popovič also refers to it as *authorized translation*. Famous autotranslators have included Beckett, Nabokov and Tagore. Further reading: Fitch 1983, 1985, 1988; Grutman 1994; Koller 1979/1992; Popovič [1976]; Sengupta 1990; Steiner 1972.

Babel, Tower of A biblical narrative explaining why man is destined to speak a multiplicity of different languages. The story takes place at a time when "the whole earth was of one language", and tells of man's attempts to build a tower "whose top may reach unto heaven". God is angered by such an act of overweening pride, as "now nothing will be restrained from them, which they have imagined to do"; to punish man's wickedness and prevent another such enterprise from ever being undertaken He proceeds to "confound their language, that they may not understand one another's speech" and then to "scatter them abroad upon the face of all the earth" (Genesis chapter 11 verses 1-9, quoted in the Authorized Version). According to Christian theology the disaster of Babel is seen as the act which completes the Fall of man into a state of sin, while the symbolic reversal of its effects at Pentecost – when Christ's apostles were filled with the Holy Ghost and "began to speak with other tongues, as the Spirit gave them utterance" (Acts of the Apostles chapter 2 verse 4) – looks forward to a time in the future where the whole of redeemed mankind will once again speak a single language. The Tower of Babel can be seen metaphysically not only as the event which gave rise to the need for translators and interpreters, but also more specifically as "the spark which set off a discussion of translation theory and method ... from a theological, philosophical, aesthetic, psychological, and ethnographic point of view" (Wilss 1982:27). In this context the confounding of mankind's speech can be viewed positively as well as negatively. Barnstone (1993), for example, talks of the world being enriched by "diverse linguistic cultures, iconic and verbal" (1993:237); he regards the destruction of the original tower as a challenge to build a second Babel by means of the act of translation (1993:3). Steiner, in a vision of the almost messianic rôle of translation, talks of it as "a teleological imperative, a stubborn searching out of all the apertures, translucencies, sluice-gates through which the divided streams of human speech pursue their destined return to a single sea" (1975/1992:256-67). In this way he looks forward to the redemption of language in much the same way that Walter Benjamin does in his discussion of the recovery of PURE LANGUAGE through the agency of translation. Rosenzweig goes even further, stating boldly that "every translation is a messianic act, which brings redemption nearer" (quoted in Steiner 1975/1992:257). Further reading: Barnstone 1993; W. Benjamin 1923/1963, 1923/1970; Derrida 1980, 1985; Eco 1995; Steiner 1975/1992; Wilss 1977, 1982.

Back-transformation See ANALYSIS.

Back-translation A process in which a text which has been translated into a given language is retranslated into SL. The procedure of back-translation has been used for various different purposes. For example, since at least the middle of the 1970s the term has been used in the literature on Bible translation to illustrate the sometimes vast structural and conceptual differences which exist between SL and TL; however, it is also sometimes simply used to refer to a GLOSS

TRANSLATION of the original Biblical text (Gutt 1991). Such back-translations are by necessity highly LITERAL, although the precise degree of literalness will vary depending on the particular feature that needs to be highlighted. Similarly, back-translation is sometimes used in contrastive linguistics as a technique for comparing specific syntactic, morphological or lexical features from two or more languages. An early use of the term in this context can be found in Spalatin (1967), while Ivir defines back-translation as "a check on the semantic content" (1981:59) which can be used to reveal instances of FORMAL CORRESPONDENCE. Casagrande (1954) proposes a similar procedure to diagnose "trouble-points in the process of transcoding" (1954:339). However, Toury is sceptical of any such apparent insights which back-translation may provide, arguing that the irreversible nature of translation makes all such general conclusions invalid (1980:23-24). Holmes (1988a), on the other hand, uses the evidence of back-translation to argue against the possibility of there being any "real" EQUIVALENCE between a poem and its translation. According to his reasoning, a hypothetical experiment in which a poem is translated by five independent translators, and then each of the five inevitably different translations are back-translated to produce 25 versions, all distinct from each other and from the original text, demonstrates that any claim of equivalence is "perverse" (1988a:53). Similar experiments have been both suggested and actually carried out to investigate certain areas of translational behaviour. For example, Levý posits that an examination of a number of parallel back-translations of a single text would provide useful insights into at least two UNIVERSALS OF TRANSLATION (1965:78-79), and also argues that "tendencies operative in the course of decision processes may be observed with great clarity, if the same text passes several times through the process of translation from language A into language B, and back again into A" (1967:1176); in support of this latter proposition he cites an experiment carried out by van der Pol (1956) into how the choice of specific lexical items varied during the (repeated) back-translation of a text. See also INTERLINEAR TRANS-LATION, PARALLEL TRANSLATION and SERIAL TRANSLATION. Further reading: Baker 1992; Brislin 1976; Holmes 1988a; Gutt 1991; Ivir 1969, 1981; Levý 1965, 1967.

Bilateral Interpreting See LIAISON INTERPRETING.

Bilingual Corpora 1 See PARALLEL CORPORA.

2 A term sometimes used to refer to both MULTILINGUAL CORPORA and PARALLEL CORPORA. Further reading: Granger 1996.

Bi-text A term introduced by Harris (1988) to refer to a construct comprising both ST and TT, which exists as a psychological reality for the translator (or the bilingual reader). Harris conceives ST and TT as being "simultaneously present and intimately interconnected" (1988:8) in the translator's mind, and defines the resulting *bi-text* as "ST and TT as they co-exist in the translator's mind at the moment of translating" (1988:8). Harris likens the concept to a "single text in two dimensions, each of which is a language" (1988:8). However, only a fragment of a bi-text will exist at any one time, as the translation process proceeds sequentially through ST. Consequently, Harris prefers the metaphor of a "roll of two laminated materials of different colours" (1988:8), which more explicitly conveys the way that individual ST and TT UNITS OF TRANSLATION are mapped onto each other throughout the length of the bi-text. There are of course problems associated with representing on paper what is essentially a psychological concept, although the most convenient format is probably that of the INTERLINEAR TRANSLATION. While reflecting a basically psychological phenomenon, the concept of bi-text was proposed with a view to its possible use in MACHINE-AIDED TRANSLATION, as a large amount of machine-readable bi-text would provide a database of translation solutions used to solve previous translation problems similar to the one in hand. A resource of this kind could provide the translator with "translations of words in context; a memory-perfect exploitation of the translator's own previous experience; near-translations of non-conventional phraseology and even longer units" (1988:9). Such practical applications are similar to some of those proposed for PARALLEL CORPORA. Further reading: Harris 1988; Toury 1995.

Blank Spaces See VOIDS.

Blank Verse Translation Presented by Lefevere (1975) as one of seven strategies for translating poetry. Lefevere's categorization relates directly to his analysis of different English translations of a single poem by Catullus. Throughout his examination of blank verse translation he highlights the extra difficulties entailed by "working with pre-selected and pre-arranged material" (Lefevere 1975:61): although this particular strategy is less restricting than other approaches such as METRICAL or RHYMED TRANSLATION, in blank verse translation the translator needs to observe the requirement of balancing a general metrical predictability with the necessity of providing some occasional rhythmic variation. Both these aims can be achieved by devices such as expansion or compression of the line, use of enjambment, and alteration of the word order. The advantages of the strategy are a greater accuracy and higher degree of literariness than is typically produced by many other strategies which entail translating into verse. On the negative side Lefevere argues that blank verse translation concentrates on only one aspect of ST to the detriment of others (such as the meaning), and can lead to TTs which are clumsy, distorted and at times even nonsensical (1975:76). See also EXTRANEOUS FORM, IMITATION 2, INTERPRETATION, LITERAL TRANS- LATION 2, PHONEMIC TRANSLATION, POETRY INTO PROSE and VERSION 2. Further reading: Lefevere 1975.

Borrowing (French *Emprunt*) One of seven translation procedures described by Vinay & Darbelnet (1958, 1958/1995). Borrowing is defined as a type of DIRECT TRANSLATION 4 in that elements of ST are replaced by "parallel" TL elements (1958:46, 1958/1995:31). Vinay & Darbelnet describe the procedure as the simplest type of translation, since it merely involves the transfer of an SL word into TT without it being modified in any way. The reason for this transfer is usually that the translator needs to overcome a *lacuna* (see VOIDS), or – more significantly – wishes to create a particular stylistic effect, or to introduce some local colour into TT. Vinay & Darbelnet cite Russian *verst* or *pood* and Spanish *tequila* or *tortillas* as words which might give a translation a Russian or Mexican flavour when introduced as borrowings (1958:47, 1958/1995:32). In a similar way they suggest that when referring to the English office of *coroner* in a French text, it is probably better to retain the English word than to struggle to find an equivalent title amongst French magistrates (1958:47, 1958/ 1995:32). Vinay & Darbelnet also point out that borrowings or loan words often enter a language after being introduced in a translation, and that many such words come to be so widely accepted in TL that they cease to be perceived as foreign items (1958:47, 1958/1995:32). See also ADAPTATION 2, CALQUE, EQUIVALENCE 2, LITERAL TRANSLA- TION, MODULATION 1 and TRANS-POSITION. Further reading: Vinay & Darbelnet 1958, 1958/1995.

Calque (or **Loan Translation**; French *Calque*) A term used to denote *attraverso il quale*

the process whereby the individual elements of an SL item (e.g. morphemes in the case of a single word) are translated literally to produce a TL equivalent. Vinay & Darbelnet classify calque as a type of DIRECT TRANSLATION 4 and list it as one of seven translation procedures (1958:47, 1958/1995:32; see also ADAPTATION 2, BORROWING, EQUIVALENCE 2, LITERAL TRANSLATION, MODULATION 1 and TRANSPOSITION). Along similar lines, Hervey & Higgins (1992) define calque as one of five types of CULTURAL TRANSPOSITION (see also COMMUNICATIVE TRANSLATION 3, CULTURAL BORROWING, CULTURAL TRANSPLANTATION, and EXOTICISM); according to them, calque differs from the similar procedure of cultural borrowing in that it appropriates only the model of SL grammatical structures, and does not borrow expressions verbatim from ST (1992:33). Some expressions which were originally examples of calque become the standard TL cultural equivalents of their SL models; examples of this are French *poids mouche*, calqued on English *flyweight*, or Spanish *rascacielos* calqued on American English *skyscraper*. Further reading: Hervey & Higgins 1992; Vinay & Darbelnet 1958, 1958/1995.

Italian = piatto e cielo .

CAT (Computer-aided Translation or **Computer-assisted Translation)** See MACHINE-AIDED TRANSLATION.

Category Shift A term used by Catford to denote one of two major types of SHIFT, or departure "from formal correspondence in the process of going from the SL to the TL" (1965:73). The term is generic, and may refer to shifts involving any of the four "fundamental categories of linguistic theory": the *class*, the *structure*, the *system* and the *unit* (1965:5-7). Category shifts will occur only in UNBOUNDED TRANSLATION, where it is possible to translate an SL item of a certain rank by a TL item of a different rank (e.g. a word by a group, a sentence by a clause, etc.). See also CLASS SHIFT, FORMAL CORRESPONDENCE, INTRA-SYSTEM SHIFT, LEVEL SHIFT, LINGUISTIC TRANSLATION 1, STRUCTURE SHIFT, UNIT OF TRANSLATION and UNIT SHIFT. Further reading: Catford 1965.

Chuchotage See WHISPERED INTERPRETING.

Class Shift A type of CATEGORY SHIFT which involves translating an SL item by means of a TL item belonging to a different grammatical class. The term *class* is understood along Hallidayan lines (Halliday

1961; see also Halliday, McIntosh & Strevens 1964) as being "that grouping of members of a given unit which is defined by operation in the structure of the unit next above" (Catford 1965:78), so that for example those adjectives which precede their noun and those which follow it would, on the basis of their function in the nominal group structure, be defined as separate classes of adjective. Consequently, the translation of *a white house* into French *une maison blanche* with its concomitant substitution of the English pre-positional adjective *white* with the French post-positional adjective *blanche* would entail a class shift. Note that instances of class shift are generally the result of differences between the linguistic systems of SL and TL, rather than representing a deliberate choice by the translator. See also INTRA-SYSTEM SHIFT, LEVEL SHIFT, MODIFICATION, SHIFTS, STRUCTURE SHIFT and UNIT SHIFT. Further reading: Catford 1965.

Close Translation A generic term used by some writers (for example Newmark 1988) to refer to translation strategies which favour exact correspondence between SL and TL linguistic units over an emphasis on conveying the overall meaning or spirit of ST. See also GLOSS TRANSLATION, INTERLINEAR TRANSLATION, LITERAL TRANS-LATION 1, METAPHRASE and WORD-FOR-WORD TRANSLATION. Further reading: Newmark 1988.

Coherence (German *Kohärenz*) Defined in general terms as "the agreement of a text with its situation" (Baker 1993:239, after Vermeer 1983). The term was introduced by Reiss & Vermeer (1984) to the study of translation; according to these authors, there are two types of coherence, *intratextual* and *intertextual*. The first of these concerns the way in which TT *per se* is received in the target situation. This depends on the "coherence rule", which states that "the message (or TT) produced by the translator must be interpretable in a way that is coherent with the target recipient's situation" (Reiss & Vermeer 1984:113, translated). If this is the case, the recipient's *feedback* (German *Rückkoppelung*), or reaction, will indicate that the text has been understood and the interaction has *succeeded* (see SUCCESS). However, the intratextual coherence of a TT may be affected by translation which is too LITERAL, by lapses on the part of the translator, or by a failure to take into consideration the different levels of knowledge which the ST and TT readers will bring to their respective texts. The second type of coherence, the intertextual – also known as *fidelity* (German *Fidelität*) – is the coherence which exists between TT and ST. It is usually subordinated to the first type, as a TT has first of all to be understood before it can be compared with its ST. Intertextual coherence depends on how the translator understands ST, and also on TT's SKOPOS, and will be judged to be present to the extent that there is consistency between a) the original ST message intended by the text producer, b) the way the translator interprets this message, and c) the way in which the translator encodes the message for the TT recipient. If there is coherence between these three factors then the "fidelity rule" is being followed. See also INFORMATION OFFER and PROTEST. Further reading: Nord 1991b; Reiss & Vermeer 1984; Vermeer 1983.

Commission (German ***Auftrag***) A term used by Vermeer (1989) within the framework of TRANSLATORIAL ACTION to refer to the specifications which the translator works with when producing a TT. A commission may come from a client or other third party as a set of explicit instructions or requirements; in this case, the translator as "expert" should be able to contribute towards its development. On the other hand, the commission is frequently simply a collection of implicit principles or preferences internalized by the translator. However, Vermeer argues that one way or another every translation should be based on a commission stating firstly the goal (or SKOPOS) of TT, and secondly the conditions under which this goal should be achieved (1989:183). Ideally these latter should include not only details of practicalities such as deadlines and fees, but also indications of TT's intended text-type, the translation strategies which the translator should use, and so forth. Further reading: Holz-Mänttäri 1984; Vermeer 1989.

Communication Load (or **Information Load**) A term used in Nida's (1964) model of the translation process, and defined by Nida & Taber as "the degree of difficulty of a message" (1969/1982:198). Nida bases his discussion of communication load (or *information load*) on a model of the communication process in which the source communicates the *information* contained by the message via the *decoder's* (or receptor's) *channel*, which will vary in capacity depending on such factors as the receptor's personal qualities, education and cultural background (Nida & Taber 1969/1982:198). Communication load consists of both formal and semantic elements and is measured by "the ratio between the number of units of information and the number of formal units (i.e. words)" (1969/1982:198). The more information that a message contains, the less predictable it is likely to be and thus the harder for the receptor to understand; therefore it is always necessary to ensure that a message contains an amount of REDUNDANCY appropriate to the audience in question, in order to prevent the receptor's channel from becoming overloaded (1964:131). In the context of interlingual communication, this means that a translation which is based on the principle of DYNAMIC EQUIVALENCE will require proper ADJUSTMENT and the addition of a certain amount of redundancy to allow for differences between the linguistic and cultural backgrounds of the two audiences; conversely, a LITERAL translation will generally be harder for TL receptors to process than ST was for its original audience, since it will be likely to contain a degree of "linguistic awkwardness" (1964:131). Further reading: Nida 1964.

Communicative Translation 1 (or **Communicative Approach**) A term used to refer to any approach which views translation as a "communicative process which takes place within a social context" (Hatim & Mason 1990:3, emphasis removed). Obviously, all approaches will to some extent consider translation as communication; however, a so-called communicative translation will typically be generally oriented towards the needs of the TL reader or recipient. Thus for example a translator who is translating communicatively will treat ST as a message rather than a mere string of linguistic units, and will be concerned to preserve ST's original function and to reproduce its effect on the new audience. In other words, a communicative translation is one which contrasts with, for example, INTERLINEAR TRANSLATION, LITERAL TRANSLATION 1 or WORD-FOR-WORD TRANSLATION in that it treats the ST wording as merely one of a number of factors which need to be borne in mind by the translator. An example of a translation model based on this type of approach is provided by Roberts, who argues that translation which adheres too closely to the original wording "does not often result in effective communication in the other language", but rather can frequently lead to "distortion of the message" (1985:158). Roberts uses Spilka's definition of a translator as a mediator between "two parties who would otherwise be unable to communicate" (Spilka 1978, quoted in Roberts 1985:142); it is the translator's function to transmit the source message (ibid), which Roberts understands as the ST words plus not only the context in which they occur, but also four non-linguistic ST parameters (1985:158). These are the *source*, or originator of the message, the *intended receptor*, the *object*, or purpose of the communication, and the *vector*, or the spacial and temporal circumstances in which the translation was produced (1985:143-45, based on Pergnier 1980:58). In the translation, depending on whether ST is expressive, informative or imperative in nature (see Nida & Taber 1969/1982:24-27), the source, object or intended receptor will be emphasized respectively in order for the translation to elicit the same reaction as ST did from the original recipients (1985:149-50). However, since "translation involves a double act of communication" (1985:146), a second set of parameters is generated in the translation process which relates specifically to the translated message (1985: 147). Roberts' model is by no means the only communicative approach, as IDIOMATIC TRANSLATION, COMMUNICATIVE TRANSLATION 2 and translation according to the principle of DYNAMIC EQUIVALENCE can all be said to be further examples of this type of translation. See also PRAGMATIC TRANSLATION 1. Further reading: Hatim & Mason 1990; Roberts 1985.

2 Defined by Newmark as one of two modes of translation (see also SEMANTIC TRANSLATION), in which "the translator attempts to produce the same effect on the TL readers as was produced by the original on the SL readers" (1981/1988:22). This means that in communicative translation the emphasis should be on conveying the message of the original in a form which conforms to the linguistic, cultural and pragmatic conventions of TL rather than mirroring the actual words of ST as closely as is possible without infringing the TL norms. When producing a communicative translation, the translator is permitted greater freedom to interpret ST and will consequently smooth over irregularities of style, remove ambiguities and even correct the author's factual errors, and in doing so will limit the semantic potential of ST by seeking to make TT fulfil one specific communicative function which is determined by the type of TL reader envisaged. Examples of text-types for which this mode of translation would be appropriate include journalistic writing, textbooks, public notices and indeed most non-literary genres. It should be noted that communicative translation is not intended to be a completely cut-and-dried category; furthermore, along with semantic translation it is intended to represent the "'middle ground' of translation practice" (Hatim & Mason 1990:7), and does not extend to the extremes of ADAPTATION and INTERLINEAR

TRANSLATION (see Newmark 1988:45). See also COVERT TRANSLA-
TION and INDIRECT TRANSLATION 2. Further reading: Newmark 1981/
1988, 1988.

3 A term used by Hervey & Higgins (1992) to describe a type of
CULTURAL TRANSPOSITION. They define communicative translation
as a style of FREE TRANSLATION which involves "the substitution for
ST expressions of their contextually/situationally appropriate cultural
equivalents in the TL", or in other words, a strategy in which "the TT
uses situationally apt target culture equivalents in preference to literal
translation" (1992:248, emphasis removed). Hervey & Higgins point
out that, although this is a technique which should not be freely used,
it is often obligatory in situations where LITERAL TRANSLATION is
impossible, such as in the translation of notices and conversational
clichés; as examples they cite translating *Objets Trouvés* as *Lost
Property*, and *Je vous en prie* as *Don't mention it*. See also CALQUE,
CULTURAL BORROWING, CULTURAL TRANSPLANTATION and EXOTICISM.
Further reading: Hervey & Higgins 1992.

Community Interpreting (or **Dialogue Interpreting**, or **Public
Service Interpreting**) A form of INTERPRETING which is distinguished by the contexts in which it is employed. Its purpose is to
provide access to a public service for a person who does not speak the
majority language of the community in which he or she lives; the
settings in which it is used include "police and (non-courtroom) legal
encounters, schools (parent-teacher conferences), public safety,
employment interviews, and community agency services, as well as
health and mental health care settings" (Downing & Helms Tillery
1992:2). It is most frequently used in countries such as Sweden,
Germany, Britain and the USA, where there are large ethnic minorities.
While a few decades ago community interpreting was regularly
performed by untrained bilinguals it is now acquiring a more
professional profile in response to the increasingly multicultural and
multilingual nature of many modern societies. Community interpreting
normally occurs in a one-to-one setting, and tends to be bi-directional;
it is generally performed consecutively, although differs from
CONSECUTIVE INTERPRETING proper in that the message is usually
interpreted sentence by sentence and the interpreter does not therefore
generally need to take notes (see LIAISON INTERPRETING). Because of
the contexts where it typically occurs most community interpreting
involves a significant element of intercultural transcoding; there is

therefore likely to be a high level of "mismatch" not only between participants' modes of expression but also in their understanding of their own rôle in the given interaction and their expectations of how their interlocutor is going to act (Zimman 1994:218). Thus as with COURT INTERPRETING – which some would consider to be a type of community interpreting – there is a degree of controversy regarding the extent to which community interpreters should intervene in encounters in which they are mediating. The *Guide to Good Practice* (1989) suggests that the interpreter is justified in intervening if a) he or she needs further clarification, b) the client has simply not understood, c) the client seems to have missed an inference or d) the client needs to be asked to modify his or her way of speaking to facilitate the interpreting (quoted in Zimman 1994:219). However, while some of these recommendations are uncontroversial, many people believe that intervention in contexts such as those outlined in the second and third points lie beyond the community interpreter's brief; thus community interpreters need to learn to strike a balance between simply translating the words which are said, and completely dominating the interview (Zimman 1994:219). Further reading: Downing & Helms Tillery 1992; *Guide to Good Practice* 1989; Shackman 1984; Wadensjö 1992, 1995; Zimman 1994.

Commutation See TEXTUAL EQUIVALENCE 1.

Comparable Corpora A term used by Baker to refer to "two separate collections of texts in the same language", of which "one corpus consists of original texts in the language in question and the other consists of translations in that language from a given source language or languages" (1995:234). The fact that comparable corpora are monolingual collections of texts distinguishes them from other types of CORPORA used in Translation Studies. Also, unlike other corpus types, comparable corpora have no clear rôle to play in translator training, materials writing or the development of MACHINE TRANSLATION systems. However, where they promise to make a significant contribution is in the "elucidation of the nature of translated text as a mediated communicative event" (Baker 1993:243). In other words, the information which they contain is likely to yield rich insights into the kind of linguistic features which are typical of translated text, regardless of the language of ST. More specifically, it is hoped that an analysis of comparable corpora will increase our understanding of the nature of UNIVERSALS OF TRANSLATION. Little work has so far been carried out with comparable corpora. However, Gellerstam (1986) employs them in an examination of certain features of Swedish TRANSLA-TIONESE, while Laviosa-Braithwaite (1997) is the first serious attempt to investigate universals of translation using this type of methodology. It should be pointed out that since the use of corpora in Translation Studies is a relatively new development, a certain degree of fluidity still exists in the usage of this term (see Baker 1995:240 n. 7). See also MULTILINGUAL CORPORA, PARALLEL CORPORA and THIRD CODE. Further reading: Baker 1993, 1995, 1997; Gellerstam 1986; Granger 1996; Laviosa-Braithwaite 1997.

Compensation A term in general use for a number of decades, and defined by Hervey & Higgins as "the technique of making up for the translation loss of important ST features by approximating their effects in the TT through means other than those used in the ST" (1992:248, emphasis removed). Hervey & Higgins describe translation as a process "fraught with compromise" (1992:34), and present various strategies of compensation as a means of partly overcoming this situation. They list four different types of compensation. Compensation in *kind* involves "making up for one type of textual effect in the ST by another type in the TT" (1992:35); one of the examples which they cite entails the substitution of a narrative tense not available in TL by other TL features which have a similar stylistic effect (1992:35-36). Compensation in *place* makes up for the loss of a particular effect at a certain place in ST by recreating this effect at a different place in TT (1992:37); Hervey & Higgins cite as an example of this the omission of an untranslatable pun on one word and subsequent punning on another word. Compensation by *merging* "[condenses] ST features carried over a relatively long stretch of text (say, a complex phrase) into a relatively short stretch of the TT (say, a single word or a simple phrase)" (1992:38); this practice often involves substituting a TL word for a longer ST item which has no literal TL equivalent. Conversely, where there is no one TL word which covers the same range of meanings as the SL word, compensation by *splitting* may be used, for example by translating the title of a technical article on *Les papillons* as *Moths and butterflies* (1992:39). However, Harvey argues that the term *compensation* should be reserved for "essentially stylistic, text-specific features and effects" (1995:71), rather than also including features which are "systemic [and] language-specific"

(1995:71) in nature; he consequently doubts the validity of Hervey & Higgins' last two categories, which he considers to be simply reflections of "the difference between two lexical systems" (1995:76). Harvey proposes a descriptive model for compensation which is based on three axes (1995:77-85). The first of these is the *typological*; it is concerned with recognizing specific instances of compensation. The second, the *correspondence* axis, has to do with describing the "degree of linguistic correspondence between the devices used to achieve the effect in source and target texts" (1995:79), while the third, the *topographical*, provides a framework for analyzing how such devices are located relative to each other in their respective texts. In this connection Harvey also makes the point that use of a compensation device at a great distance from the ST effect which it is replacing necessarily leads to the whole text being viewed as the UNIT OF TRANSLATION (1995:83). Further reading: Harvey 1995; Hervey & Higgins 1992; Vinay & Darbelnet 1958, 1958/1995.

Competence A term used by Toury (1980, 1995) for investigating certain aspects of translation practice. Following Chomsky's (1965) famous distinction, Toury defines translational competence (as opposed to PERFORMANCE) as the total SYSTEM of ST-TT relationships which could theoretically be manifested in a translation, but which will to a large extent remain unrealized. In other words, translational competence is the linguistic (and also for example stylistic and literary) resource which a translator will draw on while searching for translational solutions, rather than those solutions which are commonly turned to (NORMS) or those which may be found in a particular translation (performance). Given the nature of translational competence as a source of *potential* solutions it is generally studied from a theoretical rather than a DESCRIPTIVE viewpoint. Further reading: Toury 1980.

Componential Analysis See ANALYSIS.

Computer-aided Translation (or **Computer-assisted Translation**) (**CAT**) See MACHINE-AIDED TRANSLATION.

Concordance See VERBAL CONSISTENCY.

Conference Interpreting A term used to refer to the type of

INTERPRETING which occurs in international conferences as well as other high-profile settings such as lectures, television broadcasts or summit meetings; as such it is one of the forms of interpreting which is defined according to the context in which it is used. Conference interpreters need to be proficient in a variety of interpreting techniques, as although SIMULTANEOUS INTERPRETING is the main mode used, there is also occasional call for CONSECUTIVE INTERPRETING or even WHISPERED INTERPRETING. For the purposes of conference interpreting, languages which interpreters know are categorized into three types: A languages, in which they have a native-like fluency and which they work both from and into; B languages, which are known to an almost native level, and which interpreters are also expected to be able to interpret into (at least in the consecutive mode); and C languages, which interpreters only interpret from (Gile 1995a:209). The rôle of conference interpreters is one of mediating between a knowledgeable speaker and his or her audience; problems therefore sometimes arise since interpreters cannot always be expected to share the knowledge background which a speaker's audience is assumed to possess. To reduce this potential knowledge shortfall conference interpreters always try to prepare carefully for each assignment; such preparation may take the form of either studying the specialist field itself, or simply concentrating on the terminology which is likely to occur (Gile 1995a:149). Conference interpreting is a relatively recent form of interpreting, with a history stretching back no more than eighty years, although it was only after the development of simultaneous interpreting techniques and the associated technology that it gained recognition as a separate category of interpreting. See also A.I.I.C., EFFORT MODELS, PIVOT LANGUAGE and RELAY INTERPRETING. Further reading: Gile 1995a & 1995b; Gran & Taylor 1990; Mackintosh 1995; Seleskovitch 1968, 1968/1978.

Consecutive Interpreting A term used to refer to one of the two basic modes of INTERPRETING (see also SIMULTANEOUS INTER-PRETING). While some forms of interpreting (such as COMMUNITY INTERPRETING and LIAISON INTERPRETING) are performed in a manner which may be loosely designated "consecutive", strictly speaking the term should be reserved for the more rigorous set of procedures used when interpreting for large audiences in formal settings such as conferences or courtrooms (see CONFERENCE INTERPRETING and COURT INTERPRETING). Consecutive interpreting understood in this way proceeds as follows. The interpreter listens to a (sometimes fairly lengthy) section of a speech delivered in SL, and makes notes; such notes tend to serve simply as a brief memory aid rather than being a shorthand transcription of all that is said. The speaker then pauses to allow the interpreter to render what has been said into TL; when the section has been interpreted the speaker resumes with the next section, until the whole speech has been delivered and interpreted into TL. Consecutive interpreting thus entails a number of different abilities and skills, including a high level of SL comprehension, advanced notetaking skills, excellent general knowledge, an accurate memory and a confident manner of delivery (see also EFFORT MODELS). The procedure differs from simultaneous interpreting in that the comprehension and production of speech are separated (Gile 1995a:180); furthermore, since the speaker and the interpreter do not talk at the same time it is clearly a more prolonged process than the simultaneous variety. See also WHISPERED INTERPRETING. Further reading: Gile 1995a & 1995c; Seleskovitch & Lederer 1989.

Constitutive Translational Conventions According to Nord (1991b), one of two types of translational CONVENTION. Nord bases the term on Searle's (1969) notion of *constitutive rules*; such rules not only regulate, but "create or define new forms of behavior" (1969:33), as would be the case, for example, with the rules of a game. By analogy, Nord defines constitutive translational conventions as those conventions which "determine what a particular culture community accepts as a *translation* (as opposed to an *adaptation* or *version* or other forms of intercultural text transfer)" (1991b:100; see ADAPTATION and VERSION). In other words, the constitutive translational conventions determine the expectations with which the reader is likely to approach the text, as well as the way in which the translator will typically tackle specific translational problems. As a possible way of determining the particular constitutive translational conventions obtaining in a given cultural context, Nord suggests analyzing the solutions to concrete translation problems which are generally adopted by translators working within that context. See also EXPECTANCY NORMS and REGULATIVE TRANSLATIONAL CONVENTIONS. Further reading: Nord 1991b.

Content-derivative Form (or Organic Form) A term used by Holmes (1988d) to denote one of four possible approaches open to a translator when faced with the problem of rendering verse form in TL. A content-derivative form is one which is created when a translator "starts from the semantic material, allowing it to take on its own unique poetic shape as the translation develops" (1988d:27). In other words, such a TL form is in no way a reflection of the ST form, but is rather a form which has been allowed to develop "organically" from "the inward workings of the text itself" (1988d:28). See also ANALOGICAL FORM, EXTRANEOUS FORM, FORM-DERIVATIVE FORMS, MAPPING, METAPOEM and MIMETIC FORM. Further reading: Holmes 1988d.

Content-focused Texts (German *Inhaltsbetonte Texte*) See INFORMATIVE TEXTS.

Contextual Consistency A term used by Nida & Taber to describe "the quality which results from translating a source language word by that expression in the receptor language which best fits each context rather than by the same expression in all contexts" (1969/1982:199). In other words, a translator who adopts a policy of contextual consistency – rather than its opposite, VERBAL CONSISTENCY– is merely recognizing the fact that the words in different languages do not necessarily mesh together in terms of the semantic areas which they cover, and therefore cannot be translated without regard for the context in which they occur (1969/1982:15). As an example of the application of this principle Nida & Taber consider the translation of the Greek word *soma* in different passages of the Bible, and observe that in one English-language version it is variously translated as *body, herself, corpse, your very selves* and *lower nature* (1969/1982:15). Nida & Taber consider that such a strategy has priority over verbal consistency, and point out that contextual consistency is one aspect of DYNAMIC EQUIVALENCE. Further reading: Nida & Taber 1969/1982.

Controlled Language Defined by Arnold et al. as "a specially simplified version of a language" (1994:211). While originally conceived as "partial solution[s] to ... perceived communication problem[s]" (1994:211), such languages are now commonly used as a means of improving the performance of MACHINE TRANSLATION systems. Within this context a controlled language is in essence a variant of SL a) in which texts are composed according to a set of rules designed to enhance the clarity and readability of what is said, and b) which uses only a limited number of basic words (including a clearly circumscribed technical vocabulary), each of which typically has only one meaning. For example, Basic English, the original controlled language dating from the 1920s, is based on a very limited number of grammatical forms and a vocabulary of 850 words which can be extended as appropriate to include specialized terms from a particular field. Writing or PRE-EDITING machine translation input so that it conforms to the parameters of a controlled language considerably enhances the performance of most systems as it removes many of the ambiguities which ST would otherwise contain and which the computer might be unable to analyze. See also SUBLANGUAGE. Further reading: Arnold et al. 1994.

Conventions A term used by Nord (1991b). Starting from a general definition of the word *convention*, Nord reasons that translation, like any other form of social behaviour, will necessarily take place within parameters which are socially and culturally determined. Nord recognizes three levels of parameter: rules, NORMS and conventions. These three concepts form a hierarchy, with each term implying a level of obligation less binding than the previous one. Nord defines conventions as "specific realizations of norms" (1991b:96); they are "not explicitly formulated, nor are they binding" (1991b:96), but are based simply on common knowledge and shared expectations (1991b:96). Any one act of translation represents a careful juggling of three distinct sets of conventions: those related to the source-culture, the target-culture and the translation process itself. Depending on their precise function, translational conventions will be either CONSTITUTIVE or REGULATIVE in nature. As a concrete example of a translational practice governed by conventions Nord describes how English relative clauses are regularly replaced by other, more natural-sounding constructions when translated into German (1991b:98-99). See also LOYALTY. Further reading: Hermans 1991; Nord 1991b; Sager et al. 1980.

Corpora (singular **Corpus**) A term traditionally used in Translation Studies to refer to relatively small-scale collections of texts, (parts of) which are searched manually for examples of features which are of interest. In MACHINE TRANSLATION a corpus is defined as "the finite collection of grammatical sentences that is used as a basis for the descriptive analysis of a language" (Newton 1992:223); in other words, it is a set of examples from which the software analogizes when producing a translation (Schubert 1992:87-88). In DESCRIPTIVE TRANSLATION STUDIES the term is now frequently understood to mean "a collection of texts held in machine-readable form and capable of being analysed automatically or semi-automatically in a variety of ways" (Baker 1995:225). However, while in linguistic research corpora of this kind typically contain many millions of words, there has as yet been little or no research in Translation Studies based on corpora of similar size. See also COMPARABLE CORPORA, MULTI-LINGUAL CORPORA and PARALLEL CORPORA. Further reading: Baker 1993, 1995.

Correctability (German ***Korrigierbarkeit***) According to Reiss & Vermeer (1984), one of two features which need to apply to a given act of translation in order for it to be considered an instance of *ÜBERSETZEN* (i.e. TRANSLATION) rather than *DOLMETSCHEN* (i.e. IN-TERPRETING). The notion of correctability is dependent on the entire ST and TT being available to the translator during and after the actual process of translation so as to permit correction of TT by the translator; it is considered to be present in those cases where the translator is able to correct his or her work, for example by cross-referencing with other parts of ST. See also VERIFIABILITY. Further reading: Kade 1968; Reiss & Vermeer 1984.

Correspondence A term used to refer to the relationship which exists between elements of SL and TL that are in some way considered to be counterparts of each other. Correspondence is usually presented as a somewhat weaker notion than the perhaps more frequently encountered concept of EQUIVALENCE (Hermans 1991: 157), although the relationship between the two terms varies from author to author. Nida (1964), for example, uses the term *correspondence* to denote a broad concept which covers both DYNAMIC and FORMAL EQUIVALENCE. For him correspondence represents the relationship not only between individual SL and TL symbols, but also between the ways such units are arranged within the structures of the two languages (1964:156). Nida (1964:193) distinguishes two main types of correspondence, structural (which is of a purely formal, decontextualized nature) and dynamic (where account is also taken of factors such as context and effect). However, he states that "there can be no absolute correspondence between languages" (1964:156), and talks about correspondences and contrasts as complementary aspects of the same phenomenon (1964:193). Turk, on the other hand, sees correspondence as one of two alternative criteria which can determine the type of equivalence which is created through the translator's decisions (1990:68; see also ADEQUACY 1). He describes correspondence as a "progressive homogeneity" between ST and TT (1990:68, translated), and defines it as a "symmetrical or complementary relationship, without reference to a third entity" (Turk 1990:78-79, translated). Holmes, in a discussion of the translation process, talks about how a translator uses *correspondence rules* in order to determine "the way in which he develops his target-text map from his source-text map" (1988b:84; see MAPPING). For Holmes, the correspondences – or instances of ST-TT *matching* (1988b:84) – which occur can be of various types, depending on the level on which the translator is trying to establish similarity between ST and TT. He suggests three basic kinds: *homologues*, which correspond in form but not function, *analogues*, where correspondence is on the level of function, not form, and the half-joking coinages *semantologues* or *semasiologues*, which correspond in neither form nor function, but in meaning (1988b:85; see also HIERARCHY OF CORRESPONDENCES). Finally, Koller suggests that the term correspondence is better suited for contrastive linguistics, and reserves the term *equivalence* for use in TRANSLATION STUDIES (1979/ 1992:217). This is because – for Koller at least – the establishing of correspondence means assigning SL items to specific and fixed TL items with which they are structurally parallel (1979/ 1992:223-24), whereas Translation Studies concerns itself with describing "all possible denotatively equivalent TL variants, as well as the various linguistic, textual and situational conditions in which they are possible" (1979/1992:223, translated). In other words, correspondence for Koller is a matter of "formal similarity" (1979/ 1992:223, translated) rather than one-off appropriateness. See also FORMAL CORRESPONDENCE, IDENTITY and INVARIANCE. Further reading: Holmes 1988b; Koller 1979/1992; Nida 1964; Turk 1990.

Correspondences, Hierarchy of See HIERARCHY OF CORRESPONDENCES.

Court Interpreting A type of INTERPRETING which is defined by the context in which it occurs. Although the term most typically designates interpreting which takes place in a courtroom, it also covers the interpreter's activity in other legal settings, such as a prison or a police station. The client is usually the defendant or a witness, and generally belongs to an immigrant community. The basic purpose of court interpreting is to enable the client to participate in proceedings; such interpreting therefore needs to be bi-directional. Court interpreting is generally CONSECUTIVE or LIAISON, although other modes – such as SIMULTANEOUS (e.g. for high-profile televised trials) and WHISPERED – may also be employed. The court interpreter is bound by a code of ethics which requires, among other things, secrecy and impartiality (Edwards 1995:63-71). He or she is also required to swear to interpret accurately and faithfully. However, this in practice raises a number of important issues which concern the very nature of interpreting. For example, a common expectation on the part of members of the legal professions is that the interpreting process should be "performed in a mechanical fashion by a transparent presence" (Morris 1995:27). Thus interpreters are not permitted to offer an "interpretation" – in the sense of "decoding and attempting to convey their understanding of speaker meanings and intentions" (Morris 1995:26) – and any discretion or latitude which they exercise can be perceived as intrusiveness (Shlesinger 1991:147). This situation is, however, in tension with the fact that "the product of the interpreting process is almost always treated as a legally valid equivalent of the original utterance" (Morris 1995:29) and indeed with the fact that it is the interpreted rather than original utterances which are kept on record. Thus the court interpreter often finds him or herself caught in a dilemma, on the one hand being required to transmit information as literally as possible (and to include prosodic features such as hesitations), yet on the other aware of the fact that linguistic and cultural differences between the client and the court mean that adhering to this policy can potentially lead to one or other side being seriously misrepresented. Further reading: Barsky 1996; Berk-Seligson 1990; Colin & Morris 1996; Edwards 1995; González et al. 1991; Morris 1995; Shlesinger 1991.

Covert Translation A term introduced by House (1977) to refer to one of two contrasting modes of translation (see also OVERT TRANSLATION). The purpose of covert translation is to produce a TT which is "as immediately and 'originally' relevant as it is for the source language addressees" (1986:188). The production of a covert translation can therefore be viewed as an attempt to conceal the translated nature of a TT by producing a text which is FUNCTIONALLY

EQUIVALENT to ST. According to House's model, such an approach is appropriate for STs which have no independent status in the source culture, or in other words which are not inextricably associated with the language, traditions, history or any other aspect of the source culture. Because of this lack of rootedness in any particular culture it is argued that the original function of a text (the purpose which it serves) can in such instances be reproduced in translation, although the application of a "cultural filter" is required in order to produce a cultural configuration in TT which is equivalent to that found in ST; however, unjustified use of a cultural filter will result in a *covert version*, which is defined as being an inadequate translation. Advertising, journalistic and technical material are all examples of text-types for which covert translation is held to be appropriate; furthermore, most Bible translators will employ something like this approach in order to make the message which they are seeking to convey maximally relevant to new audiences. See also COMMUNICA-TIVE TRANSLATION 2, INSTRUMENTAL TRANSLATION and SEMANTIC TRANSLATION. Further reading: House 1977, 1986; Gutt 1991.

Cross-temporal Theories of Translation See TIME-RESTRICTED THEORIES OF TRANSLATION.

Cross-temporal Translation See INTERTEMPORAL TRANSLATION.

Cultural Approach See CULTURAL TRANSLATION 1.

Cultural Borrowing A term used by Hervey & Higgins (1992) to describe the type of CULTURAL TRANSPOSITION in which an SL expression is transferred verbatim into TL because it is not possible to translate it by a suitable TL equivalent (1992:31). The borrowed term may remain unaltered, or it may undergo minor alteration; however, what is important is that the meaning of the borrowed expression should be made clear by the TT context (1992:31). As examples of cultural borrowing Hervey & Higgins cite items such as *joie de vivre*, *sauerkraut* and *taboo* (1992:31). Cultural borrowing differs from CALQUE in that it takes the whole SL expression over into TL, whereas calque borrows only the model of the SL grammatical structure (1992:33). See also COMMUNICATIVE TRANSLATION 3, CULTURAL TRANSPLANTATION and EXOTICISM. Further reading: Hervey & Higgins 1992.

Cultural Substitution A term used by Beekman & Callow (1974) i
the context of Bible translation to describe a possible strategy for
dealing with objects or events which are unknown in the target culture. Beekman & Callow define cultural substitution as "the use of a
real-world referent from the receptor culture for an unknown referent
of the original, both of the referents having the same *function*"
(1974:201, emphasis original); they present the strategy as an alternative to using a more general term or loan-word to translate such an
SL item. However, they also point out that the strategy should be used
with great caution, since a) it is clearly inappropriate with words
which are making a historical reference rather than a didactic point
(1974:203), b) it is important to choose the most relevant rather than
simply the most obvious function (1974:204), and c) there is a risk of
causing a clash between the functions of the source and target items
(1974:205). Finally, Beekman & Callow do not recommend translators to use a cultural substitute if the distortion in DYNAMIC FIDELITY
caused by not using it would only be slight (1974:207). See also
DIDACTIC FIDELITY and HISTORICAL FIDELITY. Further reading:
Beekman & Callow 1974.

Cultural Translation 1 (or **Cultural Approach**) A term used informally to refer to types of translation which function as a tool for
cross-cultural or anthropological research, or indeed to any translation
which is sensitive to cultural as well as linguistic factors. Such
sensitivity might take the form either of presenting TL recipients with
a transparent text which informs them about elements of the source
culture, or of finding target items which may in some way be considered
to be culturally "equivalent" to the ST items they are translating.
Thus a translator who uses a cultural approach is simply recognizing
that each language contains elements which are derived from its culture
(such as greetings, fixed expressions and REALIA), that every text is
anchored in a specific culture, and that conventions of text production
and reception vary from culture to culture (Koller 1979/1992:59-60).
An awareness of such issues can at times make it more appropriate to
think of translation as a process which occurs between cultures rather
than simply between languages. SKOPOS THEORY, THICK TRANSLATION
and TRANSLATORIAL ACTION are all examples of this type of approach.
Further reading: Snell-Hornby 1988/1995; Toury 1987.

2 Defined by Nida & Taber in the context of Bible translation as a
"translation in which the content of the message is changed to conform

to the receptor culture in some way, and/or in which information is introduced which is not linguistically implicit in the original" (1969/ 1982:199). In other words, a cultural translation is one in which additions are made which cannot be directly derived from the original ST wording; these might take the form of ideas culturally foreign to ST, or even elements which are simply included to provide necessary background information. An example of a cultural translation of the Bible might thus be one which transposed the narrative to a contemporary setting, or one which expanded the text in an attempt to explain the meaning. According to Nida & Taber, translation of this type cannot be considered FAITHFUL, an epithet which they reserve for its opposite, LINGUISTIC TRANSLATION 3 (1969/1982:134). Thus for them cultural translation is in some ways synonymous with what other writers term ADAPTATION 1 (1969/1982:134). See also DYNAMIC EQUIVALENCE. Further reading: Gutt 1991; Nida & Taber 1969/1982.

Cultural Transplantation A term used by Hervey & Higgins (1992) to denote the highest degree of CULTURAL TRANSPOSITION, in which details of the source culture contained in ST are replaced by target culture elements with the result that the text is partially rewritten in a target culture setting. The technique can be successful, but Hervey & Higgins suggest that it is not to be considered normal translation practice, as in some cases it approximates more to ADAPTATION 2 than to translation (1992:30). See also CALQUE, COMMUNICATIVE TRANS-LATION 3, CULTURAL BORROWING and EXOTICISM. Further reading: Hervey & Higgins 1992.

Cultural Transposition A general term used by Hervey & Higgins to describe "the various degrees of departure from literal translation that one may resort to in the process of transferring the contents of a ST into the context of a target culture" (1992:28). Hervey & Higgins point out that all types of cultural transposition are alternatives to a LITERAL TRANSLATION 1, and any degree of cultural transposition selects TL and target culture features rather than those of SL and the source culture. The overall effect is a TT which contains a limited number of SL features and thus appears less foreign, and closer to the TL culture. See also CALQUE, COMMUNICATIVE TRANSLATION 3, CUL-TURAL BORROWING, CULTURAL TRANSPLANTATION, EXOTICISM and REALIA. Further reading: Hervey & Higgins 1992.

Decision-making, Translation as A term used to characterize part of the process which the translator goes through in the course of formulating a TT. Levý (1967) describes the act of translation as one of *decision-making* because he sees it as "a series of a certain number of consecutive situations – moves, as in a game – situations imposing on the translator the necessity of choosing among a certain (and very often exactly definable) number of alternatives" (1967:1171). Thus by the term *decision* Levý means a choice which needs to be taken between a number of possible solutions to a given problem encountered while translating a text, and which will influence subsequent choices by opening up or closing off other options dependent on the initial selection made. Such decisions, whether necessary or unnecessary, motivated or unmotivated, are hierarchical rather than merely sequential in nature, although little work has so far been done on investigating the hierarchical structures to which they belong. Levý argues that subjective factors (such as the translator's aesthetic standards) play a part in the making of decisions. This notion is built on by Wilss, who suggests four main factors involved in the process: the translator's cognitive system, his or her knowledge bases, the task specification agreed with the client or SL author, and problems specific to the particular text-type (1994:148). Wilss argues that, as well as generating some insights of its own through such approaches as THINK-ALOUD PROTOCOLS, the discipline of TRANSLATION STUDIES could benefit greatly from some of the work which has been done on decision theory in other fields; issues which could be profitably addressed include such questions as why certain decisions are sometimes postponed or avoided, or how our knowledge of the decision-making process should influence the way translations should be assessed. The answers to questions of this type might improve the quality of translation performance, and in particular help in the task of translator training. See also GAMES (TRANSLATION AND THE THEORY OF), MAPPING, MINIMAX PRINCIPLE, OPERATIONAL NORMS and SHIFTS. Further reading: Gorlée 1994; Levý 1967; Wilss 1988, 1994.

Definitions of Translation See TRANSLATION.

Degree of Differentiation (or **Degree of Precision**) (German *Differenzierungsgrad*) A term used by Hönig & Kussmaul (1982) to refer to a strategy for translating words denoting items of the

source culture (see REALIA). It is well known that such items represent particularly severe problems for the translator, since their cultural
significance in SL can never be fully reproduced in TT. As a classic
example of this Hönig & Kussmaul cite the English expression *public school*, which has a cultural background so rich and complex that
not even a "note of several pages" (1982:53, translated) would suf-
fice to provide an exhaustive description of the sociological
significance of the institutions it refers to. However, Hönig &
Kussmaul contend that such a procedure should never be necessary,
since the function of a text will determine the most appropriate translation in terms of how much of the socio-cultural background implicit
in the item needs to be verbalized in TT on any particular occasion
(1982:58). Thus in one place the term *public school* might be glossed
as *elite English school* but in another as *expensive private school*
(1982:53). However, the inclusion of too much or too little detail on
any one occasion will respectively lead to OVERTRANSLATION 2 or
UNDERTRANSLATION. Because this translation strategy is sensitive to
contextual requirements, it is also sometimes referred to as the *necessary* degree of differentiation (1982:63). Using this technique Hönig
& Kussmaul present a way of looking at translation which is dependent not on the notion of EQUIVALENCE – or in other words on the
extent to which TT matches the "visible" verbalized part of ST
(1982:62) – but rather on the importance of supplying the amount of
detail called for by the context and function of the translation. However, like any other, such an approach has its limitations. As argued
by Frank (1991), for example, it is most effective when applied to
journalistic and other text-types which can be said to possess a single, unifying function. In the case of poetic or other literary texts, on
the other hand, the text function is not usually so clear-cut, and words
may be chosen precisely because of the socio-cultural resonances
which they set in motion; consequently, in such cases it is possible to
argue that it is always necessary to include in TT every shade of
meaning which is present in the original (1991:117-18). Further reading: Hönig & Kussmaul 1982; Lehmuskallio et al. 1991; Snell-Hornby
1988/1995.

Descriptive Translation Studies (DTS) Defined by Holmes (1988e)
as one of the two subdivisions of PURE TRANSLATION STUDIES (the
other being THEORETICAL TRANSLATION STUDIES). According to
Holmes, the aim of this area of the discipline of TRANSLATION STUD-

IES is "to describe the phenomena of translating and translation(s) as they manifest themselves in the world of our experience" (1988e:71). Holmes' article has proved to be highly influential in certain circles, and the new approach it has engendered has led to "a considerable widening of the horizon, since any and all phenomena relating to translation, in the broadest sense, become objects of study" (Hermans 1985a:14). Thus for the purposes of Descriptive Translation Studies, a translation is taken to be "any target-language utterance which is presented or regarded as such within the target culture, on whatever grounds" (Toury 1985:20). It is Toury who has developed the notion of Descriptive Translation Studies to the greatest extent, arguing that "no empirical science can make a claim for completeness and (relative) autonomy unless it has a proper *descriptive branch*" (Toury 1995:1, emphasis original). Toury argues that translations are "*facts of one system only*: the target system" (Toury 1985:19, emphasis original). Thus Descriptive Translation Studies is for him a TARGET TEXT-ORIENTED discipline consisting of "carefully performed studies into well-defined corpuses, or sets of problems" (Toury 1995:1). Studies of this type are able to examine such areas as DECISION-MAKING in translation, translation NORMS, the THIRD CODE and UNIVERSALS OF TRANSLATION (see for example Toury 1995). Toury argues that such investigations "constitute the best means of testing, refuting, and especially modifying and amending the very *theory*, in whose terms research is carried out" (Toury 1995:1, emphasis original); thus he stresses the interrelatedness of the various branches of Translation Studies. Holmes' original model divides Descriptive Translation Studies into three areas: FUNCTION-ORIENTED TRANSLATION STUDIES, PROCESS-ORIENTED TRANSLATION STUDIES and PRODUCT-ORIENTED TRANSLATION STUDIES. Toury argues that the most important of the considerations which these reflect is function, and the least important process, as the purpose of a translation will determine its characteristics as a concrete TL product, which in turn will influence the procedures which the translator follows when producing the translation (1995:13-14). Toury also distinguishes between Descriptive Translation Studies and isolated descriptive studies of translation; he argues that it is only the former that has a coherent methodology of its own and is therefore able to make verifiable generalizations about translation (see 1991:181-82 and 1995:11). See also APPLIED TRANSLATION STUDIES, MANIPULATION SCHOOL, NORMS and PRESCRIPTIVE TRANSLATION STUDIES. Further reading: Hermans 1985; Holmes

1988e; Koller 1979/1992; van Leuven-Zwart 1991; Toury 1985, 1991, 1995.

Diagrammatic Translation (French *Traduction Diagrammatique*) According to Gouadec (1990), one of seven types of translation (or translation-like processes) which serve to meet the various translation needs which occur in a professional environment. In diagrammatic translation the content of ST is transferred to TL by means of a diagram rather than by text. Sager comments that this way of providing information "exceeds what is [by many] considered translation" (1994:184). See also ABSOLUTE TRANSLATION, ABSTRACT TRANSLATION, KEYWORD TRANSLATION, RECONSTRUCTIONS (TRANSLATION WITH), SELECTIVE TRANSLATION and SIGHT TRANSLATION. Further reading: Gouadec 1990; Sager 1994.

Dialogue Interpreting See COMMUNITY INTERPRETING.

Didactic Fidelity According to Beekman & Callow (1974), one of two complementary principles of fidelity which are used in the translation of Biblical texts (see also HISTORICAL FIDELITY). Didactic fidelity is defined as the strategy of adapting the text where necessary to fit in with the different culture of the target audience; it is used to translate instructive rather than narrative passages. Translation according to this principle thus utilizes CULTURAL SUBSTITUTION where appropriate. However, the situation is complicated by the fact that some Biblical teaching is based on cultural items which also anchor the passage in which they occur in a specific historical period, with the result that tension between didactic and historical fidelity can arise (1974:36). In situations such as this Beekman and Callow suggest that a possible solution is to use a more general term to translate the problem item (1974:37). See also FAITHFULNESS. Further reading: Beekman & Callow 1974.

Differentiation, Degree of (German *Differenzierungsgrad*) See DEGREE OF DIFFERENTIATION.

Direct Translation 1 A term used by a number of writers (e.g.Toury 1980, 1995) to refer to the type of translation procedure in which a TT is produced directly from the original ST, rather than via another, intermediate translation in another language. Direct translation tends to be the only permitted type of translation in well-established literary SYSTEMS which do not depend heavily on another system or language for literary models. See also INDIRECT TRANSLATION 1. Further reading: Toury 1980, 1995.

2 Defined as the type of translation in which the translator works into, rather than away from, his or her native language (or language of habitual use); the opposite procedure is termed INVERSE TRANSLATION or SERVICE TRANSLATION. In large, predominantly monolingual nations direct translation is the method which is most commonly used; only when a translation is being carried out from a "rare" SL for which there is a shortage of translators is the alternative method of inverse translation resorted to. However, in spite of the current predominance of direct translation in Western culture, before about the eighteenth century the direction of translation was not generally held to be of any importance. Further reading: Kelly 1979.

3 Defined by Gutt (1991) as one of two possible types of translation. Gutt works within the framework of Sperber and Wilson's (1986) relevance theory, and views translation as a special instance of the wider concept of communication. The notion of direct translation arises from the "desire to distinguish between translations where the translator is free to elaborate or summarize and those where he has to somehow stick to the explicit contents of the original" (1991:122). Treating these two types of translation as the poles of a cline, Gutt defines direct translation as the case in which the translator seeks to remain FAITHFUL to the content and form of the original to the maximum possible extent. In the terms of relevance theory, a TT is considered to be direct "if and only if it purports to interpretively resemble the original completely in the context envisaged for the original" (1991:163). The notion of the original context – which is conceived in terms of the explicit and implicit information which is available to the original audience – is vital, as translation is viewed in terms of the "interaction of context, stimulus and interpretation" (1991:188), and the new audience bears the responsibility for compensating for changes in the contextual information available. Direct translation consequently eschews explanatory interpolation in the translated text, but rather relies on such devices as introductions, notes or glossaries to provide information which the translator considers vital for a full understanding of the original context. Direct translation is likely to be the favoured strategy when, for example, the receptor audience have some knowledge of the original, and expect the translation to conform to

their preconceptions. See also DYNAMIC EQUIVALENCE, FUNCTIONAL EQUIVALENCE, INDIRECT TRANSLATION 2 and THICK TRANSLATION. Further reading: Gutt 1991.

4 (French *Traduction Directe*) A term used by Vinay & Darbelnet (1958, 1958/1995) to refer to translation procedures which are based on the use of parallel grammatical categories or parallel concepts (1958:46, 1958/1995:31); as such it contrasts with OBLIQUE TRANS-LATION. The types of direct translation which Vinay & Darbelnet identify are BORROWING, CALQUE and LITERAL TRANSLATION; in each of these cases, ST is transferred into TL "without upsetting the syntactic order, or even the lexis" (1958/1995:31). Further reading: Vinay & Darbelnet 1958, 1958/1995.

Direction of Translation (or **Directionality**) A term which refers to whether translation occurs into or out of the translator's native language (or language of habitual use). While in past centuries the issue of direction of translation was not held to be of any importance, most translation activity is today geared towards translating into the translator's native language (see DIRECT TRANSLATION 2). The NAIROBI DECLARATION, for example, states that "a translator should, as far as possible, translate into his own mother tongue or into a language of which he or she has a mastery equal to that of his or her mother tongue" (Osers 1983:182). However, such issues as the availability of translators, the relative status of the two languages, the text-type involved and the translation's function and intended audience will inevitably play a rôle in determining whether a particular translation is performed into or out of the translator's first language. Furthermore, it should be pointed out that in certain countries (mainly in Central and Eastern Europe) the preferred direction of translation for INTERPRETING is out of the interpreter's language of habitual use. See also ETHNOLINGUISTIC MODEL OF TRANSLATION, INVERSE TRANSLA-TION and SERVICE TRANSLATION. Further reading: Beeby Lonsdale 1996; Kelly 1979.

Disambiguation See SEMANTIC DISAMBIGUATION.

Discourse-type Restricted Theories of Translation See TEXT-TYPE RESTRICTED THEORIES OF TRANSLATION.

Documentary Translation According to Nord (1991a), one of two types of translation defined according to how TT is intended to function in the target culture (see also INSTRUMENTAL TRANSLATION). A documentary translation is a translation which serves as "a document of [a source culture] communication between the author and the ST recipient" (1991a:72). Thus in this type of translation the TT recipient becomes a mere observer of a "past communicative action" (1991a:72), as ST (or possibly only certain aspects of ST) is reproduced without any attempt to make adjustments in the light of the target context. WORD-FOR-WORD and other types of LITERAL translation, as well as "exoticising translation", which tries to preserve the "local colour" of ST, are all examples of documentary translation; what all such types of translation have in common is that they focus on certain aspects or features of ST (e.g. its wording or grammatical structures, or the local colour which it contains), while ignoring others (1991a:73). While Nord's notions of documentary and instrumental translation are similar to House's (1977) OVERT and COVERT TRANSLATION, she points out that the assignment of a TT to one of her types is not simply dictated by the text-type which ST belongs to, as is the case with House's categories (1991a:72 n. 36). See also OBSERVATIONAL RECEIVER. Further reading: Nord 1988, 1991a, 1997.

Dolmetschen (**Interpreting**) (German) The standard German word for INTERPRETING. *Dolmetschen* has traditionally been used to denote the oral translation of spoken messages and to distinguish this process from that of *ÜBERSETZEN*, or written TRANSLATION. However, the existence of certain intermediate procedures along with the advent of modern recording techniques has caused the line between the two procedures to become blurred and has led to Kade (1968) suggesting alternative, more rigorous lines on which to define the term. According to Kade, the most important criterion should not be that the communication is spoken, but rather that the presentation of ST occurs only once and is immediately followed by the production of the finished TT. This means that *Dolmetschen* should be distinguished from *Übersetzen* in that the output from the former process can be neither corrected nor checked by the translator on a subsequent occasion (see CORRECTABILITY and VERIFIABILITY). Consequently the process of translating a written document at sight should be considered an example of *Dolmetschen* rather than *Übersetzen*. Further reading: Kade 1968, Reiss & Vermeer 1984.

Domesticating Translation (or **Domestication**) A term used by Venuti (1995) to describe the translation strategy in which a transparent, fluent style is adopted in order to minimize the strangeness of the foreign text for TL readers. Venuti traces the roots of the term back to Schleiermacher's famous notion of the translation which "leaves the reader in peace, as much as possible, and moves the author towards him" (Schleiermacher 1838/1963:47, 1838/1977:74; Venuti 1995:19-20). However, for Venuti the term *domestication* has negative connotations as it is identified with a policy common in dominant cultures which are "aggressively monolingual, unreceptive to the foreign", and which he describes as being "accustomed to fluent translations that invisibly inscribe foreign texts with [target language] values and provide readers with the narcissistic experience of recognizing their own culture in a cultural other" (1995:15). The notion of *invisibility* is important here, as this is the term used to describe the translator's rôle in preparing a TT likely to be acceptable in a culture where domesticating translation is standard; indeed, it is the translator's very invisibility which simultaneously "enacts and masks an insidious domestication of foreign texts" (1995:16-17). An approach based on domestication will thus involve such steps as the careful selection of texts which lend themselves to being translated in this manner, the conscious adoption of a fluent, natural-sounding TL style, the adaptation of TT to conform to target discourse types, the interpolation of explanatory material, the removal of SL REALIA and the general harmonization of TT with TL preconceptions and preferences. Venuti argues that domestication is the predominant translation strategy in Anglo-American culture, and that this is consistent with the asymmetrical literary relations which generally exist between this and other cultures. He further argues that, since domestication serves broader domestic agendas, it is necessary to challenge its domination by consciously adopting other translation strategies. See also FOREIGNIZING TRANSLATION and RESISTANCY. Further reading: Venuti 1995.

DTS See DESCRIPTIVE TRANSLATION STUDIES.

Dubbing A term used to refer to one of the two main techniques used in the translation of audio-visual material such as films and television programmes (see also SUBTITLING). The term *dubbing* is used in two ways. Firstly, it can refer to any technique of "covering the original voice in an audio-visual production by another voice" (Dries 1995:9). This broad definition has the advantage of including other types of *revoicing*, such as voice-over, narration or free commentary (Luyken et al. 1991:71). However, the term usually refers more narrowly to *lip-sync* dubbing, which is defined as the process in which "the foreign dialogue is adjusted to the mouth movements of the actor in the film" (Dries 1995:9) and which is designed to give the impression that the actors whom the audience sees are actually speaking in TL; this is the definition which will be used here. (It should be added that the term can also sometimes refer to occasions on which the original dialogue needs to be re-recorded in the same language.) Like subtitling, dubbing has until recently been largely ignored by the discipline of TRANSLATION STUDIES. This can be explained partly by the fact that dubbing is a process which involves many stages besides that of language transfer, so that a large number of additional factors (such as the use of up-to-date equipment, the choice of actors, the skill of the editor and standard of the sound engineering) also contribute to the quality of the dubbing (Dries 1995:12; see also Luyken et al. 1991:73-76, 78-79 for a detailed discussion of the mechanics of dubbing). A further, possibly more fundamental reason, suggested by Fawcett (1996:69), is the existence of the synchronization constraint, which can force dubbers to introduce major changes to the original wording simply in order to match sounds to lip movements (and indeed physical gestures: see Delabastita 1989:203). However, it would be wrong to think that the synchronization constraint is of overriding importance in all situations. Dubbing should not be seen as a rigid kind of PHONOLOGICAL TRANSLATION, in which ST is translated sound by sound. Rather it is more helpful to view it as an exercise in what has been termed *visual phonetics* (Fodor 1976:85), since the synchronization which is required needs to be visual rather than acoustic (Goris 1993:182). Furthermore, the level of synchronization needed in a particular shot will depend for example on the distance of the camera from the speaker (see Delabastita 1989:203). Thus Goris observes that even in close-up shots it is only ever necessary to match those consonants which require the mouth to be closed (i.e. labials and semi-labials), while in shots where the speaker's mouth is not clearly visible no synchronization is needed at all (1993:180-82). In a number of European countries, such as France, Germany, Italy and Spain, dubbing is the standard method of translating film and television (Dries 1995:10). However, there are perceived to be both advantages and disadvantages in using dubbing rather than subtitling. On the negative side, a dubbed film can be said to be less "authentic" than one with subtitles. Furthermore, dubbing is less flex-ible than subtitling in that it is harder to add explanations (Goris 1993:171). Finally, dubbing is considerably more expensive than subtitling and also takes longer to perform. On the other hand, an obvious advantage is that a dubbed film demands less cognitive effort from the viewer than one with subtitles (Delabastita 1989:205). Fur-thermore, dubbing generally involves less compression of the message than subtitling (Luyken et al. 1991:74). However, it is also some-times argued that the choice of dubbing over subtitles has "cultural, ideological and linguistic" implications, in that larger countries with basically monolingual cultures tend to prefer dubbing (Ballester 1995:159; see also Danan 1991). Furthermore, in certain societies dubbing is favoured for nationalistic reasons as a way of "naturaliz-ing" an imported film and at the same time somehow minimizing its foreign, possibly subversive influence by completely concealing the original dialogue; as an example of this Ballester describes how in Franco's Spain a policy was for many years in operation which pro-moted dubbing for those films which were screened as part of the permitted quota of foreign imports (1995:166-70; 175-77). Further reading: Danan 1991; Delabastita 1989, 1990; Dries 1995; Fawcett 1996; Gambier 1996; Goris 1993; Herbst 1994; Luyken et al. 1991; Whitman-Linsen 1992.

Dubrovnik Charter A Translators' Charter adopted by the F.I.T. in 1963 at the Fourth International Translators' Conference in Dub-rovnik. The general purpose of the Dubrovnik Charter was to delineate the responsibilities and rights of translators, and it included a number of important recommendations. It stressed the moral involvement of the translator in the translation and urged translators not to give a text an interpretation with which he or she did not agree; it also emphasized the need for FAITHFULNESS in translation, although distinguished between this and LITERALISM. Working conditions were also covered, and translators were adjured not to enter into unfair competition with each other. On the other hand, it affirmed that the translator should be the copyright holder of his or her work, and required that publishers should clearly mention the translator's name in the appropriate places, and should not make alterations to his or her work without permission (Haeseryn 1994:212-13). See also A.I.I.C. and NAIROBI DECLARATION. Further reading: Haeseryn 1994; Osers 1983.

Dynamics See DYNAMIC FIDELITY.

Dynamic Equivalence A term introduced by Nida (1964) in the context of Bible translation to describe one of two basic orientations found in the process of translation (see also FORMAL EQUIVALENCE). Dynamic equivalence is the quality which characterizes a translation in which "the message of the original text has been so transported into the receptor language that the response of the receptor is essentially like that of the original receptors" (Nida & Taber 1969/1982:200, emphasis removed). In other words, a dynamically equivalent translation is one which has been produced in accordance with the threefold process of ANALYSIS, TRANSFER 2 and RESTRUCTURING (Nida & Taber 1969/1982:200); formulating such a translation will entail such procedures as substituting TL items which are more culturally appropriate for obscure ST items, making linguistically implicit ST information explicit, and building in a certain amount of REDUNDANCY (1964:131) to aid comprehension. In a translation of this kind one is therefore not so concerned with "matching the receptor-language message with the source-language message"; the aim is more to "relate the receptor to modes of behavior relevant within the context of his own culture" (Nida 1964:159). Possibly the best known example of a dynamically equivalent solution to a translation problem is seen in the decision to translate the Biblical phrase "Lamb of God" into an Eskimo language as "Seal of God": the fact that lambs are unknown in polar regions has here led to the substitution of a culturally meaningful item which shares at least some of the important features of the SL expression (see Snell-Hornby 1988/1995:19). Nida & Taber argue that a "high degree" of equivalence of response is needed for the translation to achieve its purpose, although they point out that this response can never be identical with that elicited by the original (1969/1982:24). However, they also issue a warning about the limits within which the processes associated with producing dynamic equivalence remain valid: for example, a comparison with the broadly similar category of LINGUISTIC TRANSLATION 3 reveals that only elements which are *linguistically* implicit in ST – rather than any additional contextual information which might be necessary to a new audience – may legitimately be made explicit in TT. The notion of dynamic equivalence is of course especially relevant to Bible translation, given the particular need of Biblical translations not only to inform readers but also to present a relevant message to them and hopefully elicit a response (1969/1982:24). However, it can clearly also be applied to other genres, and indeed in many areas (such as literary translation) it has arguably come to hold sway over other approaches (Nida 1964:160). See also FUNCTIONAL EQUIVALENCE. Further reading: Gutt 1991; Nida 1964, 1995; Nida & Taber 1969/1982.

Dynamic Fidelity A term used by Beekman & Callow to describe a Bible translation which is "both natural in structure and meaningful in content" (1974:40). In other words, according to Beekman & Callow a dynamically faithful translation must firstly be characterized by the NATURALNESS of the TL forms and structures which it uses, and secondly must be easily understood by those who receive it. If these two criteria are met, then a translation is said to be preserving the *dynamics* of the original. Beekman & Callow also point out that such a translation will explicate information which is implicit in ST as and when the "stylistic and discourse structures" of TL require it (1974:60), and indeed, will also in appropriate circumstances do the reverse (1974:66). See also CULTURAL SUBSTITUTION, EXEGETICAL FIDELITY, FAITHFULNESS and IDIOMATIC TRANSLATION. Further reading: Beekman & Callow 1974.

Effort Models A term coined by Gile to refer to a set of models of the INTERPRETING process, which he developed in the late 1970s and early 1980s. The effort models represent an attempt to explain the considerable difficulties inherent in interpreting in a way that "should facilitate the selection and development of strategies and tactics toward better interpreting performance" (Gile 1995a:159); they are designed to account for the observed fact that interpreting errors are found not only in the output of beginners, but also that of experienced professionals. According to Gile, the act of interpreting consists of a number of *non-automatic* operations, each of which (unlike *automatic* operations) takes up a certain amount of the brain's limited processing capacity (1995a:161). Gile introduces the term *efforts* to refer to these individual components of the interpreting process, each of which makes its demands on the available processing capacity and thus occupies a share of the interpreter's attention. The first and most developed of the models concerns the process of SIMULTANEOUS INTERPRETING. According to Gile, this type of interpreting comprises a *listening and analysis effort* (or *comprehension effort*), which accounts for all mental operations aimed at deriving the meaning of ST, a *speech production effort*, which covers the various stages of TL output formulation, a *short-term memory effort*, which involves the operations which occur because of the time-lag between hearing and speaking, which may vary according to the difficulty of the speech being interpreted, and finally, a *co-ordination effort*, which regulates the way the interpreter's processing capacity is apportioned among the other three at any given moment (1995a:162-70). If at any point the total processing requirements of the various efforts exceed the available capacity then interpreting performance begins to deteriorate (1995a:161). Such a situation can be caused by a variety of "triggers", such as rapid or high-density speech, idiosyncratic linguistic usage, the occurrence of numbers or unfamiliar or short names, or simply a high level of incompatibility between SL and TL (1995a:172-74). Gile has also proposed effort models for other types of interpreting (and also for written translation). In the case of CONSECUTIVE INTER-PRETING, for example, he distinguishes two phases, the *listening and note-taking phase* and the *speech production phase* (1995a:178); the first of these consists of *listening and analysis*, *note-taking*, *short-term memory* and *co-ordination* efforts, and the second of *remembering*, *note-reading* and *production* efforts (1995a:178-83). Further reading: Gile 1985, 1988, 1995a, 1995b.

Emprunt See BORROWING.

Equivalence (or **Translation Equivalence**) 1 A term used by many writers to describe the nature and the extent of the relationships which exist between SL and TL texts or smaller linguistic units. As such, equivalence is in some senses the interlingual counterpart of synonymy within a single language, although Jakobson's famous slogan "equivalence in difference" (1959/1966:233) highlights the added complications which are associated with it. The issues lurking behind the term are indeed complex and the concept of equivalence has consequently been a matter of some controversy; Hermans, for example, has described it as a "troubled notion" (1995:217). Part of the problem stems from the fact that the term is also a standard polysemous English word, with the result that the precise sense in which *translation* equivalence is understood varies from writer to writer. For example, some commentators have by analogy with the mathematical notion of equivalence implied that translational equivalence – and consequently translation itself – is both symmetrical and reversible. Furthermore, it is in practice impossible to use the term with the level of precision assumed by some writers. Catford, for example, defines translation as the "replacement of textual material in one language (SL) by equivalent textual material in another language (TL)" (1965:20), and argues that one of the central tasks of translation theory is "that of defining the nature and conditions of translation equivalence" (1965:21). Catford's view of equivalence as something essentially quantifiable – and of translation as simply a matter of replacing each SL item with the most suitable TL equivalent, chosen from a list of all the potential equivalents – has been described as "an allegory of the limitations of linguistics at that time" (de Beaugrande 1978:11); similarly, according to Snell-Hornby such a view "presupposes a degree of symmetry between languages" (1988/1995:16) and even "distorts the basic problems of translation" (1988/1995:22), in that it reduces the translation process to a mere linguistic exercise, ignoring cultural, textual and other situational factors, which it is now agreed play an essential rôle in translation. This perception has led a number of scholars to subdivide the notion of equivalence in various ways. Thus some have distinguished between the equivalence found at the levels of different UNITS OF TRANSLATION, while others have formulated a number of complete equivalence typologies, such as Nida's (1964) influential DYNAMIC and FORMAL EQUIVALENCE, Kade's (1968) *total* (one-to-one), *facultative* (one-to-many), *approximative* (one-to-part) and *zero* (one-to-none) equivalence, Koller's (1979/1992, 1989) more wide-ranging *denotative, connotative, text-normative* (i.e. text type-based), *pragmatic* and *formal-aesthetic* equivalence, and Popovič's ([1976]) LINGUISTIC, PARADIGMATIC, STYLISTIC and TEXTUAL EQUIVALENCE 2. Each of these individual categories of equivalence encapsulates a particular type of ST-TT relationship, although few can be said to be complete in themselves, while some (for example dynamic and formal equivalence) are mutually exclusive; consequently, the term, which had originally been introduced in order to define translation scientifically, has become increasingly complex and fragmented. Many writers, seeing the difficulties which have been assailing the concept of equivalence, have suggested alternative, weaker notions, such as *similarity, analogy,* CORRESPONDENCE or *matching* (Hermans 1991:157). Toury, on the other hand, insists on viewing every translation as "a concrete act of performance" (1980:28; see PERFORMANCE) and proposes that each TT should be approached via the particular NORMS under which it was produced, arguing that these norms determine "the (type and extent of) equivalence manifested by actual translations" (1995:61).

Thus he turns the order of priorities on its head. Equivalence is no longer a set of criteria which translations have to live up to, but is rather the group of features (termed the *equivalence postulate*) which characterizes the particular relationships linking each individual TT with its ST: "when considered from TT's point of view, equivalence is not a postulated requirement, but an empirical fact, like TT itself" (1980:39). Similarly, in another area of TRANSLATION STUDIES, Reiss & Vermeer (1984) also reinterpret equivalence on the basis of each individual text, but, unlike Toury, in terms of function and communicative effect. For them, there are no particular features of ST which automatically need to be preserved in the translation process; however, they reserve the term *equivalence* for those instances in which ST and TT fulfil the same communicative function (1984: 139-40; see SKOPOS THEORY). See also ADEQUACY 1, DEGREE OF DIFFERENTIATION, FORMAL CORRESPONDENCE, FUNCTIONAL EQUIVALENCE, INDETERMINACY, INVARIANCE, SHIFTS, TEXTUAL EQUIVALENCE 1, TERTIUM COMPARATIONIS and TRANSLATABILITY. Further reading: van den Broeck 1978; Kade 1968; Koller 1979/1992, 1989; Pym 1992a; Reiss & Vermeer 1984; Sturrock 1991; Toury 1980; Turk 1990; Wilss 1977, 1982.

2 (French *Equivalence*) A term used by Vinay & Darbelnet (1958, 1958/1995) to refer to one of seven translation procedures. Equivalence is a kind of OBLIQUE translation, which means that it does not rely on the use of parallel categories existing in SL and TL (1958:46-47, 1958/1995:31). According to Vinay & Darbelnet, equivalence is a procedure which "replicates the same situation as in the original, whilst using completely different wording" (1958/1995:342). It is thus used for instance to translate fixed expressions such as idioms, proverbs or clichés where SL and TL units which bear little or no external resemblance are used to translate each other; thus for example English *like a bull in a china shop* would probably be translated into French as *comme un chien dans un jeu de quilles* (1958/1995:38). See also ADAPTATION 2, BORROWING, CALQUE, LITERAL TRANSLATION, MODULATION 1 and TRANSPOSITION. Further reading: Vinay & Darbelnet 1958, 1958/1995.

ESIT (Ecole Supérieure d'Interprètes et de Traducteurs) See INTERPRETIVE THEORY OF TRANSLATION.

Ethnographic Translation One of four classifications of translation proposed by Casagrande (1954). The aim of an ethnographic translation is to explicate the cultural background and anthropological significance of ST and the differences in meaning between "apparently equivalent elements of messages in the two languages" (1954:336); this may be achieved in the translation itself, or in explanatory annotations. Explication would also be needed, for example, on occasions when SL and TL contain terms which are analogous rather than equivalent (such as the German word *Schadenfreude* and English "pleasure in another's misfortune"), or when dealing with SL words which have no satisfactory TL equivalent (1954:336). See also AESTHETIC-POETIC TRANSLATION, LINGUISTIC TRANSLATION 2, PRAGMATIC TRANSLATION 2 and THICK TRANSLATION. Further reading: Casagrande 1954.

Ethnolinguistic Model of Translation A term used by Nida (1964) to describe the situation, common in Bible translation, in which the translator translates between two languages both of which he or she has acquired, namely the Greek or Hebrew of the original, and a modern, often non-Indo-European language. According to Nida, this situation usually requires the translator to work through his or her native language, which is usually English or another Western European language. Such a situation is of course less than ideal, although is frequently inevitable, since the knowledge which translators have of SL is rarely perfect, and has generally been acquired through grammars and bilingual dictionaries intended for speakers of the mediating language (1964:148). Translation in such a context is a particularly complex process, as the problems involved in translating between languages and cultures are intensified by the presence of a significant INTERTEMPORAL element; furthermore, the mediating language and culture will tend to exert an influence on the way in which TT takes shape. However, Nida argues that, while such "contamination" is virtually inevitable, the ultimate criterion for the success of this type of translation is the extent to which the response which it elicits in the target audience matches that of the original SL readers to ST (see DYNAMIC EQUIVALENCE). See also DIRECTION OF TRANSLATION. Further reading: Nida 1964.

Excluded Receiver A term used by Pym (1992b) to denote a reader (or listener) who is unable to participate in the message of a text because it is explicitly not addressed to him or her; the most obvious instance of this is when a document is written in an unknown language and is therefore clearly addressing a different audience. See also OBSERVATIONAL RECEIVER and PARTICIPATIVE RECEIVER. Further reading: Fawcett 1995; Pym 1992b.

Exegetic Translation Defined by Hervey & Higgins as "a style of translation in which the TT expresses and explains additional details that are not explicitly conveyed in the ST", or in other words one in which "the TT is, at the same time, an expansion and explanation of the contents of the ST" (1992:250). As such it contrasts sharply with the strategy of GIST TRANSLATION in terms of the amount of information that is conveyed. See also REPHRASING. Further reading: Hervey & Higgins 1992.

Exegetical Fidelity According to Beekman & Callow (1974), a term used to describe the principle of basing a translation strictly on a correct understanding of the original message. Beekman & Callow are Bible translators, and so for them the notion of correct *exegesis* – or determining the "meaning intended by the original author" (1974: 60) by means of a careful study of ST and of reference works such as lexicons, grammars and commentaries – is of central importance. The term is introduced in the context of a discussion of when information which is implicit in ST should be made explicit in TT. They argue that explication is not to be adopted at the whim of the translator, but is permissible only if the grammar, meanings or *dynamics* (see DYNAMIC FIDELITY) of TL require it "in order that the information conveyed will be the same as that conveyed to the original readers" (1974:58). Regarding the first of these three categories, information necessitated by the grammar of TL has to be expressed whether it is explicit in the original or not. As an example of this Beekman & Callow cite the fact that some languages have two first person plural pronouns, where one indicates that the speaker or writer is including those who are being addressed, and the other that they are excluded; when translating into such a language the translator is constantly required to make decisions about which pronoun to use, on the basis of the meaning of the original (1974:58-59). The second category – that of correcting wrong implications which may emerge in TT – involves problems which can be resolved not only by relying on correct exegesis but also by gauging the reaction of the TL audience. Finally, in line with the requirements of dynamic fidelity ST elements can be made explicit in the interests of resolving ambiguities and clarifying points which are obscure, but once again only as long as the information introduced is exegetically justifiable. See also FAITHFULNESS. Further reading: Beekman & Callow 1974.

Exoticism A term defined by Hervey & Higgins (1992) as the lowest degree of CULTURAL TRANSPOSITION. Linguistic and cultural features of ST are taken over into TT with little or no adaptation, so that TT has an obvious "foreign" appearance. This may be deliberate, in order to make TT more attractive to the TL audience, but it affects the TL audience in a way that ST did not affect the SL audience, for whom the text was in no way foreign (1992:30). See also CALQUE, COMMUNICATIVE TRANSLATION 3, CULTURAL BORROWING and CULTURAL TRANSPLANTATION. Further reading: Hervey & Higgins 1992.

Expectancy Norms A term used by Chesterman (1993) to refer to one of two types of translational NORM (see also PROFESSIONAL NORMS). According to Chesterman, expectancy norms are established by TT readers' expectations of what translations should be like and how they should compare or contrast with native texts (1993:9). Chesterman understands the function of norms as being not only to reflect translational practice but also to regulate it (1993:4); in this respect expectancy norms are the norms which govern the translation product rather than the process of production (1993:9). Expectancy norms are of a "higher-order" than professional norms (1993:9), and thus govern the form which these latter norms assume as professional translators will generally attempt to design TTs to conform with the relevant expectancy norms (1993:10). However, unlike professional norms, they are not validated by a "norm-authority" as such, but rather simply reflect the views, assumptions and expectations of the TL community (1993:10). Chesterman illustrates the relationship between expectancy and professional norms by positing a professional norm which might state that "in certain text types, source-language culture-bound terms should be expanded or explained in translation" (1993:14, emphasis removed); according to Chesterman, this would be governed by the corresponding expectancy norm which stated that "readers do not expect unknown concepts in a text of this type" (1993:14). Chesterman comments that the notion of expectancy norms is in many ways parallel with Nord's (1991b) concept of CONSTITUTIVE TRANSLATIONAL CONVENTIONS. Further reading: Chesterman 1993.

Explicitation A term introduced by Vinay & Darbelnet (1958, 1958/ 1995). Explicitation can be characterized in general terms as the phenomenon which frequently leads to TT stating ST information in a more explicit form than the original. Such a process is brought about by the translator filling out ST, for example by including additional explanatory phrases, spelling out implicatures or adding connectives to "help" the logical flow of the text and to increase readability. This process may be avowedly philanthropic, motivated by the translator's conscious desire to explain the meaning to the TT reader, or may sometimes simply be an inevitable result of the act of mediation. However, whatever the reason, the result is that "the translator simply expands the TL text, building into it a semantic redundancy absent in the original" (Blum-Kulka 1986:21). Commentators on translation have long been paying attention to the phenomenon, as can be seen for example in Güttinger's (1963) general observation that TTs tend to be longer than their originals, or Nida's claim that translated messages are more comprehensible if "drawn out" by the addition of a certain amount of REDUNDANCY (1964:131). However, it is only relatively recently that researchers have started taking serious notice of it. For example, Blum-Kulka (1986), in a study of cohesion and coherence in translation, finds a greater concentration of cohesive devices in translated text, *irrespective of differences between SL and TL* (1986:19); she concludes that "it might be the case that explicitation is a universal strategy inherent in the process of language mediation, as practiced by language learners, non-professional translators and professional translators alike" (1986:21). Similarly, Baker, commenting on explicitation of a rather different kind, cites the example of how a translator adds several lines explaining to Arab readers the significance of an allusion to American President Harry Truman (1992:246-8). Furthermore, on the stylistic level it has been pointed out by van Leuven-Zwart that "a limited degree of explicitness is characteristic of modern prose" (1990:81), so that a translator seeking to make a TT seem dated may well consider increasing the level of explicitness in the text. Toury posits the phenomenon as being one of a number of UNIVERSALS OF TRANSLATION (1980:60); however, serious investigation of this phenomenon has not yet progressed very far, although it is hoped that new avenues of research will be opened up through the study of computerized CORPORA. See also NORMS. Further reading: Baker 1992, 1993; Blum-Kulka 1986; Güttinger 1963; Levý 1965; Newman

1980; Toury 1980, 1995; Vinay & Darbelnet 1958, 1958/1995.

Expressive Texts (German *Expressive Texte*) (formerly **Form-focused Texts**; German *Formbetonte Texte*) A term used by Reiss (1977/1989) to refer to one of three main text-types (see also IN-FORMATIVE TEXTS and OPERATIVE TEXTS). According to Reiss, each text-type is identified by its semantic, lexical, grammatical and stylistic features (see Nord 1996:84), which influence the way a text is translated and also serve as a basis for translation criticism. In the case of each text-type, these features reflect the primary function which the text serves, and which, she argues, should be preserved in the translation. The major characteristic of texts of the expressive type is that they include an aesthetic component, as the author "exploits the expressive and associative possibilities of the language in order to communicate his thoughts in an artistic, creative way" (Reiss 1977/1989:109). This means that when translating such texts the main concern of the translator should be to try to produce an analogous aesthetic effect (Nord 1996:83), as well as reproducing the semantic content of the original. The expressive text-type is exemplified to different extents by poetry, novels and biographies. However, like the other text-types which she describes, it is not a watertight category, as many texts also contain a subsidiary function, as in the case for example of a didactic poem or a satirical novel (Reiss 1977/1989:111). See also MULTI-MEDIAL TEXTS and SKOPOS THEORY. Further reading: Nord 1996; Reiss 1971, 1976, 1977, 1977/1989; Reiss & Vermeer 1984; Zimmer 1981.

External Transfer See TRANSFER 1.

Extraneous Form A term suggested by Holmes (1988d) to describe one of four strategies for rendering verse form in TL. According to Holmes, the translator who opts for this approach "casts the metapoem [i.e. ST] into a form that is in no way implicit in either the form or the content of the original" (1988d:27). Holmes describes this strategy as "deviant" as it does not derive from the original poem in any way; he comments that it is often the favoured strategy of translators whose work can be described as IMITATION. See also ANALOGICAL FORM, CONTENT-DERIVATIVE FORM, FORM-DERIVATIVE FORMS, MAPPING, METAPOEM and MIMETIC FORM. Further reading: Holmes 1988d.

Faithfulness (or **Fidelity**) General terms used to describe the extent to which a TT can be considered a fair representation of ST according to some criterion; while a given writer will tend to consistently use either one term or the other, any distinction between the two would be artificial. In traditional discussions of translation the concept of fidelity has probably been the most basic and widely used yardstick for measuring translation quality; however, partly because of a certain in-built vagueness and partly because of a perceived emotiveness (Sager 1994:121) it has more recently been replaced by notions such as EQUIVALENCE, while these in turn are in many quarters now giving way to methodologies which do not rely so heavily on such concepts (see Snell-Hornby 1988/1995:13-22). Traditionally a faithful translation has been understood as one which bears a strong resemblance to its ST, usually in terms of either its LITERAL adherence to source meaning or its successful communication of the "spirit" of the original; not surprisingly therefore, the terms *fidelity* and *faithfulness* have frequently been used by writers on Bible translation. However, contemporary writers have made use of the terms in a number of different and often innovative ways. For Nida & Taber, for example, faithfulness is a property of a text which displays DYNAMIC EQUIVALENCE; a faithful translation is one which "evokes in a receptor essentially the same response as that displayed by the receptors of the original message" (1969/1982:201). This is an approach which is refined by Gutt, who defines faithfulness in terms of "resemblance in *relevant respects*" (1991:111), whether those be semantic, or purely formal as in the case of the verse by the German poet Morgenstern which he cites. Popovič appeals to the notion of faithfulness in order to justify the translator's use of SHIFTS, which according to him "do not occur because the translator wishes to 'change' a work, but because he strives to reproduce it as faithfully as possible and to grasp it in its totality, as an organic whole" (1970:80). Finally, Frawley advocates abandoning notions of fidelity and of good and bad translations, and suggests replacing the faithful/free dichotomy with one of *moderate* vs. *radical* (1984:173). See also ABUSIVE TRANSLATION, ACCURACY, DIDACTIC FIDELITY, DYNAMIC FIDELITY, EXEGETICAL FIDELITY, HISTORICAL FIDELITY and RESISTANCY. Further reading: Beekman & Callow 1974; Gile 1995a; Gutt 1991.

False Friends (or **Faux Amis**) A standard term used to describe SL and TL items which have the same or very similar form but different meanings, and which consequently give rise to difficulties in translation (and indeed interlingual communication in general). As stated by Wandruszka (1978), the phenomenon of false friends is caused by historical chance, as cognate words may have developed differently in closely related languages. While some false friends have meanings which are quite distinct in the two languages (for example English *to assist* and French *assister* "to be present", or English *sensible* as opposed to French *sensible* and German *sensibel* "sensitive"), the greatest danger of interference arises where the difference is more subtle (for instance English *grin* and the more restricted German *grinsen*). It should be added that sometimes false friends differ from each other only connotatively, as is the case with English *let us* and the more elevated German "equivalent" *lasst uns*. Although the existence of false friends is largely restricted to languages which are closely related, examples can also be found in languages which are much more distant. According to Wandruszka, if a TL false friend is used frequently enough in the SL sense it can eventually become a "true friend" by taking on that SL meaning in addition to its own (1978:228). Koller (1979/1992) notes that the process of translator training should include raising students' awareness of matters of interlingual interference, of which false friends are an important example. Further reading: Baker 1992; Vinay & Darbelnet 1958, 1958/1995; Wandruszka 1978.

Faux Amis See FALSE FRIENDS.

Fictitious Translation See PSEUDOTRANSLATION 1.

Fidelität See COHERENCE.

Fidelity See FAITHFULNESS.

F.I.T. (International Federation of Translators, French *Fédération Internationale des Traducteurs*) An association of translators' organizations founded in Paris in 1953. Translators had begun to form their own associations after World War II, and the charter establishing F.I.T. was signed by pioneer societies of translators from France, West Germany, Italy, Norway, Denmark and Turkey. F.I.T. was authorized to operate as an international association by a ministerial order of 18 March 1954. In 1955, the journal *Babel* started to appear as the official organ of the federation. In 1963, the DUBROVNIK CHAR-TER was adopted; it contained directives and recommendations on the rights and duties of translators, and thus contributed to the recognition of translation as a distinct and autonomous profession. See also A.I.I.C.. Further reading: Haeseryn 1994; Osers 1983.

Foreignizing Translation (or **Minoritizing Translation**) A term used by Venuti (1995) to designate the type of translation in which a TT is produced which deliberately breaks target conventions by retaining something of the foreignness of the original. Venuti sees the origin of such a concept in Schleiermacher, who discusses the type of translation in which "the translator leaves the author in peace, as much as possible, and moves the reader towards him" (Schleiermacher 1838/1963:47, 1838/1977:74; Venuti 1995:19). Commenting that Schleiermacher viewed this as the preferred translation strategy, Venuti proposes its adoption in "aggressively mono-lingual" cultures (such as the Anglo-American) where the standard approach is that of DOMESTICATING TRANSLATION. Adopting the strategy in this way would represent "a strategic cultural intervention in the current state of world affairs" (Venuti 1995:20), as it would challenge the mentality of the dominant culture which sought to suppress the foreignness (or "otherness") of translated texts. Describing foreignizing translation as an "ethnodeviant pressure" (1995:20), Venuti thus sees its rôle as being to "register the linguistic and cultural difference of the foreign text, sending the reader abroad" (1995:20). In concrete terms such a strategy would entail not only a freedom from absolute obedience to target linguistic and textual constraints, but also where appropriate the selection of a non-fluent, opaque style and the deliberate inclusion of SL REALIA or TL ARCHAISMS; the cumulative effect of such features would be to provide TL readers with an "alien reading experience" (1995:20). However, since even the construction of the foreign "depends on domestic cultural materials" (1995:29), Venuti concedes that foreignizing translations are "equally partial [as domesticating translations] in their interpretation of the foreign text", yet points out that they "tend to flaunt their partiality instead of concealing it" (1995:34). Examples of a foreignizing strategy in English include many of Ezra Pound's translations, and Nabokov's (1964/1975) famous LITERAL translation of Pushkin's *Eugene Onegin*. See also ABUSIVE TRANSLATION and RESISTANCY. Further reading: Venuti 1995.

Form-derivative Forms A general term devised by Holmes (1988d) to refer to the two strategies of verse form translation which he terms ANALOGICAL FORM and MIMETIC FORM. When using a form-derivative approach the translator selects a target verse form which in some way reflects that of ST; thus these two strategies are distinguished from those denoted by the terms CONTENT-DERIVATIVE FORM and EXTRANEOUS FORM. See also BLANK VERSE TRANSLATION, MAPPING, METAPOEM, METRICAL TRANSLATION and RHYMED TRANSLATION. Further reading: Holmes 1988d.

Form-focused Texts (German *Formbetonte Texte*) See EXPRESSIVE TEXTS.

Formal Correspondence According to Catford's model, a formal relationship which exists when a TL category can be found which occupies "the 'same' place in the 'economy' of the TL as the given SL category occupies in the SL" (1965:27). In contrast to TEXTUAL EQUIVALENCE 1, this is a theoretical, systemic category which is established on the basis of a formal comparison of SL and TL. Because of inevitable incompatibilities between the systems of the two languages, formal correspondence is nearly always approximate rather than absolute, although it is easier to establish at higher levels of linguistic abstraction. For example, both French and English are languages which operate with grammatical units at five ranks (sentence, clause, group, word and morpheme); it is consequently reasonable to say that there is formal correspondence between these two hierarchies of units, even though not every instance of one rank in one language will be translated by an item of the same rank in the other. However, it is important not to confuse similar grammatical nomenclature with formal correspondence; thus for example, the term *gerund* denotes different word-classes in Russian and Latin, while to some extent the English category of indefiniteness and Russian sentence-final position can be said to be formal correspondents of each other. In a development of Catford's idea, Ivir (1969, 1981), who approaches the concept from the discipline of contrastive linguistics, argues that formal correspondence between SL and TL items should be seen as a one-to-many relationship which can only be posited on the basis of an examination of pairs of "translationally equivalent" texts (1981:55). It should also be noted that the term *formal correspondence* is used by Nida & Taber (1969/1982) to refer to what

they elsewhere term FORMAL EQUIVALENCE. See also CORRESPOND-
ENCE and EQUIVALENCE. Further reading: Catford 1965.

Formal Equivalence (or **Formal Correspondence**) Defined by Nida
as one of "two different types of equivalence" (see also DYNAMIC
EQUIVALENCE), which "focuses attention on the message itself, in
both form and content" (1964:159). Formal equivalence is thus the
"quality of a translation in which the features of the form of the
source text have been mechanically reproduced in the receptor
language" (Nida & Taber 1969/1982:201). Nida proposed his catego-
risation in the context of Bible translation, and in many respects it
offers a more useful distinction than the more traditional notions of
FREE and LITERAL translation (Hatim & Mason 1990:7). The aim of a
translator who is striving for formal equivalence is to allow ST to
speak "in its own terms" rather than attempting to adjust it to the
circumstances of the target culture; in practice this means, for example,
using FORMAL rather than FUNCTIONAL EQUIVALENTS wherever
possible, not joining or splitting sentences, and preserving formal
indicators such as punctuation marks and paragraph breaks (Nida
1964:165). The frequent result of such strategies is of course that,
because of differences in structure between SL and TL, a translation
of this type "distorts the grammatical and stylistic patterns of the
receptor language, and hence distorts the message" (Nida & Taber
1969/1982:201). For this reason it is frequently necessary to include
explanatory notes to help the target reader (Nida 1964:166). Like its
converse, dynamic equivalence, formal equivalence represents a
general orientation rather than an absolute technique, so that between
the two opposite extremes there are any number of intervening grades,
all of which represent acceptable methods of translation (1964:160).
However, a general tendency towards formal rather than dynamic
equivalence is characterized by, for example, a concern for accuracy
(1964:159) and a preference for retaining the original wording
wherever possible. In spite of its apparent limitations, however, formal
equivalence is sometimes the most appropriate strategy to follow:
besides frequently being chosen for translating Biblical and other
sacred texts, it is also useful for BACK-TRANSLATION and for when the
translator or interpreter may for some reason be unwilling to accept
responsibility for changing the wording of TT (see Hatim & Mason
1990:7). It should be noted that when Nida & Taber (1969/1982)
discuss this concept they use the term *formal correspondence* to refer

to it. See also GLOSS TRANSLATION. Further reading: Nida 1964; Nida & Taber 1969/1982; Tymoczko 1985.

Formal Equivalent A term used by Nida (1964) to refer to a TL item which represents the closest decontextualized counterpart to a word or phrase in SL. Clearly, not all items in one language will have formal equivalents in another, for example because many apparent equivalents in fact refer to objects which are subtly different (as is for example the case with words for *bread* even in different Western European languages), and also because many words refer to cultural or geographical phenomena which do not necessarily have any equivalent in other languages (1964:167; see also REALIA and VOIDS for examples). Nida argues that, in a translation which is aiming for a high degree of FORMAL rather than DYNAMIC EQUIVALENCE, there will be a tendency to use formal equivalents wherever possible, even in contexts like those described above. This will of course frequently result in a translation which is not easily understood, and which will need to be supplemented, for example by means of footnotes. An example of this would be if the Western European use of the word *heart* to represent the seat of the emotions were transposed into another language where a different part of the body (such as the *liver* or *abdomen*) normally served that function (adapted from Nida 1964:172). Nida points out that certain ST elements, such as puns and other strictly formal features, will almost inevitably lie beyond the reach of formal equivalents (1964:165). See also FUNCTIONAL EQUIVALENT. Further reading: Nida 1964.

Forward-transformation See RESTRUCTURING.

Free Translation A type of translation in which more attention is paid to producing a naturally reading TT than to preserving the ST wording intact; also known as SENSE-FOR-SENSE TRANSLATION, it contrasts with LITERAL and WORD-FOR-WORD TRANSLATION. Linguistically it can be defined as a translation "made on a level higher than is necessary to convey the content unchanged while observing TL norms" (Barkhudarov 1969:11, translated). In other words, the UNIT OF TRANSLATION in a free translation might be anything up to a sentence (or more) even if the content of the ST in question could be reproduced satisfactorily by translating on the word or group level. Furthermore, according to Catford it is a prerequisite of free translations that they should also be UNBOUNDED (1965:25) as regards the rank (or level) on which they are performed. Free translations are thus generally more "TL-oriented" than literal translations. The free/ literal dichotomy is probably the one most frequently encountered in traditional accounts of translation; however, it has been developed in various ways. For example, some writers have redefined the contrast in different terms without significantly altering the underlying concepts: e.g. Nida's (1964) DYNAMIC and FORMAL EQUIVALENCE. Others have suggested alternative contrasts based on related though different notions: e.g. House's (1977) COVERT and OVERT TRANSLATION, Gutt's (1991) DIRECT TRANSLATION 3 and INDIRECT TRANSLATION 2 or Toury's (1980, 1995) ACCEPTABILITY and ADEQUACY 2. A third tendency has been to attempt to get away from binary contrasts altogether: e.g. Dryden's (1680/1989) IMITATION 1, METAPHRASE and PARAPHRASE. Some writers have furthermore chosen to side-step the issue, an approach which is probably most strongly associated with TARGET TEXT-ORIENTED TRANSLATION STUDIES. However, it is generally agreed nowadays that free and literal translation do not form a binary contrast, and that the most appropriate translation strategy will vary according to the text-type being translated and the purpose of the translation (see for example SKOPOS THEORY). See also IDIOMATIC TRANSLATION, PRESCRIPTIVE TRANSLATION STUDIES and SENSE-FOR-SENSE TRANSLATION. Further reading: Catford 1965.

Full Translation According to Catford's model, a term used to refer to the kind of translation in which the entire text is translated, or in other words, "every part of the SL text is replaced by TL text material" (1965:21). Such a TT will consequently contain no SL elements at all, whether extended passages or single lexical items. See also PARTIAL TRANSLATION. Further reading: Catford 1965.

Function-oriented Translation Studies (or Function-oriented Descriptive Translation Studies) Defined by Holmes (1988e) as one of three types of DESCRIPTIVE TRANSLATION STUDIES. This approach is concerned with analyzing the function of translations in the context of the recipient cultural and social setting, and typically addresses such questions as which texts were or were not selected for translation by a particular culture, and what influences were exerted as a result of such selection. Greater systematizing of this area might possibly lead to the establishment of *translation sociology* as a separate field of study (1988e:72). See also PROCESS-ORIENTED TRANSLATION STUDIES and PRODUCT-ORIENTED TRANSLATION STUDIES. Further reading: Holmes 1988e.

Functional Equivalence A term used to refer to the type of EQUIVALENCE reflected in a TT which seeks to adapt the function of the original to suit the specific context in and for which it was produced. According to Gutt, the function that a text is intended to fulfil is now probably the "most widely accepted frame of reference for translation equivalence" (1991:10). However, while the term is used by a number of writers, it is perhaps defined most systematically by House (1977). House's aim is to develop a methodology for assessing translation quality, and so her concept of functional equivalence is basically evaluative. She presents (1977:42) a detailed, "multi-dimensional" analysis of text function in which she distinguishes three dimensions of linguistic usage relating to the language user (*geographical origin, social class* and *time*), and five reflecting language use (*medium, participation, social rôle relationship, social attitude* and *province,* or general area of discourse). Using this framework it is possible to build up a "text profile" for both ST and TT, and House argues that a translated text "should not only match its source text in function, but employ equivalent situational-dimensional means to achieve that function" (1977:49). This means that there should be a high level of matching between ST and TT in the dimensions which are particularly relevant to the text in question if TT is to be considered functionally equivalent to ST (1977:49). Within House's wider model, functional equivalence is only attainable in cases of COVERT TRANSLATION (1977: 204), although even here it is difficult to achieve "because differences of the socio-cultural norms have to be taken into account" (1977:205). However, according to Gutt, problems remain in the case of texts which possess more than one function (1991:10); indeed, it would be extremely difficult to construct a model which could accommodate such texts. It should be noted that the term *functional equivalence* is also used by de Waard & Nida (1986) to replace what Nida elsewhere refers to as DYNAMIC EQUIVALENCE; according to de Waard & Nida, the new term is less open to misinterpretation, and its use serves to "highlight the communicative functions of translating" (1986:viii). Further reading: Gutt 1991; House 1977; de Waard & Nida 1986.

Functional Equivalent According to Nida (1964), a TL item chosen to translate an ST word or phrase not for its formal similarity to this ST item but because it offers target readers a clearer understanding of the contextual meaning of the original. Such a translation might be settled upon either in preference to a more LITERAL translation, or because no such phenomenon – and hence no FORMAL EQUIVALENT – exists in TL. Nida cites the example of how people to whom the concept of *snow* was unknown might have a phrase such as *white as kapok down*, which could be used as a functional equivalent of the English *white as snow* (1964:171). Use of functional rather than formal equivalents (with or without the formal equivalent being supplied in a footnote) tends to be a feature of translations which aim for a high degree of DYNAMIC EQUIVALENCE (1964:172). Further reading: Nida 1964.

Games, Translation and the Theory of A concept based on a parallel between the translation process and the activity of game-playing originally suggested by Wittgenstein, who includes "translating from one language into another" (1953: I: 23) in a list of examples of language games. However, the idea was first exploited in a discussion specifically devoted to translation by Levý (1967). In the course of his analysis of TRANSLATION AS DECISION-MAKING, Levý draws on the concepts of game theory invented by Luce & Raiffa (1957), and applies them to the process of translation in order to highlight the nature of the decisions which a translator typically has to make when translating a literary text. On the basis of the earlier work Levý distinguishes two basic types of game, respectively typified by chess and card-games, and argues that translation resembles the former, since "every succeeding move is influenced by the knowledge of previous decisions and by the situation which resulted from them" (1967:1172). In this way, each time a decision is made the translator creates the context for a number of subsequent decisions. One further important parallel between the translation process and this type of game (termed *games with complete information*) is that, while the decisions are non-random, they may still be inspired by subjective preferences (Gorlée 1986:99). Levý argues that an analysis of the hierarchy of the translational decisions contained in a given TT will cast light on the "degree of importance of various elements in the literary work" (1967:1172). Gorlée describes the translation process as "a kaleidoscopic, never-ending game of creative mental skill" (1986:103); however, in contrast to Levý she argues that translation is more akin to assembling a jigsaw than to a game of chess (although with the one significant difference that in translation there is no one pre-existing solution which needs to be discovered). See also MAP-PING. Further reading: Gorlée 1986, 1994; Levý 1967.

Gaps See VOIDS.

***Gemeinte, Das* (Intended Meaning)** See TERTIUM COMPARATIONIS.

General Theories of Translation A term used by Holmes (1988e) to refer to one of two branches of THEORETICAL TRANSLATION STUD-IES (see also PARTIAL THEORIES OF TRANSLATION). A general theory of translation is defined as "a full, inclusive theory accommodating so many elements that it can serve to explain and predict all phenom-ena falling within the terrain of translating and translation, to the exclusion of all phenomena falling outside it" (1988e:73). Given the diverse, multifaceted nature of the discipline of TRANSLATION STUD-IES, it is understandable that such a theory "will necessarily be highly formalized and ... also highly complex" (1988e:73). Such a theory (if it is attainable at all) has yet to be arrived at; as Holmes points out, although a number of possible candidates have from time to time been proposed, they are all strictly speaking either a) merely a dis-cussion of some of the initial considerations which such a theory will need to take account of, or b) a list of axioms or hypotheses which either fail to explain all the phenomena associated with translation or take in other phenomena besides, or c) simply too partial or specific to be considered as general theories (1988e:73). See also PURE TRANSLATION STUDIES and TRANSLATION THEORY. Further reading: Holmes 1988e.

Generalization 1 (or **Modulation/Generalization**) A term used in van Leuven-Zwart's (1989, 1990) model for comparing a literary text with its translation. Generalization is defined as the type of MODU-LATION 2 in which the dissimilarity between ST and TT TRANSEMES is characterized by a SHIFT towards greater generality in TT; as such it contrasts with the opposite phenomenon of SPECIFICATION. See also ARCHITRANSEME, INTEGRAL TRANSLATION, MODIFICATION and MU-TATION. Further reading: van Leuven-Zwart 1989, 1990.

   2 See GENERALIZING TRANSLATION.

Generalizing Translation (or **Generalization**) A term used by

Hervey & Higgins (1992) to describe a situation where TL uses an expression which is wider and less specific than the SL expression it translates, as is for example the case when translating English *daughters* by French *filles*: *filles* is less specific than *daughters*, since it could also mean *girls*. According to Hervey & Higgins, generalizing translation is acceptable if TL has no suitable alternative, or if the omitted detail may be gleaned from the TT context or is just not important (1992:95). However, they consider this strategy unacceptable in circumstances contrary to the above, or if the omitted detail cannot be COMPENSATED for elsewhere in TT (1992:95-96). See also OVERLAPPING TRANSLATION, PARTICULARIZING TRANSLATION and UNDERTRANSLATION. Further reading: Hervey & Higgins 1992.

Gist Translation A term common in discussions of translation, and used by Hervey & Higgins to refer to "a style of translation in which the TT expresses a condensed version of the contents of the ST" (1992:250); in other words, a gist translation is one which provides "a synopsis of the ST" (1992:250). Within Hervey & Higgins' framework gist translation contrasts with EXEGETIC TRANSLATION in terms of the amount of detail which it provides. See also REPHRASING. Further reading: Hervey & Higgins 1992.

Gloss Translation According to Nida, the kind of translation in which the translator tries "to reproduce as literally and meaningfully as possible the form and content of the original" (1964:159). As such, gloss translation typifies the approach usually associated with FORMAL EQUIVALENCE. Nida points out that the production of such a WORD-FOR-WORD translation will probably necessitate the inclusion of numerous footnotes in order to make the text comprehensible to the TL reader. A gloss translation might be of use as a study aid, and has the advantage of giving the TL reader deeper insight into elements of source language and culture (1964:159). See also INTERLINEAR TRANSLATION. Further reading: Nida 1964.

Glücken See SUCCESS.

Goal Language See TARGET LANGUAGE.

Grammatical Analysis See ANALYSIS.

Grammatical Translation Defined by Catford as a type of RE-
STRICTED TRANSLATION in which "the SL grammar of a text is replaced
by equivalent TL grammar, but with no replacement of lexis"
(1965:71). For example, the English sentence *This is the man I saw*
might be grammatically translated into French as *Voici le man que
j'ai see-é*; here everything except the two lexical items (*man* and *see*)
is replaced by French equivalents (1965:71). It should be noted that
grammatical and LEXICAL translation are the converse of each other,
since grammatical translation from language A into language B arrives
at the same result as lexical translation in the other direction. See also
GRAPHOLOGICAL TRANSLATION and PHONOLOGICAL TRANSLATION.
Further reading: Catford 1965.

Grammatical Transposition A term used by Hervey & Higgins to
refer to "the replacement or reinforcement of given parts of speech in
the ST by other parts of speech in the TT, whenever this is made
necessary by significant differences of syntactic configuration between the SL and the TL" (1992:200). For example, in translating *Je
persiste à croire qu'ils ont raison* as *I still think they're right*, the
adverb *still* is used in TT to convey what is expressed in ST by the
verb *persiste*. Hervey & Higgins point out that while they use the
term *grammatical* transposition in order to distinguish the phenomenon from CULTURAL TRANSPOSITION, some other writers refer to
it simply as TRANSPOSITION. Further reading: Hervey & Higgins 1992.

Graphological Translation According to Catford (1965), a type of
RESTRICTED TRANSLATION. Catford argues that it is possible to reduce
letters (or other graphological units such as ideograms) to a description
in terms of a number of distinctive features. Thus for example, all the
letters of the Roman and Cyrillic alphabets can be seen as consisting
of a number of vertical, horizontal, oblique and semicircular
components. On the basis of such a description, it is possible to set up
EQUIVALENCE relations between letters from these two alphabets. For
instance, the Russian word СПУТПИК can be graphologically
translated into the Roman form CHYTHNK by substituting Cyrillic
letters not with their nearest Roman sound equivalents, but with
those Roman letters which most closely resemble them *in appearance*. An approximation to graphological translation is sometimes
practised by typographers in order to give a text an "exotic"
flavour; instances of this are particularly common in advertising.

See also GRAMMATICAL TRANSLATION, LEXICAL TRANSLATION, PHONOLOGICAL TRANSLATION and TRANSLITERATION. Further reading: Catford 1965.

Hermeneutic Motion A model introduced by Steiner (1975/1992) to describe the process of literary translation. Considering the act of translation in the context of human communication across barriers of language, culture, time and personality, Steiner subdivides the "hermeneutic motion" represented by the translation process into four stages (or *moves*); throughout his argument he famously eschews a fixed terminology, preferring a multiple designation of each stage. The first move is termed *trust* or *faith*, and consists of the translator's assumption that ST contains "a sense to be extracted and retrieved ... into and via his own speech" (1975/1992:372); although this is generally an instantaneous, unconscious action, Steiner argues that it represents a vital assumption which underlies every act of translation. Next comes *aggression, penetration* or *decipherment*, in which the translator "invades, extracts and brings home" (1975/1992:314) the meaning of the original. Steiner here refers to St. Jerome's image of the ST meaning being led home captive by the translator; the imagery of aggression is appropriate, he argues, because "decipherment is dissective, leaving the shell smashed and the vital layers stripped" (1975/1992:314). The third move is termed *incorporation, embodiment* or *appropriative use*. "Acts of translation add to our means" (1975/1992:315) by introducing new elements into the target linguistic and cultural system. Furthermore, such importation frequently brings change: "no language, no traditional symbolic set or cultural ensemble imports without risk of being transformed" (1975/1992:315). Steiner elucidates the stage of *incorporation* by means of two images: such an intake of new elements into the system can be viewed in terms of either receiving the sacrament or becoming infected. Such an action, however, causes a disequilibrium within the system, which can only be rectified by the fourth and final stage, which is termed *compensation, restitution* or *fidelity*. Here, since an act of plunder has taken place, Steiner argues that both the translator *and the translation* need to make recompense: "translation fails where it does not compensate" (1975/1992:417). Translations commonly misrepresent their STs by either failing to do justice to all the aspects of the original, or by augmenting the original's effect; the translator needs to be aware of this and attempt to rectify TT's imbalances. On one level this process is of course linguistic: "translators must now work to restore in their own language what they failed to recover from the original text" (Leighton 1991:23). However, Steiner presents the translator's task almost as one of moral obligation to the original: "The translator ... is *faithful to* his text, makes his response responsible, only when he endeavours to restore the balance of forces, of integral presence, which his appropriative comprehension has disrupted" (1975/ 1992:318, emphasis original). In this way Steiner suggests an alternative to the traditional linking of the notion of FAITHFULNESS to the FREE/LITERAL dichotomy. The *translation*, on the other hand, may be said to compensate the original by bringing it to life in a new cultural context: "Translation recompenses in that it can provide the original with a persistence and geographical-cultural range of survival which it would otherwise lack" (1975/1992:416). It is in this final stage that Steiner's ultimately philosophical aims are most clear: while his scheme does relate to individual acts of translation, his main concern is with the elucidation of the nature of translation in the light of broader philosophical, cultural and even metaphysical considerations. Further reading: Kelly 1979; Leighton 1991; Steiner 1975/1992.

Hierarchy of Correspondences Defined by Holmes (1988b) as the order of priorities set up by the translator, who has to decide which ST features to "preserve" in TT, possibly at the expense of other features. Holmes argues that what is achieved in a translation – and particularly in the case of literary translation – is "not textual *equivalence* in any strict sense of the term, but a network of *correspondences*, or *matchings*, with a varying closeness of *fit*" (1988g:101). He lists various kinds of CORRESPONDENCE, such as formal, semantic or functional (1988g:101), which can form the basis of a translation solution. However, as he points out, the translator finds that "the choice of a specific kind of correspondence in connection with one feature of the source-text map determines the kind of correspondence available for another" (1988b:86). For this reason the translator establishes a *hierarchy of correspondences*, by giving priority, for example, to a strict *formal* correspondence and as a result having to reduce correspondence requirements in regard to the semantic content. According to Holmes, while semantic correspondence receives priority in many less complex texts, the establishment of a hierarchy of correspondence for literary texts is much more difficult (1988b:86). See also MAPPING. Further reading: Holmes 1988b.

Historical Fidelity A term used by Beekman & Callow (1974) to refer to one of two complementary principles of fidelity which should guide the translation of Biblical texts (see also DIDACTIC FIDELITY). Historical fidelity is defined as the strategy of not transplanting historical narratives into a target setting, and is based on the conviction that the Christian faith is rooted in history. Beekman & Callow thus argue that "objects, places, persons, animals, customs, beliefs, or activities which are part of a historical statement must be translated in such a way that the same information is communicated by the translation as by the original statements" (1974:35). The principle of historical fidelity can be violated by the inappropriate use of CULTURAL SUBSTITUTION (1974:203). As pointed out by Gutt, it should be noted that the principle of historical fidelity does not follow so much from TRANSLATION THEORY as from the "high importance attached to matters of history in the Christian faith" (1991:114-15). See also FAITHFULNESS. Further reading: Beekman & Callow 1974.

Homophonic Translation See PHONEMIC TRANSLATION.

Horizontal Translation A term coined by Folena (1973/1991) to refer to one of two types of translation used in the Middle Ages (see also VERTICAL TRANSLATION). Folena defines horizontal translation as translation "between languages with a similar structure and a strong cultural affinity" (1973/1991:13, translated). In other words, in horizontal translation both SL and TL have a similar value as languages in that neither has any special prestige. Thus translation from Provençal into Italian, or Norman French into English, would both be examples of this particular strategy since all of these languages are vernaculars (see Bassnett 1980/1991:52). Horizontal translation, however, is also characterized by a blurring of the distinction between translation, IMITATION, unacknowledged borrowing and original creation; this is because, as Bassnett points out, "originality of material was not greatly prized and an author's skill consisted in the reworking of established themes and ideas" (1980/1991:53). Further reading: Bassnett 1980/1991; Folena 1973/1991.

Hyperinformation (German *Hyperinformation*) Defined by Reiss & Vermeer (1984) as information which is interpolated by the interpreter in order to compensate for the hearer's possible lack of any cultural background knowledge which is necessary for a proper understanding of the message. Further reading: Reiss & Vermeer 1984.

IA See INFORMATION OFFER.

Identity One of a series of terms used to refer to the way ST and TT meaning (and other features) relate to each other. However, identity contrasts with such notions as ADEQUACY, CORRESPONDENCE, EQUIVALENCE and INVARIANCE in that it implies a much closer relationship than these other terms. For this reason most writers have shied away from using the term. Nida & Taber, for example, distinguish between identity and equivalence, and argue that the translator should strive for the latter rather than the former, as for them identity implies "conservation of the form of the utterance", rather than "reproduction of the message" of the original (1969/1982:12). Wilss also objects to the term, since its use can lead to the mistaken impression that linguistic communication is "computable in a rigorous mathematical sense" (1982:152). Frawley, who understands identity as "exactness in recoding" (1984:163), argues that it can only exist in trivial cases (1984:163). Interlingual identity cannot be equated with absolute synonymy, as the meaning of items belonging to a given linguistic system depends just as much on their relationships with other items in the system as it does on those with the reality which is being represented (1984:163). Frawley also discusses the possible relevance to interlingual identity of linguistic universals – or features of language which are thought to be present in all human languages – and concludes that their existence can only establish "point-to-point identity" (1984:166), while their use in translation "has the effect of changing translation into copying across codes" (1984:166). Thus Frawley concludes that "identity may be granted across linguistic codes, but this identity is actually useless in translation" (1984:167). See also FORMAL CORRESPONDENCE. Further reading: Frawley 1984.

Idiomatic Translation (or **Idiomatic Approach**) A term used by Beekman & Callow (1974) in the field of Bible translation, and by Larson (1984) more generally, to refer to a translation strategy which aims for a TT which reads as naturally as possible. The approach is similar to that of DYNAMIC EQUIVALENCE, in that it stresses the importance of reproducing the original's impact on the target audience. An idiomatic translation is thus defined as one "which has the same meaning as the source language but is expressed in the natural form of the receptor language", and one in which "the meaning, not the form, is retained" (Larson 1984:10, emphasis removed). The aim of such a meaning-based method is to reproduce the same message for a new audience in the form of a translation which reads like a text originally composed in TL. This is achieved not only by careful linguistic reformulation and paraphrase, but also by paying close attention to the need to make explicit for target readers information which, for example, was generally available to the source audience and thus only implicitly contained in ST. This is, however, a high aim, and Gutt argues that it will only meet with limited success, since it fails to take full account of the "inferential nature of communication and its strong dependence on context" (1991:99). See also FREE TRANSLATION and NATURALNESS. Further reading: Beekman & Callow 1974; Larson 1984.

Idiomaticity See IDIOMATIC TRANSLATION.

Imitation 1 According to the seventeenth century writer Dryden, one of three possible methods of translating. Dryden uses the term *imitation* to refer to what is otherwise known as FREE TRANSLATION; he does not invent the term himself, but rather borrows it from Cowley, whose (1656/1905) translations of the Greek poet Pindar's *Odes* are cited as an example of the procedure. Dryden characterizes the approach as a process in which the translator "assumes the liberty, not only to vary from the words and sense, but to forsake them both as he sees occasion" (1680/1989:8). Indeed, for Dryden this process represents such extreme deviation from the original that he questions whether it can with any legitimacy be thought of as translation at all; instead, he likens it to creating a variation on a theme or giving a present when what is expected is the repayment of a debt. Yet Dryden's view of imitation is clearly somewhat ambivalent, as he concedes that Cowley's translations of Pindar are not as extreme in practice as his theoretical depiction may suggest, and even states that in the case of such a difficult and idiosyncratic writer as Pindar imitation was the only possible technique to adopt. However, while Dryden acknowledges that the practice of imitation can allow the "translator" to show himself advantageously by creating something new, he in general views it as "the greatest wrong which can be done to the memory and reputation of the dead" (1680/1989:10). See also METAPHRASE and PARAPHRASE. Further reading: Dryden (1680/1989); Frost 1955.

2 According to Lefevere (1975), one of two sub-types of the translation strategy which he terms INTERPRETATION. In all, Lefevere describes seven different strategies for translating poetry on the basis of his analysis of different English translations of a single poem by the Roman writer Catullus. Strictly speaking, however, Lefevere does not consider imitation – or VERSION 2, the other sub-type of inter- pretation – to be translation at all. He accordingly defines imitation as the creation of a "new" poem, which "has only title and point of departure, if those, in common with the source text" (1975:76). Thus ST will simply serve as a source of inspiration for the imitation- writer, who produces a text which must be considered a "different work" (1975:103). The text thus produced represents a radically new interpretation of the original, which, in contrast to a version, is governed purely by the imitator's personal aesthetic inclinations. See also BLANK VERSE TRANSLATION, LITERAL TRANSLATION 2, METAPOEM, METRICAL TRANSLATION, PHONEMIC TRANSLATION, POETRY INTO PROSE and RHYMED TRANSLATION. Further reading: Lefevere 1975.

Indeterminacy A concept used in philosophical discussions of meaning and translation. Broadly speaking, the term *indeterminacy* refers to the unavoidable ambiguity which arises in both interlingual and intralingual communication; however, it has been used by different writers in different ways. The concept was originally formulated by Quine (1959/1966, 1960), and was illustrated through his notion of RADICAL TRANSLATION. Quine argues that "translation manuals" (i.e. systems of interlingual equivalences) present only one of a potentially unlimited number of mutually incompatible, yet internally consistent mappings between the totality of SL and TL items, and consequently suggests that it would be at least theoretically possible to formulate a new set of correspondences which would challenge the one which had been traditionally accepted (1960:72). Indeterminacy of this type originates in the fact that sentences which are sufficiently free of situational or cultural implicatures to be translated with confidence are too sparse to provide a fixed, reliable basis from which one single, unchallengeable set of translational equivalences for the entire language could be developed. However, for Quine the type of indeterminacy which is revealed by the case of translation is simply a graphic demonstration of the more general phenomenon of *intralingual* indeterminacy. This can be described through the observation that the sentences of a language could be mapped onto each other in different permutations in such a way that, although the "overall pattern of associations of sentences with one another and with non-verbal stimulation" (Quine 1960:27) was maintained, there would be many sentences whose meaning drastically diverged from that of their respective correlates. In other words, according to Quine, not even synonymy – the intralingual counterpart of interlingual EQUIVALENCE – can avoid containing a certain element of arbitrariness. Furthermore, as can be seen from the above, Quine is not interested in the translation of individual words or sentences; for him, the basic unit of meaning (and therefore of translation) is the entire language (Harrison 1979:114). Consequently, it is meaningless to ask what the *real* TL equivalent of an SL sentence would be, unless one is working within "some total scheme of translation which matches up *all* the sentences of [SL] with *all* the sentences of [TL]" (Harrison 1979:108, emphasis original). However, a number of writers have commented on the pessimistic nature of Quine's notion of indeterminacy. Pym, for example, observes that it is "widely thought to be a theory not of translation but of untranslatability" (1992a:181). Davidson's (1984) version of indeterminacy, on the other hand, represents a less extreme notion than Quine's. One of the main reasons for this is Davidson's advocacy of a "principle of charity", which dictates that, faced with a problem of interpretation, one is generally best advised to "prefer theories of interpretation that minimize disagreement" (1984:xvii) and by so doing to maximize one's chances of understanding what the SL speaker is trying to communicate. Davidson reduces the notion of indeterminacy to the idea that it is ultimately impossible to decide whether an SL speaker has "used words as we do but has more or less weird beliefs, [or whether] we have translated him wrong" (Davidson 1984:101). He observes that the concept of indeterminacy includes the recognition that certain apparent distinctions are not important, and concludes by saying that "If there is indeterminacy, it is because when all the evidence is in, alternative ways of stating the facts remain open" (Davidson 1984:154). Such ambiguities do not, however, inhibit the ability of the TL hearer or reader to make sense of the message. Mutual comprehension is never out of reach; indeed, according to Andrew Benjamin, in Davidson's way of looking at things it is "almost

inescapable" (Benjamin 1989:61). See also TRANSLATABILITY. Further
reading: Davidson 1984; Harrison 1979; Malmkjær 1993; Quine
1959/1966, 1960.

Indirect Translation 1 (or **Intermediate Translation**, or **Mediated
Translation**, or **Retranslation**, or **Second-Hand Translation**) A
term used to denote the procedure whereby a text is not translated
directly from an original ST, but via an intermediate translation in
another language. According to Toury (1980, 1995), such a procedure is of course NORM-governed, and different literary SYSTEMS
will tolerate it to varying extents. For example, it is frequently encountered in weak POLYSYSTEMS which depend on other, stronger
systems for literary models and precedents, particularly where the
language of the dominant system is widely spoken; in stronger
polysystems it can be seen in the practice of established TL poets
"translating" an ST (in an SL of which they have no knowledge) with
the aid of a TL crib. Another situation in which indirect translation is
turned to is where there is no suitable bilingual dictionary in existence.
TTs produced in this manner have a greater tendency towards
ACCEPTABILITY, as the original ST is frequently not even available to
be consulted, and the parameters of an ST which is a translation in its
own right are less likely to be held to be inviolable. In spite of the fact
that indirect translation is relatively widespread in some parts of the
world, it is not a procedure which is generally approved of; the NAIROBI
DECLARATION, for example, states that recourse should be had to it
"only where absolutely necessary" (Osers 1983:182). See also DIRECT
TRANSLATION 1, PIVOT LANGUAGE, PRELIMINARY NORMS and RELAY
INTERPRETING. Further reading: Toury 1980, 1995.

2 According to Gutt (1991), one of two possible types of translation (see also DIRECT TRANSLATION 3). Gutt introduces the notion in
the framework of Sperber and Wilson's (1986) relevance theory, and
uses it to investigate the theoretical implications of the concepts of
DYNAMIC and FUNCTIONAL EQUIVALENCE which originate within the
Bible-translating tradition. Indirect translation is defined as the strategy
used by the translator when the dilemma between "the need to give
the receptor language audience access to the authentic meaning of the
original, unaffected by the translator's own interpretation effort"
(1991:177) and "the urge to communicate as clearly as possible"
(1991:177) is resolved in favour of the latter. An indirect translation
will typically expand upon and elucidate ST so that implicit information

which it contains and which is easily retrievable by the SL audience in the original context envisaged by the ST writer will be equally available to the TL audience. Consequently an indirect translation created for a communicative context which differs significantly from the original context is likely to include large amounts of additional interpolated explanatory information; such a translation is, however, considered FAITHFUL inasmuch as it resembles the original in "relevant respects" (1991:111). A strategy of indirect translation is frequently employed when translating the Bible into languages which are rooted in cultures and world-views radically different from those presupposed by the original, or from the translator's own. Gutt argues that the distinction between this approach and direct translation throws new theoretical light on the FREE versus LITERAL TRANSLATION debate. Further reading: Gutt 1991.

Industrial Process, Translation as A term used by Sager (1994) to refer to the use of automatic and semi-automatic routines to facilitate, accelerate or lower the cost of the translation process, as for example in MACHINE and MACHINE-AIDED TRANSLATION. The expression "industrial process" is used even though the "substance" being processed – language – is "man-made and symbolic", unlike other industrial materials (1994:19). However, Sager points out that, while there are models in theoretical and applied linguistics which are designed to account for the characteristics of language, the specification of the *automated* translation process presents difficulties, because work which has been done on TRANSLATION THEORY is based on human rather than machine translation (1994:19-20); Sager thus argues that the design specifications for machine translation systems need to be based on theoretical models specifically created to account for this type of translation (1994:20). See also READER-ORIENTED and WRITER-ORIENTED MACHINE TRANSLATION. Further reading: Sager 1994.

Information Load See COMMUNICATION LOAD.

Information Offer (or **Offer of Information**) (German *Informationsangebot* or *IA*) A term suggested by Vermeer (1982) as an alternative to Stein's (1979, 1980) description of a text as a collection of *instructions* to the recipient. Vermeer argues that the term *instruction* is not a helpful way of designating an act of communication, preferring to view all communication in "more democratic"

(1982:99, translated), "more evaluatively neutral" (Reiss & Vermeer 1984:73, translated) terms as an *offer* (1982:99), whereby it is the responsibility of the reader or listener to interpret the multivalent, potentially ambiguous message in the way that makes greatest sense in the given context and with the given purpose of the communication. However, with such multivalence in the original message, it is inevitable that every reception of a message will only realize some of the possible meanings which it contains, while producing further possible meanings not present in the original (Reiss & Vermeer 1984:62); consequently, each interpretation of a message may be seen as a new *information offer* in its own right, or "information offer about an information offer" (*"Informationsangebot über ein Informationsangebot"*, 1984:67). Vermeer argues that there are at least two types of such "secondary" information offers: commentary and translation (1982:99). In this way translation is characterized as a *special type* (*"Sondersorte"*) of *information offer* (Reiss & Vermeer 1984:103) which *simulates* the original text or message by interpreting it in a different linguistic and cultural context. Vermeer thus rejects notions of translation as a two stage process in which the translator acts as a kind of "relay station" (Reiss & Vermeer 1984:77, translated), receiving a message, recoding it and transmitting it to the target audience; instead he aligns himself with scholars such as Neubert (1970), House (1977; see COVERT TRANSLATION and OVERT TRANSLATION) and Diller & Kornelius (1978; see PRIMARY TRANSLATION and SECONDARY TRANSLATION), who argue that the process of translation is one which involves providing the target audience with "information" about ST, and therefore one which allows the translator to make responsible, creative decisions (Reiss & Vermeer 1984:75). Central to Vermeer's argument is the claim that the translator's decisions are made not on the basis of the text-type (see EXPRESSIVE TEXTS, INFORMATIVE TEXTS, MULTI-MEDIAL TEXTS and OPERATIVE TEXTS) of the original, but rather in line with the particular purpose (or SKOPOS) which the translation is designed to serve. In the light of such considerations translation is seen as achieving not something less than the original text, but something new and different. Further reading: Reiss & Vermeer 1984; Vermeer 1982.

Informationsangebot See INFORMATION OFFER.

Informative Texts (German *Informative Texte*) (formerly **Content-focused Texts**; German *Inhaltsbetonte Texte*) According to Reiss

(1977/1989), one of three main text-types (see also EXPRESSIVE TEXTS and OPERATIVE TEXTS). Reiss' typology is intended as a set of guidelines for translators and translation critics, and the three types which she proposes are distinguished from each other in terms of their major function, which is reflected in the language they contain, and which needs to be preserved in TT. In the case of informative texts the primary aim is one of conveying information to the receiver. This means that a translator should concentrate on establishing semantic EQUIVALENCE, and only then turn to other kinds, such as connotative or aesthetic (see Reiss & Vermeer 1984:157). Similarly, a translation which is deemed to fulfil this function of reproducing in TL the informative content of SL should be judged to be successful. Reiss makes the point that her text-types represent tendencies rather than clearly delineated categories, and that it is possible for texts to have secondary, more subsidiary functions; however, reference works, business letters, official documents and academic articles all represent this text-type to varying degrees. See also MULTI-MEDIAL TEXTS and SKOPOS THEORY. Further reading: Nord 1996; Reiss 1971, 1976, 1977, 1977/1989; Reiss & Vermeer 1984.

Initial Norm Defined by Toury (1980, 1995) as one of a number of basic types of NORM which guide the production of a TT. In spite of the name, this type of norm does not *precede* other norms, but has *logical* priority over them, in that the functioning of other types depends on how this norm operates. In other words, the initial norm refers to "the translator's (conscious or unconscious) choice as to the main objective of his translation, the objective which governs all decisions made during the translation process" (van Leuven-Zwart 1989:154). Interpreting the statement that "translation, especially literary translation, always involves an encounter, if not a confrontation, between two sets of norms" (1980:55), Toury defines the initial norm as reflecting whether the translator attempts to remain as FAITHFUL as possible to the parameters of the original text, or seeks to adapt the emerging TT to the linguistic and literary norms active in TL to as great an extent as possible (a choice between ADEQUACY 2 and ACCEPTABILITY). However, it is clear that these alternatives represent extremes, and that in most TTs the translator will compromise between the two tendencies. As is the case with most other norms, the initial norm is not directly observable, but may be inferred by identifying the SHIFTS contained in TT (van Leuven-Zwart 1989:154). See also

MATRICIAL NORMS, OPERATIONAL NORMS, PRELIMINARY NORMS and TEXTUAL NORMS. Further reading: Toury 1980, 1995.

Instrumental Translation A term used by Nord (1991a) to refer to one of two types of translation defined according to how TT is intended to function in the target culture (see also DOCUMENTARY TRANS-LATION). According to Nord, an instrumental translation is intended to fulfil a new communicative purpose in the target culture "without the recipient being conscious of reading or hearing a text which, in a different form, was used before in a different communicative action" (1991a:73). As such it is "a communicative instrument in its own right" (1991a:72) rather than merely a *documentary* record of the ST author's act of communication with the source culture recipients (1991a:72). An instrumental translation can have "the same or a similar or analogous function as the ST" (1991a:72); depending on the precise relationship between source and target functions, it can be classified as belonging to one of three types. If it serves the same function(s) as ST it is termed a *function-preserving* translation, as for example in the case of operating instructions or business correspondence. If on the other hand the original function cannot be meaningfully realized in the new context, it will have to be *adapted* by the translator in a way that is at least compatible with the author's intentions; an example of such a text would be a translation of *Gulliver's Travels* which was also adapted for children. Finally, a *corresponding translation* is a literary translation intended to fulfil in the target literary context a "homologous" function to that which it achieved in the source culture; much translated poetry can be said to belong to this type (1991a:73). According to Nord, instrumental translation differs from House's (1977) comparable concept of COVERT TRANSLATION in that it only requires the TT function to be compatible, rather than identical or equivalent, with that of ST (1991a:72 n. 36). See also PARTICIPATIVE RECEIVER. Further reading: Nord 1988, 1991a, 1997.

Integral Translation A term used by van Leuven-Zwart (1989, 1990) to refer to a translation which "contains no additions or deletions transcending the sentence level" (1989:154). The term is used in the context of an investigation into the similarities and differences between fictional narrative texts and their translations. Van Leuven-Zwart argues that in integral translations translational SHIFTS occur on two levels, the microstructural (i.e. involving sentences, clauses and phrases) and the macrostructural (including for example changes in characterization, style or narrative viewpoint), and presents a complex model for analyzing how consistent patterns of shifts observed on the former level influence the broader categories associated with the latter, and hence the overall "feel" of TT as compared to ST. In view of its basic reliance on a close comparison of the microstructural features of ST and TT, such a method is clearly only applicable to integral translations and their STs. See also ARCHITRANSEME, GENERALIZATION, MODIFICATION, MODULATION 2, MUTATION, SPECIFICATION and TRANSEME. Further reading: van Leuven-Zwart 1989, 1990.

Intercultural Cooperation See TRANSLATORIAL ACTION.

Interlanguage See TRANSLATIONESE.

Interlineal Translation A term coined by Hervey & Higgins (1992) to refer to the type of translation which is at the extreme of SL bias (as opposed to FREE TRANSLATION, which is at the extreme of TL bias). Hervey & Higgins suggest that an interlineal translation "does not necessarily respect TL grammar, but has grammatical units corresponding to every grammatical unit of the ST" (1992:20). It thus differs from the less extreme strategy of LITERAL TRANSLATION 1, which usually respects the TL grammar, although also commonly uses the decontextualized meaning of words. According to Hervey & Higgins, interlineal translation is rare, and is normally only used in language teaching or in descriptive linguistics (1992:20). It should be pointed out that interlineal translation is basically the same as INTERLINEAR TRANSLATION except that it does not require the TL units to appear directly above or below the ST units to which they correspond. Further reading: Hervey & Higgins 1992.

Interlinear Translation A type of extremely LITERAL translation in which TL words are arranged line by line below (or above) the ST items to which they correspond. As with a GLOSS TRANSLATION, the purpose of an interlinear translation is to provide access to a text – frequently but not invariably sacred – for people who would linguistically speaking otherwise be inadequately equipped to tackle it. According to Steiner, an interlinear translation thus "sets a dictionary equivalent from the target-language above each word in the source-language" and is therefore strictly speaking "nothing else but a total glossary, set out horizontally in discrete units" (1975/1992:324). In other words, in contrast to most other types of translation, an interlinear version is meant to be read in conjunction with the original, and so is explicitly intended to function as a crib. Nida argues that such a rendering "can scarcely be called a translation in the usual sense of the term" (1964:23), and indeed in some respects it resembles a kind of semantic TRANSCRIPTION, as the closest TL equivalent is automatically chosen for each ST item. However, it is not only the words themselves which are copied; as Gutt points out, interlinear translations are also intended to preserve syntactic categories such as word order "with as little change as possible" (1991:137). As a result of using this type of translation, what frequently happens is that the linguistic norms of TL are violated. Because of this consideration, Gutt argues that "the feasibility of this approach will be strongly determined by the degree of structural similarity between the two languages in question", since "the more they differ in structure, the less it will be possible to combine the demand for resemblance in structure with that for intelligibility" (1991:169). Much has also been said about interlinear translations on a more metaphysical level, following Walter Benjamin's assertion – in his famous discussion of PURE LANGUAGE – that "the interlinear version of the Scriptures is the prototype or ideal of all translation" (1923/1963:195, 1923/1970: 82). However, while many writers have speculated about what he meant by this enigmatic statement, it is clear that he was referring to an "ideal" interlinear translation in which the ST meaning is not obscured but enhanced by its extreme literalism. See also BACK-TRANSLATION, BI-TEXT and INTERLINEAL TRANSLATION. Further reading: W. Benjamin 1923/1963, 1923/1970; Gutt 1991; Steiner 1975/1992.

Interlingua See TERTIUM COMPARATIONIS.

Interlingual Translation According to Jakobson (1959/1966), one of three types of translation (see also INTERSEMIOTIC TRANSLATION and INTRALINGUAL TRANSLATION). For the purposes of this classification, Jakobson uses a broad definition of translation, as of the three types, interlingual translation – or *translation proper* – is the only one which corresponds to what is normally understood by the word *translation.* Working within a semiotic framework, Jakobson defines interlingual translation as "an interpretation of verbal signs by means of some other language" (1959/1966:233). Because of the lack of full EQUIVALENCE between words of different languages, however, translation from one language into another usually substitutes one entire message for another; hence Jakobson views the process of interlingual translation as a kind of *reported speech* in which the translator "recodes and transmits a message received from another source" (1959/1966:233). The problems involved in this kind of recodification are of course considerable. As stated by Gorlée, interlingual translation is "primarily concerned with breaking up and dislocating familiar sign-structures and relationships between signs, and with rearranging them meaningfully in the light of the new system" (1994:161); it thus becomes "a semiotic encounter between two *Weltanschauungen*" (1994:161). The outcome of this is that the two linguistic codes "meet, interact, and (eventually and ideally) interconnect, creating a new contextual structure", and the different languages "demonstrate their similarities and ... aim to overcome their differences" (1994:160). It should be pointed out that Jakobson's categories are not watertight; the case of *interdialectal* translation, for example, is suggested by Toury (1986:1113) as lying on the border between interlingual and intralingual translation. See also TRANSFER 1 and TRANSLATION. Further reading: Gorlée 1994; Jakobson 1959/1966.

Intermediate Translation See INDIRECT TRANSLATION 1.

Internal Transfer See TRANSFER 1.

Interpretation According to Lefevere (1975), one of seven possible strategies for translating poetry. Lefevere distinguishes two types of interpretation, IMITATION 2 and VERSION 2. He considers both procedures to be distinct from translation proper, arguing that "the difference between translation, version, and imitation lies in the degree of interpretation" (1975:76). See also BLANK VERSE TRANSLATION, LITERAL TRANSLATION 2, METAPOEM, METRICAL TRANSLATION, PHONEMIC TRANSLATION, POETRY INTO PROSE and RHYMED TRANSLATION. Further reading: Lefevere 1975.

Interpreting A term used to refer to the oral translation of a spoken message or text. The history of interpreting is not well documented, although it is generally agreed that as an activity it is older than written TRANSLATION. It differs from this latter in a number of important respects. Firstly, the communication skills which it requires are clearly different, as interpreters need to be expert oral communicators. Secondly, while translators often have relatively unlimited opportunity to make alterations and improvements before submitting a final version, interpreters are required to create a finished product in "real time" without the possibility of going back and making revisions; in other words, interpreting, unlike written translation, is both non-CORRECTABLE and non-VERIFIABLE. Thirdly, interpreters must ensure that any background knowledge which they are likely to need has been acquired in advance; seeking colleagues' advice or consulting reference works is not generally possible during the actual process of interpreting. Fourthly, interpreters are "performers" who are constantly making split-second decisions and taking communicative risks; consequently they typically experience higher stress levels while "on the job" than most translators (see Gile 1995a:111-14). Various types of interpreting can be distinguished, either by the context in which it occurs (e.g. COMMUNITY INTERPRETING, CONFERENCE INTERPRETING and COURT INTERPRETING) or the way in which it is carried out (e.g. CONSECUTIVE INTERPRETING, LIAISON INTERPRETING, SIMULTANEOUS INTERPRETING and WHISPERED INTERPRETING), although clearly there is a considerable amount of overlap between some of these categories; however, one further type which is significantly different from the others is SIGNED LANGUAGE INTERPRETING, since this involves both oral and visual-gestural modalities. It should be pointed out that while the term *interpretation* is often used interchangeably with *interpreting*, some writers insist that the former term should be avoided in this context. The retention of a distinction between these two notions is particularly necessary in the case of court interpreting, where interpretation in the sense of "conveying one's understanding of meanings and intentions" (Morris 1995:25) is an activity which interpreters are supposed to avoid. See also *DOLMETSCHEN*, EFFORT MODELS, INTERPRETIVE THEORY OF TRANSLATION, PIVOT LANGUAGE and RELAY INTERPRETING. Further reading: Gerver & Sinaiko 1977; Gile 1995a; *Target* 7:1; Seleskovitch 1976; Seleskovitch & Lederer 1989; Tommola 1995.

Interpretive Theory of Translation (or Interpretative Theory of Translation or Theory of Sense) A term used to designate a model originally designed to reflect the processes which are involved in CONFERENCE INTERPRETING. The interpretive theory of translation is associated with a group of scholars based at ESIT (École Superieure d'Interprètes et de Traducteurs), who are sometimes known as the Paris School. First presented by Seleskovitch and Lederer in the late 1960s, the interpretive theory of translation is a reaction against some of the restricted views of language proposed by the linguistics of the time. The proponents of the theory argue that interpreters do not work merely with linguistic meaning, but also need to take into account such factors as the cognitive context of what has already been said, the setting in which the interpreting is taking place and the interpreter's own world knowledge (Lavault 1996:97). As a consequence of this, one of the theory's principle tenets has been that interpreting should be based on a deverbalized, intended meaning (the sense or *sens*) derived from the overall context, rather than on the words of ST as such (Seleskovitch 1976:92). Thus according to the model interpreting ignores the need to identify direct translation equivalents for ST items and instead "concentrates on finding the appropriate wording to convey a given meaning at a given point in time and in a given context, whatever that wording ... or the original wording may mean under different circumstances" (1976:93). The approach also focuses on the mental and cognitive processes involved in interpreting, which is seen as comprising the three stages of *interpretation, de-verbalization* and *reformulation* (Seleskovitch 1977). While concepts such as deverbalization are easier to apply to conference or SIMULTANEOUS interpreting, the theory has latterly been extended to include (non-literary) written TRANSLATION as well (see for example Lederer 1994). Another important extension has been suggested by Delisle (1980, 1993), who introduces insights from text linguistics and discourse analysis. Further reading: Delisle 1980, 1988, 1993; Lavault 1996; Lederer 1994; Seleskovitch 1976, 1977; Seleskovitch & Lederer 1984, 1989.

Intersemiotic Translation (or **Transmutation**) A term coined by Jakobson (1959/1966) to refer to one of three types of translation (see also INTERLINGUAL TRANSLATION and INTRALINGUAL TRANSLATION). In Jakobson's framework, in which translation is understood as the conversion of a sign into "some further, alternative sign" (1959/1966:232), intersemiotic translation is defined as "an interpretation of verbal signs by means of signs of nonverbal sign systems" (1959/

1966:233). Jakobson cites the reinterpretation of verbal art by "music, dance, cinema or painting" (1959/1966:238) as examples of this process. What is thus meant by the term is not translation in the standard sense, but *transmutation* of a verbal message into another medium of expression, or in other words translation in a *figurative* sense, since the target code is a language "only in a metaphorical manner of speaking" (Gorlée 1994:162). Indeed, it is clear that intersemiotic translation is in many ways set apart from Jakobson's other two types. For example, as pointed out by Gorlée, information loss is at its highest here (1994:168). Furthermore, intersemiotic translation is a one-way process, while the other two types are at least potentially reversible (Sturrock 1991:310). However, some commentators have strong misgivings about the appropriateness of the term, simply because of its counter-intuitive nature; Sturrock, for example, comments that it is "a semiotic change so radical as to depart from what we normally understand by *translation*" (1991:310). Yet Jakobson's categorization does have the advantage of placing translation within a wider context by comparing it with similar processes and thus enabling one to generalize about how signs can be changed into other signs. Thus he observes that in intersemiotic translation "certain structural features ... are preserved despite the disappearance of their verbal shape", and concludes that "many poetic features belong not only to the science of language but to the whole theory of signs, that is, to general semiotics" (1960:350-51). See also TRANSFER 1. Further reading: Gorlée 1994; Jakobson 1959/1966; Sturrock 1991.

Intertemporal Translation (or **Cross-temporal Translation**) A term used to refer to the translation of a text by an author writing in (or about) an earlier time (see Vladova 1993:15-16). Presumably formulated on the basis of Jakobson's (1959/1966) INTERLINGUAL, INTERSEMIOTIC and INTRALINGUAL TRANSLATION, the term can be understood as including the simple modernizing of a text dating from an earlier stage of a language; however, it is usually taken to refer to a process which also contains an interlingual element. Intertemporal translation is in fact a very widespread phenomenon; indeed, Steiner points out that all translation, except SIMULTANEOUS INTERPRETING, contains an intertemporal element (1975/1992:351), although in many cases this can basically be ignored since it is so small. However, when ST is the Bible or a text of classical literature it is clear that it will sometimes be necessary to confront vast differences in language, culture and mentality caused by the amount of time which has elapsed since ST was composed. Furthermore, in the case of intertemporal translation across major spans of time there is frequently the problem of the work losing its original contextual significance, or indeed of the genre in which it was written becoming defunct (Bassnett 1980/ 1991:83). Such loss of defining context has meant that, in the absence of a translation which has become a classic in its own right, successive generations have generally felt the need to retranslate works, since translations more than original texts have a tendency to "shift in value and significance as [the] world itself changes and develops" (Snell-Hornby 1987:102). The practical approaches to this type of translation which translators have adopted have varied. Some writers (e.g. Popovič [1976]:18) have identified the two basic strategies of *historization* and *modernization*. However, Holmes (1988h) argues that this simple choice is not sufficient to reflect the range of approaches adopted, at least by translators of verse. According to Holmes, intertemporal translation of poetry involves shifting between linguistic, socio-cultural and literary systems (1988h:36), while in each of these three areas, independently of each other, the translator may choose between equivalents which are a) roughly contemporary with ST, b) representative of a kind of "standard archaic usage" (see Leech 1969:13), or c) broadly modern in nature (1988h:38-39). While his study is fairly small-scale, Holmes observes that there seems to be a general unwillingness to produce a TT "that is completely modern on all levels, with nothing in it to indicate its ties with an earlier time" (1988h:41-42). See also ARCHAISM and VERTICAL TRANSLATION. Further reading: Holmes 1988h; Steiner 1975/1992; Vladova 1993.

Intralingual Translation (or Rewording) A term used by Jakobson (1959/1966) to refer to one of three types of translation (see also INTERLINGUAL TRANSLATION and INTERSEMIOTIC TRANSLATION). Within a semiotic framework Jakobson defines the process of intralingual translation as "an interpretation of verbal signs by means of other signs of the same language" (1959/1966:233). In other words, intralingual translation is not translation in the strict sense, but rather relies either on the use of synonyms (although these will of course always be approximate, at least to some degree) or circumlocution in order to reword a message in the language of the original. For example, simplifying a technical text for a non-specialist readership, adapting a classic for a children's audience or producing a version of Chaucer in modern English are all processes which can be classified as intralingual translation. Of course, it can be difficult to determine whether reformulations which span great distances of time or dialect should be considered intralingual or interlingual, for as Pym points out there is "no strict cut-off point at which wholly intralingual rewriting can be said to have become wholly interlingual" (1992a:25). However, Jakobson's widening of the definition of translation to include intralingual "rewording" is less controversial than is the case with intersemiotic translation, and is mirrored by Steiner's slogan that "inside or between languages, human communication equals translation" (1975/1992:49, emphasis removed). Indeed, by producing his categorization he is simply suggesting that translation belongs to a group of interlinked phenomena between which one can find "family resemblances". Thus there is arguably more that these two types of translation have in common than there is that separates them; for example, one of the problems central to translation – that of determining synonymy – according to Sturrock "remains the same whether the translation be effected between two natural languages or within one language" (1991:309). Furthermore, there is much which intralingual translation can teach us about the more "standard" interlingual variety, and indeed about the "conventional but never static, nature of verbal language", which "highlights the ability of one linguistic sign system to stand in more than one fashion for something else" (Gorlée 1994:159). On the other hand, there are of course specific features – besides the obvious ones – that set intralingual translation apart from Jakobson's other two categories; an example of this is the fact that the amount of information which is lost during the recodification process is lower here than with the other types (Gorlée 1994:168). See also TRANSFER 1. Further reading: Gorlée 1994; Jakobson 1959/1966.

Intra-system Shift According to Catford, a type of CATEGORY SHIFT which occurs when "SL and TL possess systems which approximately correspond formally as to their constitution, but when translation involves selection of a non-corresponding term in the TL system" (1965:80). For example, although English and French largely correspond on a formal level in their use of the singular-plural distinction, there are many occasions when this FORMAL CORRESPONDENCE is departed from, so that the translation equivalent of a *singular* item in one language is a *plural* item in the other, as is the case in such correspondences as *advice = des conseils, the contents = le contenu* and so forth (1965:80). Like other types of category shift, intra-system shifts are generally forced on the translator by the conflicting demands of SL and TL structure. See also CLASS SHIFT, LEVEL SHIFT, STRUCTURE SHIFT, SHIFT and UNIT SHIFT. Further reading: Catford 1965.

Invariance A term used to denote the concept of the immutability of (elements of) ST in the translation process; the related term *invariant* is defined along similar lines as the features or elements common to ST and TT. The notion behind these terms is closely connected with that of EQUIVALENCE, and many of the issues raised in the discussion of that concept are of relevance here too. Many early statements on invariance were formulated with a view to developing effective procedures for MACHINE TRANSLATION, and tended to overlook aspects of the translation process which could not be described as simple replacement of linguistic units. Thus Oettinger, for example, writes that "keeping significance invariant is the central problem in translating between natural languages" (1960:104, quoted in Koller 1979/ 1992:90). This view persisted past the period of optimism about the possibilities of machine translation, so that Popovič, for example, writes that the invariant core of a text is "represented by stable, basic and constant semantic elements" ([1976]:11) which, he argues, can be arrived at through *semantic condensation*, a process akin to that of back-transformation (see ANALYSIS). However, many writers have argued that denotative meaning is not the only textual element in terms of which it is possible to talk of invariance. Thus Bassnett, for example, uses the term *invariant* to refer in general terms to "that which exists in common between all existing translations of a single work" (1980/1991:27). Kade, on the other hand, understands invariance more specifically in terms of the potentially equal communicative value of ST and TT which is realized in an "approximately equal effect on ST and TT recipients" (Kade 1968:63, translated). Similarly, Neubert answers the question of what makes one text a translation of another by saying that "translation always alters ST in such a way as to make it impossible to speak of an invariance between SL and TL which takes no account of pragmatics" (1973:15, translated). He thus argues that truly ADEQUATE translation should be characterized by invariance not only on the semantic level, but also within the parameters dictated by pragmatic considerations such as the need to conform to the conventions of a given text-type within both SL and TL (1973:18-19). Toury, who takes a more relative view of translation, understands invariance as something which can only be defined in relation to a specific act of translation, in the light of the particular NORMS and strategies which have been followed by the translator; he thus talks of "invariance conditions", which arise from the relationships found to exist between a particular TT and ST (see for example 1980:28). See also CORRESPONDENCE, IDENTITY and TERTIUM COMPARATIONIS. Further reading: Kade 1968; Neubert 1973.

Invariant See INVARIANCE.

Inverse Translation A term used to describe a translation, either written or spoken, which is done from the translator's native language (or language of habitual use). Inverse translation has clear pedagogical applications (such as the traditional *prose translation*, in which an English-speaking student would translate a passage from English, usually into Latin or Greek). In previous ages the direction of translation was not considered important. Today, however, apart from in the context of language learning, the use of inverse translation in English-speaking countries is limited, as here the relatively small volume of translation from English can easily be handled by native speakers of the relevant TL. However, in other parts of the world translators turn to inverse translation with rather greater frequency, for example to cope with the huge amount of translation into English which needs to be performed. This is particularly true for certain text-types (such as material for tourists) where the need for perfect style is not so pressing, although even when other, more sensitive text-types are involved many of the shortcomings of this technique can be overcome by team translating or by having TTs edited by a TL native speaker. Furthermore, in some countries (such as Russia) inverse translation is the preferred DIRECTION OF TRANSLATION for interpreters (see INTERPRETING). A similar, though more complicated, procedure is described by Nida (1964) in his discussion of the ETHNOLINGUISTIC MODEL OF TRANSLATION. An alternative term for inverse translation is SERVICE TRANSLATION. See also DIRECT TRANSLATION 2. Further reading: Beeby Lonsdale 1996; Kelly 1979; Snell & Crampton 1983.

Invisibility See DOMESTICATING TRANSLATION.

Kernel (or **Kernel Sentence**) See ANALYSIS.

Keyword Translation (French *Traduction Signalétique*) According to Gouadec (1989, 1990), one of seven types of translation (or translation-like processes) which serve to meet the various translation needs which arise in a professional environment. This particular type involves keywords in ST being translated into TL to determine whether or not the information contained in ST requires fuller translation and, if so, how it should be translated. The keywords indicate the basic concepts of ST, and by placing them in decreasing order of frequency in ST the translator can indicate which concepts are the most important. The result is a TL index of the SL document which enables the TL reader to identify the sections of the text which will be of most use to him or her (1989:23). See also ABSOLUTE TRANSLATION, ABSTRACT TRANSLATION, DIAGRAMMATIC TRANSLATION, RECONSTRUCTIONS (TRANSLATION WITH), SELECTIVE TRANSLATION and SIGHT TRANSLATION. Further reading: Gouadec 1989, 1990; Sager 1994.

Kohärenz See COHERENCE.

Kontrollierbarkeit See VERIFIABILITY.

Korrigierbarkeit See CORRECTABILITY.

Lacunes See VOIDS.

Leipzig School An influential group of translation scholars based in the Department of Theoretical and Applied Linguistics at the University (formerly the Karl Marx University) of Leipzig. The Leipzig School have been active since the 1960s, and have made a major contribution to one of the two main schools of translation theory which now "dominate the scene in Europe" (see Snell-Hornby 1988/1995:14). The Leipzig School is characterized by a linguistic, scientific approach to the study of translation, and most of their work has centred around the problems of scientific and technical translation (Koller 1979/1992:130). The best-known scholars within the Leipzig school are probably Otto Kade and Albrecht Neubert, whose main publications include Kade (1968), an important work coining the terms *TRANSLAT* and *TRANSLATION* and containing a much-quoted discussion of types of EQUIVALENCE, and Neubert (1985), which broadens the linguistic approach to include factors of a text-linguistic nature. See also SCIENCE OF TRANSLATION. Further reading: Snell-Hornby 1988/1995.

Level Shift A term used by Catford (1965) to denote one of two major types of SHIFT, or departure from FORMAL CORRESPONDENCE "in the process of going from the SL to the TL" (1965:73). An SL item which undergoes a level shift in the process of translation will have a TL translation equivalent at a different linguistic level from its own. Following Halliday (1961), Catford identifies a total of four possible levels on which linguistic phenomena may occur: the grammatical, the lexical, the graphological and the phonological. In practice, however, level shifts only occur between the levels of *grammar* and *lexis*, and so entail the use of lexical means in TT to express a meaning which in ST is grammatically encoded, and vice versa. For example, the notion of *completion* is expressed in Russian by the grammatical category of *perfectivity*. However, in certain contexts it is more expedient to render this concept lexically in English by using an alternative verb, so that for instance Russian *on sdelal* "he has done" might become "he has *achieved*" if this conveyed the particular emphasis required by the context. It should be noted that the notion of the level shift includes not only instances of incompatibility between the SL and TL linguistic systems, but also occasions where the translator has simply decided to translate an SL item in a certain way. See also CATEGORY SHIFT. Further reading: Catford 1965.

Lexical Translation A term used by Catford to refer to a type of RE-STRICTED TRANSLATION in which "the SL lexis of a text is replaced by equivalent TL lexis, but with no replacement of grammar" (1965:71-72). For example, the English sentence *This is the man I saw* might be lexically translated into French as *This is the homme I voi-ed*; here the English grammar is preserved, while the lexical items *man* and *see* are replaced by their French equivalents. A more famous example of (partial) lexical translation is Burgess' *A Clockwork Orange*, which is written throughout in a kind of futuristic slang which contains a large number of Russian lexical items; an example of this, taken from the opening of the novel, is the sentence

"There was me ... and my three droogs ..., and we sat in the Korova Milkbar making up our rassoodocks what to do ...." (1962/1972:5). It should also be pointed out that lexical and GRAMMATICAL translation are the converse of each other, since lexical translation from language A into language B produces the same type of text as grammatical translation in the other direction. See also GRAPHOLOGICAL TRANSLATION and PHONOLOGICAL TRANSLATION. Further reading: Catford 1965.

Liaison Interpreting (or **Bilateral Interpreting**) Defined by Keith as a type of INTERPRETING in which "an individual who speaks two languages mediates in a conversation between two or more individuals who do not speak each other's tongue" (1985:1). While most closely associated with COMMUNITY INTERPRETING, liaison interpreting is used in any small-scale context, such as for example business meetings, official visits or informal conversations. Liaison interpreting is bi-directional, and is usually performed sentence by sentence in a consecutive manner; however, it is not generally classified as CONSECUTIVE INTERPRETING proper, as this term is generally reserved for a procedure which is more closely defined and which involves notetaking. The practice of liaison interpreting is probably found in all multilingual societies; however, according to Ozolins, as a profession it is still "embryonic", and is frequently performed by anyone who happens to know the two languages in question, including in some cases a family member of one of the parties involved (1995:154). Further reading: Gentile et al. 1996; Ozolins 1995.

Lingua Universalis See TERTIUM COMPARATIONIS.

Linguistic Approach See LINGUISTIC TRANSLATION 1.

Linguistic Equivalence According to Popovič ([1976]), one of four types of EQUIVALENCE. Popovič defines linguistic equivalence as "homogeneity of elements upon the linguistic (phonetic, morphological, and syntactic) levels of the original and the translation" ([1976]:6). The linguistic levels of a text are considered to be the lowest ([1976]:11), and are concerned with "stylistic purity and linguistic correctness" ([1976]:14); "homogeneity" between ST and TT upon this level is established by the "search for and evaluation of correspondence between the elements of the original language and those of the recipient language" ([1976]:14), and helps to determine equivalence on the higher, expressive level of the text ([1976]:6). See also PARADIGMATIC EQUIVALENCE, STYLISTIC EQUIVALENCE and TEXTUAL EQUIVALENCE 2. Further reading: Popovič [1976].

Linguistic Translation 1 (or **Linguistic Approach**) A term used to refer to any approach which views translation as simply a question of replacing the linguistic units of ST with "equivalent" TL units without reference to factors such as context or connotation. It should be pointed out that the term is strictly speaking misleading, as modern linguistics seeks to account for these areas too. The term is akin to CLOSE TRANSLATION, as it can be used as a kind of superordinate covering strategies like INTERLINEAR TRANSLATION, LITERAL TRANSLATION 1 and WORD-FOR-WORD TRANSLATION. While such strategies are of limited applicability, it is commonly agreed that they are appropriate for certain purposes, such as illustrating SL structure (for example in the context of language teaching); however, they are also frequently used for translating sacred texts, where the original wording is often considered to be in some way inviolable. See also EQUIVALENCE, RANK-RESTRICTED THEORIES OF TRANSLATION and UNIT OF TRANSLATION.

2 One of four classifications of translation proposed by Casagrande (1954). The term is used to describe a WORD-FOR-WORD or even morpheme-for-morpheme translation in which ST segments are translated sequentially into the most closely corresponding TL units. According to Casagrande, the aim of such a translation is "to identify and assign equivalent meanings to the constituent morphemes of the source language" (1954:337); thus structural or grammatical form is the central concern. When an ST has been translated in this way, the result will be a LITERAL or even an INTERLINEAR TRANSLATION. Morphemes and words are translated into their nearest equivalents, and the original word order is frequently adhered to, so that the translation remains as close to ST as possible. Although linguistic translation has its uses, in Casagrande's opinion it may lead to a kind of false translation which "can be as misleading as an overly free translation" (1954:337). See also AESTHETIC-POETIC TRANSLATION, ETHNOGRAPHIC TRANSLATION and PRAGMATIC TRANSLATION 2. Further reading: Casagrande 1954.

3 A term used by Nida & Taber in the context of Bible translation to refer to a translation "in which only information which is linguistically implicit in the original is made explicit and in which all changes

of form follow the rules of back transformation and transformation and of componential analysis" (1969/1982:203; see also ANALYSIS and RESTRUCTURING). In other words, a linguistic translation is one which only contains elements which can be directly derived from the ST wording, avoiding any kind of explanatory interpolation or cultural adjustment which cannot be justified on this basis; in this way linguistic translation contrasts with CULTURAL TRANSLATION 2. According to Nida & Taber, linguistic translation is the only legitimate strategy for Bible translation (1969/1982:134), and only a linguistic translation can be considered FAITHFUL (1969/1982:203). See also DYNAMIC EQUIVALENCE. Further reading: Gutt 1991; Nida & Taber 1969/1982.

Linguistically Creative Translation (German *Sprachschöpferische Übersetzung*) A term used by Reiss & Vermeer (1984) to denote the translation of an ST which contains cultural terms, concepts or other items which are not native to TL and for which new TL labels consequently need to be designed. Religious, philosophical and technical writing are all examples of genres in which such a procedure tends to be common. However, it should be pointed out that TTs which contain a high level of such new lexical items cannot be considered to be ADEQUATE (1984:136). Further reading: Reiss & Vermeer 1984.

Literal Translation 1 A notion which has for many centuries been at the heart of most translation controversies, where it has been either staunchly defended against or vigorously attacked in favour of its rival, FREE TRANSLATION (see PRESCRIPTIVE TRANSLATION STUDIES). However, there is a certain amount of variation in the way this term is applied, as literal translation is sometimes understood as including the related notion of WORD-FOR-WORD TRANSLATION. A literal translation can be defined in linguistic terms as a translation "made on a level lower than is sufficient to convey the content unchanged while observing TL norms" (Barkhudarov 1969:10, translated). In a similar vein Catford also offers a definition based on the notion of the UNIT OF TRANSLATION: he argues that literal translation takes word-for-word translation as its starting point, although because of the necessity of conforming to TL grammar, the final TT may also display group-group or clause-clause EQUIVALENCE (1965:25). Thus the term is a relative one, as for any ST "there are as many degrees of literalness and freedom of translation as there are levels of hierarchical structure"

(Hockett 1954:313). As a translation strategy, literal translation clearly has its uses; a fairly literal approach is, for example, generally appropriate for translating many types of technical text, while in a different context the technique can also provide language learners with useful insights into TL structures. In literary translation, too, the approach has its champions. Nabokov, for example, describes it as "rendering, as closely as the associative and syntactical capacities of another language allow, the exact contextual meaning of the original", and claims that only this strategy can be considered true translation (Nabokov 1964/1975:viii). On a more philosophical level, Walter Benjamin reasons that the kinship of languages is more clearly highlighted in a literalist approach to translation (1923/1963, 1923/1970; see PURE LANGUAGE). However, amongst modern literary translators there are few who would consider literal translation to be a suitable vehicle for their work. One of the main reasons for this is stated by Nida as follows: "Since no two languages are identical, either in the meanings given to corresponding symbols or in the ways in which such symbols are arranged in phrases and sentences, it stands to reason that there can be no absolute correspondence between languages. Hence there can be no fully exact translations" (1964:156). Furthermore, to this could be added the near-impossibility of reproducing in TT meanings which are only implicitly present in ST (see Gutt 1991). Literal translation frequently fails to make sufficient allowance for such factors, or is sometimes resorted to because SL or ST is considered in some way superior or sacred (Shen 1995:571); moreover, its adoption frequently leads to a "complete distortion of the meaning of the original" (Chukovsky 1966:242, 1984:6). The notion of literal translation has been formalized by Nida as FORMAL EQUIVALENCE (1964), while Vinay & Darbelnet (1958, 1958/1995) categorize it as a type of DIRECT TRANSLATION 4, listing it as one of seven translation procedures (1958:48, 1958/1995:33; see also ADAPTATION 2, BORROWING, CALQUE, EQUIVALENCE 2, MODULATION 1 and TRANSPOSITION). See also BACK-TRANSLATION, INTERLINEAR TRANSLATION, LITERALISM, METAPHRASE and RANK-BOUND TRANS-LATION. Further reading: Gutt 1991; Nabokov 1964/1975; Shen 1989, 1995.

2 Defined by Lefevere (1975) in the course of an analysis of English translations of a poem by Catullus as one of seven possible strategies for translating poetry. Clearly when it is poetry that is being translated, use of a literal approach is particularly problematic,

as the translator is "working with pre-selected and pre-arranged material" (Lefevere 1975:61). Lefevere consequently considers that the method has severe limitations. However, he also concludes that because of the impossibility of finding direct TL equivalents for SL items a literal approach to translating poetry is in practice unworkable, at least on an artistic level; in this connection he argues that the work of the literal translator is "the record of a long series of more or less strategic retreats from the principle that he ... pay[s] lip service to" (1975:28). See also BLANK VERSE TRANSLATION, IMITATION 2, INTERPRETATION, METRICAL TRANSLATION, PHONEMIC TRANSLATION, POETRY INTO PROSE, RHYMED TRANSLATION and VERSION 2. Further reading: Lefevere 1975.

Literalism A term used in the same way as LITERAL TRANSLATION 1 (or to refer to a single occasion in which this type of approach is applied). While literalism is appropriate to the translation of certain types of text (such as legal documents), most modern commentators condemn the literal translation of literature. For example, Steiner comments that "far from being the most obvious, rudimentary mode of translation, 'literalism' or as Dryden called it, *metaphrase*, is in fact the least attainable" (1975/1992:324; see METAPHRASE), while Barnstone in a similar vein describes the strategy as operating like "an interlingual photocopier of meaning, giving automatic, predictable, and repeatable versions" (1993:31). Further reading: Barnstone 1993; Shen 1989, 1995.

Loan Translation See CALQUE.

Logeme A term used by Radó to refer to a unit which "corresponds to the character and tasks of translation" (1979:189). A logeme is defined as the "element of the ST [the translator] has to *distinguish* and then to *reproduce* while composing the TT" (1979:189). The term is more or less synonymous with UNIT OF TRANSLATION, although Radó's concept is perhaps slightly broader. Thus, not only items such as morphemes, words or phrases may be considered logemes, but also – in a cultural setting where translation conventions require their reproduction – textual features such as verse metre (1979:191). According to Radó, the concept of the logeme is useful not only to translators and interpreters, but also in translator training and translation criticism, and as a "tool of analysis" (1979:189) in TRANSLATOLOGY. Further reading: Radó 1979.

Logos See PURE LANGUAGE.

Low Countries Group See MANIPULATION SCHOOL.

Loyalty (German *Loyalität*) A term introduced by Nord (1991a) to describe the attitude which should ideally characterize the translator's relationship to the ST author and sender, and the TT reader. Nord describes loyalty as "a moral principle indispensable in the relationships between human beings, who are partners in a communication process" (1991a:29). Such a concept is necessary because "in normal intercultural communication, neither the initiator nor the recipient of the translated text is able to check on whether or not the TT really conforms to their expectations" (1991b:94); whenever this is the case, they have to trust the translator to do a good job. Nord suggests the term to supplement the framework provided by SKOPOS THEORY, consequently terming her new revised model "functionality plus loyalty". In accordance with this model, a translator is free to focus on particular ST aspects to the detriment of others, if this is in line with the *skopos*; however, the principle of loyalty then requires him or her to explain to the ST sender how ST has been changed, if such changes conflict with the prevailing translational CONVENTIONS and consequently also with the sender's expectations. Failure to do this amounts to misleading the ST sender as to the nature of the TT produced. The notion of loyalty is totally distinct from that of fidelity (see FAITHFULNESS), which is "a rather technical relationship between two texts" (Nord 1991a:29). See also TRANSLATORIAL ACTION. Further reading: Nord 1988, 1991a, 1991b, 1997.

Machine-aided Translation (MAT) (or Computer-aided Translation, or Computer-assisted Translation, or Machine Aided Human Translation, or Machine-assisted Human Translation, or Machine-assisted Translation) Defined by Sager as "a translation strategy whereby translators use computer programs to perform part of the process of translation" (1994:326). As such it contrasts with MACHINE TRANSLATION in that the computer is simply used as an aid for the human translator rather than actually performing the translation itself. However, it is in reality difficult to draw a clear distinction between these two modes of operation as there is a considerable area of overlap in which automated or semi-automated processes are combined with varying amounts of human intervention (Arnold et al. 1994:35).

There are many types of computer application which are nowadays commonly used by professional translators, and with the IT explosion the potential for their exploitation has grown rapidly. Of course many non-specialist applications frequently find a place in a translator's "workstation", such as for example word processing (including the multilingual variety), CD-ROM resources, optical character recognition (OCR), concordancing and e-mail; however, many would question whether the use of such facilities alone would justify employing the term MACHINE-AIDED TRANSLATION. Contrasting with these are an increasing number of dedicated "translation tools" – frequently combined as a single "package" – such as CORPORA of pre-existing or pre-translated text segments, on-line dictionaries (with or without an automatic look-up facility) and a variety of more specialized computerized aids designed to help develop and store TERM BANKS and to perform a number of other tasks connected with TERMINOLOGY management. However, the main purpose of all such systems is to accelerate the process of human translation (Sager 1994:276); they are thus all highly interactive in nature and require a large amount of human intervention. Furthermore, it should be pointed out that applications of this type work more satisfactorily if the translation can be limited to a specialist area with its own range of vocabulary (1994:276). See also BI-TEXT. Further reading: Arnold et al. 1994; Clark 1994; Melby 1992; Neubert 1991b; Sager 1994.

Machine Translation (or **Automatic Translation**) **(MT)** A term used to refer to translation which is performed wholly or partly by computer. As implied by this definition, such translation may be carried out with or without human intervention; however, if there is a considerable level of intervention, or if computer applications are simply used as "translation tools", then it is more common to talk of MACHINE-AIDED TRANSLATION, although the boundary between these two approaches is not always completely clear-cut. It must be said that there has been much cynicism about machine translation in some quarters, and wags have been quick to recite some of the direr howlers which machine translation systems have produced. Furthermore, on a more scholarly level, Snell-Hornby expresses a common perception when she states that "now there is no longer any doubt that the product of technology, however sophisticated, cannot compete with the creative power of the human mind" (1988/1995:66). However, the fact is that modern approaches to machine translation tend to be more realistic and level-headed than those which arose from the initial euphoria of the 1950s, and the previously-held assumption that machine translation should eventually replace human translation has given way to a more sober appraisal of its potential. It is indeed clear that humans are considerably more adept at analyzing and interpreting natural language than even the most sophisticated machines, and that genres such as literary texts, advertising and promotional material are not generally suited to translation by machine (Newton 1992a:7). Fully automatic, high quality machine translation (FAHQMT) may indeed be impossible (Arnold et al. 1994:13-14), but on the other hand, there are areas where the machine wins out, such as for example in spelling and TERMINOLOGICAL consistency (Newton 1992a:5). The approach can usefully be employed for translating more restricted text-types (such as financial reports or weather forecasts), and is particularly efficient within an organization which has "a large, constant flow" of texts of a certain type which need to be translated (Melby 1992:149; see also SUBLANGUAGES). Its performance can be improved by ensuring that the input is in a form which the system will find easy to analyze (see CONTROLLED LANGUAGE and PRE-EDITING). Furthermore, the raw output from machine translation does not need to be perfect in order to serve a useful purpose (Newton 1992a:4), as it can be POST-EDITED to the extent that is appropriate to the purpose it is to serve; however, one of the main criteria for determining the usefulness of the approach in a given context is that it should be quicker or cheaper than performing the task by hand. Another common misconception is that machine translation systems exist as a "single, stand-alone, black box" (Sager 1994:16). In reality, while the system itself is actually made up of two main components, the *translation engine* and the *dictionary*, it usually forms part of a suite of document processing software. As regards the design (or "architecture") of the translation engine, older systems have generally used a *direct* system, in which SL sentences are converted directly into TL sentences, while more modern designs tend to favour an *indirect* architecture, in which SL material is converted into TL via an underlying representation, which in some cases is termed an *interlingua* (see Arnold et al. 1994). Much research is still being carried out into machine translation, and significant advances are being made. However, it needs to be recognized that the approach continues to suffer from unfair comparison with human translation, partly because, as Sager argues, the discipline as a whole does not offer an adequate model for it

(1994:20); after all, it may be that rather than TRANSLATING, the computer "does something else, which may be similar in some respects, and the outcome of which is a derived document for which we have yet to find another name" (1994:119-20). See also INDUSTRIAL PROCESS (TRANSLATION AS), READER-ORIENTED MACHINE TRANSLATION and WRITER-ORIENTED MACHINE TRANSLATION. Further reading: Arnold et al. 1994; Hutchins & Somers 1992; Newton 1992; Sager 1994; Wilss 1977, 1982.

Manipulation See MANIPULATION SCHOOL and REWRITING.

Manipulation School (or **Low Countries Group**) A term used by some to refer to the group of scholars associated with a particular approach to the study of translated literature. First coined as a word-play (Lambert 1991:33), it is now used almost as a nickname; however, the school's own preferred terms are either TRANSLATION STUDIES or the Low Countries group, although this latter term is misleading to the extent that the group includes scholars from countries other than Belgium and the Netherlands, most notably former Czechoslovakia and Israel. The group has also been known as the *descriptive*, *empirical* or *systemic* school (Hermans 1995:217); however, the name *manipulation school* arose because of the group's conviction that from the target perspective, "all translation implies a degree of manipulation of the source text for a certain purpose" (Hermans 1985a: 11), so that the process of translating will "bring the Target Text into line with a particular model and hence a particular correctness notion, and in so doing secure social acceptance, even acclaim" (Hermans 1991:166). According to one of their best known programmatic statements, the members of the school have in common

> a view of literature as a complex and dynamic system; a conviction that there should be a continual interplay between theoretical models and practical case studies; an approach to literary translation which is descriptive, target-oriented, functional and systemic; and an interest in the norms and constraints that govern the production and reception of translations, in the relation between translation and other types of text processing, and in the place and role of translations both within a given literature and in the interaction between literatures.
>
> (Hermans 1985a:10-11)

Their basic approach thus contrasts with that of the SCIENCE OF TRANSLATION, firstly since their starting-point is "not intended equivalence but admitted manipulation" (Snell-Hornby 1988/1995:22), and secondly because of their concentration on literary rather than technical translation. The group's most important texts include Even-Zohar (1990), Hermans (1985), Holmes et al. (1978), Holmes (1988), van Leuven-Zwart & Naaijkens (1991) and Toury (1980, 1995), while their most important contributions to the discipline are probably the use of a TARGET TEXT-ORIENTED approach, and the notions of NORMS, REWRITING and the literary POLYSYSTEM. See also DESCRIPTIVE TRANSLATION STUDIES and NITRA SCHOOL. Further reading: Hermans 1985a; Lambert 1991; Snell-Hornby 1988/1995.

Mapping A concept used by Holmes (1988) for two separate purposes. Firstly, as a commentary on how different translations of a single poem will each provide the TL reader with an accurate reflection only of certain features of ST, Holmes observes that "all translations are maps, the territories are the originals" (1988a:58); in the same way as no map is definitive, but will serve only the specific purpose for which it was made, it is necessary to have a variety of translations of a poem in order to achieve a fuller understanding of the original. Secondly, Holmes (1988b) argues that translation (particularly the translation of poetry) is a text-rank operation which simultaneously proceeds both serially and structurally, or in other words both sentence by sentence and also as the translator derives and then constantly refers to an overall mental conception (or map) of the text as a whole. However, according to Holmes, not one, but two maps are used during the translation process; the first of these reflects the features which the translator abstracts from ST, while the second is created on the basis of the choices (linguistic, stylistic, rhythmic, and so forth) which he or she makes from the available options and reflects the shape that TT will ultimately take. Furthermore, the second map is influenced by a HIERARCHY OF CORRESPONDENCES (1988b:86) which inevitably emerges as certain choices are ruled out simply because other, more important ones have already been made. The concept of the map could have a practical application for scholars investigating the relationship between an ST and its translation. See also ANALOGICAL FORM, CONTENT-DERIVATIVE FORM, DECISION-MAKING (TRANSLATION AS), EXTRANEOUS FORM, GAMES (TRANSLATION AND THE THEORY OF), METAPOEM and MIMETIC FORM. Further reading: Holmes 1988a, 1988b.

MAT See MACHINE-AIDED TRANSLATION.

Matricial Norms Defined by Toury (1980, 1995) as one of two kinds of OPERATIONAL NORM (see also TEXTUAL NORMS). Matricial norms regulate the decisions which the translator will make during the actual process of translation regarding the organization of the text on a level above that of the sentence. For example, the operation of such NORMS will determine to what extent the omission of ST material is permitted (*existence*), whether sections of text may be moved (*location*), and the way in which the text is subdivided (*textual segmentation*). (These categories are of course not clear-cut, as for example the moving of a section of text from one location to another is tantamount to an omission in one place and an addition in another.) Matricial norms also determine whether such changes are acknowledged by the inclusion of a statement to the effect that TT has been abridged or adapted. See also INITIAL NORM and PRELIMINARY NORMS. Further reading: Toury 1980, 1995.

Mediated Translation See INDIRECT TRANSLATION 1.

Mediating Language See TERTIUM COMPARATIONIS.

Medium-restricted Theories of Translation According to Holmes (1988e), one of six varieties of PARTIAL THEORY OF TRANSLATION. A medium-restricted theory of translation may for example be concerned only with human, MACHINE or MACHINE-AIDED TRANSLATION, or might more specifically encompass one particular medium of human translation, such as SIMULTANEOUS INTERPRETING or written TRANSLATION. See also AREA-RESTRICTED, PROBLEM-RESTRICTED, RANK-RESTRICTED, TEXT-TYPE RESTRICTED and TIME-RESTRICTED THEORIES OF TRANSLATION. Further reading: Holmes 1988e.

Metaphrase (or **Verbal Translation**) A term used by the seventeenth century poet and translator Dryden (1680/1989) to refer to one of three methods of translating. Dryden defines metaphrase as the process of "turning an author word by word, and line by line, from one language into another" (1680/1989:7). In other words, the process which this term denotes is that of LITERAL TRANSLATION. Dryden condemns such a practice in no uncertain terms by arguing that "'tis almost impossible to translate verbally, and well, at the same time"

(1680/1989:8). Indeed, his description of metaphrase is written in highly evaluative language throughout: the translation which results from such a method is characterized as pedantic (1680/1989:8) and servile (1680/1989:9), while the translator is dubbed a verbal copier (1680/1989:9). However, it is only in the following famous image that Dryden pours his fullest scorn on this type of translation: "'Tis much like dancing on ropes with fettered legs: a man may shun a fall by using caution; but the gracefulness of motion is not to be expected: and when we have said the best of it, 'tis but a foolish task; for no sober man would put himself into a danger for the applause of escaping without breaking his neck" (1680/1989:9). See also IMITATION 1 and PARAPHRASE. Further reading: Dryden (1680/1989); Frost 1955.

Metapoem A term coined by Holmes (1988c, 1988d) on the basis of Barthes' (1964) *meta-language*. Distinguishing works of literature from literary criticism, Barthes argues that while the former are intended as statements about "reality", criticism is in effect a statement about *these original works*. In other words, the relationship between literary text and reality is mirrored by that between criticism and text. Changing the term to *meta-literature*, Holmes takes up this idea and argues that criticism is not the only type of writing of which this may be said. Indeed, he suggests seven kinds of text which can function as comment on a poem: a critical essay in the language of the poem, a critical essay in another language, a prose translation, a verse translation, an IMITATION, a poem "about" the poem and a poem inspired by the poem (1988d:24). Holmes uses the term *metapoem* to designate the fourth text-type, the verse translation. To illustrate how these text-types relate to the original poem and to each other he arranges them in the shape of a *fan* around the word *poem*. One implication of such a model is that a metapoem is "a fundamentally different kind of object from the poem from which it derives" (Holmes 1988c:10), in that it does not relate directly to the reality which is ultimately being portrayed, but only via its ST. Another implication is that all kinds of translation are a critical interpretation of their ST, a metapoem specifically "enacting" (Frost 1955 cited in Holmes 1988c:11) the original by remaining as FAITHFUL as possible to the parameters of ST and at the same time having poetic integrity in TL. A metapoet must thus combine the perception of the critic, the sensibility of the poet and the special skill of resolving the confrontation of source and target NORMS. See also METATEXT. Further reading: Holmes 1988c, 1988d.

Metatext A term used by Popovič (1976, [1976]) to describe a text which has been produced using another text (or PROTOTEXT) as its starting-point or model. The term is used within the framework of an attempt to study literary interrelations – or "inter-textual continuity" (1976:225) – in a systematic way. According to Popovič, metatexts belong to the wider category of *metacommunication*, which refers to "all types of processing (manipulation) of the original literary text" (1976:226). A metatext is thus understood as being a text which results from the development or modification of "the semiotic, meaning-bearing, side of the original text" (1976:226). In this way the notion of the metatext includes text-types such as translations, paraphrases or parodies ([1976]:31), but excludes for example TRANSCRIPTIONS or new editions of existing works (1976:226). A translation is a type of metatext which serves as a substitute for another text (1976:230), and is the result of "imitative continuity" with the prototext (1976:231-32). However, it is important to point out that a translation does not merely reflect the original, but is rather "determined by the relation of the translator as creator to reality" (1976:233). In other words, the translator not only "conveys information about invariants of the original"; he or she also "discovers in the original further virtual or concealed meanings" in the light of his or her own experience of reality (1976:233). In this respect the notion of the metatext is distinct from Holmes' related concept of the METAPOEM. Further reading: Popovič 1976, [1976].

Metrical Translation Described by Lefevere (1975) as one of seven strategies for translating verse. Within an analysis of English translations of a poem by Catullus produced over a hundred-year period Lefevere uses the term *metrical translation* to refer to the type of translation in which the metre of ST is preserved in TT. Metrical translation is thus the strategy in which a kind of equivalence is pursued first and foremost on the metrical level. However, Lefevere is in agreement with Holmes that it is a "convenient fiction" (Holmes 1988d:25) that a verse form in any one language "can be entirely identical with a verse form in any other" (1988d:26), regardless of similarity between terminology or language structure. Metrical translation is thus seen as a "very rigorous straitjacket imposed on the target text" (Lefevere 1975:37), in that the translator is obliged to impose on TT a new metrical order which conflicts with and cuts across the "pre-selected and pre-arranged material" (1975:61) of ST.

In this way, argues Lefevere, metrical translation concentrates on one aspect of ST, while neglecting other more important features (such as the semantic content); in so doing, it "fails completely to make the source text available as a literary work of art in the target language" (1975:42). See also BLANK VERSE TRANSLATION, IMITATION 2, IN-TERPRETATION, LITERAL TRANSLATION 2, MIMETIC FORM, PHONEMIC TRANSLATION, POETRY INTO PROSE, RHYMED TRANSLATION and VER-SION 2. Further reading: Lefevere 1975.

Mimetic Form According to Holmes (1988d), one of four strategies for the translation of verse form, in which the form of the original is retained in TT. However, Holmes points out that verse forms in different languages cannot be identical, even if they share the same name. Use of mimetic form has the effect of "re-emphasizing, by its strangeness, the strangeness which for the target-language reader is inherent in the semantic message of the original poem" (1988d:27); this is because an imported form frequently goes beyond the bounds of what is acceptable in the target literary tradition in terms of which verse form is appropriate to which genre. However, the selection of such a form may introduce new features into the literary system, some of which may take on permanent status. Consequently the use of mimetic form is common in cultures or periods in which concepts of genre are less rigid. Along with ANALOGICAL FORM, Holmes catego-rizes mimetic form as one of two types of FORM-DERIVATIVE FORM. See also CONTENT-DERIVATIVE FORM, EXTRANEOUS FORM, MAPPING and METAPOEM. Further reading: Holmes 1988d.

Minimax Principle A term used by Levý (1967) during a discussion of the "pragmatic dimension" of translation. However, what Levý means by the term *pragmatic* is not the problem of translating the contextual aspects of a given text, but rather non-textual concerns which the translator is likely to face, such as the question of the extent to which he or she should accommodate the target audience's probable preferences and expectations. According to the minimax principle, during the DECISION-MAKING process which is involved in any translation, the translator "resolves for that one of the possible solutions which promises a maximum of effect with a minimum of effort" (1967:1179). For example, the extra effect brought about by reproducing the rhyme-scheme of an original poem is not usually felt by translators in many traditions to justify the considerable effort which it involves. Levý argues that translators typically adopt a "pessimistic strategy" (1967:1180), by rejecting all those solutions which are not likely to meet their audience's aesthetic or linguistic expectations. Translators, Levý suggests, will subconsciously predict how readers will evaluate their work; this will in turn influence decisions taken during the translation process, so that for example linguistic elements perceived as being non-native to the TL system may be deliberately avoided. The application of minimax procedures on a statistical basis may cast light on such problems as the relative importance of different stylistic devices in SL and TL, or the extent to which the linguistic purity of a particular TL is considered to be a matter of importance. Further reading: Levý 1967.

Minoritizing Translation See FOREIGNIZING TRANSLATION.

Modification In van Leuven-Zwart's (1989, 1990) model for comparing a literary work with its translation, one of three types of SHIFT which may occur between ST and TT TRANSEMES during the translation process. A shift is said to be an example of modification when each of the two transemes is hyponymically related to its corresponding ARCHITRANSEME, so that the overall relationship which obtains between them is one of contrast. For example, choosing a word with a slightly different meaning, using another part of speech or substituting a word with other stylistic overtones all qualify as instances of modification. It should be pointed out that, while many examples of modification result from a conscious decision on the part of the translator, the phenomenon is frequently caused by constraints of a language-bound or culture-bound nature. When the modification consists of supplying extra syntactic links or making vague logical connections more explicit it is termed *explanation*. Parallels exist between the notion of modification and some of Catford's categories of shift; for example, a change in part of speech, which van Leuven-Zwart would term *syntactic* or *syntactic-semantic* modification, would be classified in Catford's model as CLASS SHIFT. See also GENERALIZATION, INTEGRAL TRANSLATION, MODULATION 2, MUTATION and SPECIFICATION. Further reading: van Leuven-Zwart 1989, 1990.

Modulation 1 (French *Modulation*) A term used by Vinay & Darbelnet (1958, 1958/1995) to refer to one of seven translation methods. Modulation is a kind of OBLIQUE translation, which means that it does not involve the use of parallel SL and TL categories

(1958:46-7, 1958/1995:31). Vinay & Darbelnet define modulation in general terms as "a variation of the form of the message, obtained by a change in the point of view" (1958/1995:36). In other words, modulation involves a manipulation of mental rather than grammatical categories (as opposed to TRANSPOSITION: 1958:88, 1958/1995:88), and reflects the subtly different angles from which speakers of different languages view real-life objects and phenomena. As such it is justifiable when a LITERAL translation or a transposition would result in an expression which is grammatically correct, but which does not sound natural in TL (1958:51, 1958/1995:36). According to Vinay & Darbelnet, some modulations are fixed, or in other words "referred to in dictionaries and grammars and ... regularly taught" (1958/1995:37); others on the other hand are free, or not "sanctioned by usage" in the same way (1958/1995:37). Vinay & Darbelnet (1958:89-90, 235-40, 1958/1995:89-91, 249-54) also distinguish various types of modulation, such as "abstract for concrete" (e.g. *le dernier étage* for *the top floor*), part for whole (e.g. *to wash one's hair* for *se laver la tête*) or – most commonly – negation of the opposite (e.g. *forget it!* for *n'y pensez plus!*). See also ADAPTATION 2, BORROWING, CALQUE and EQUIVALENCE 2. Further reading: Vinay & Darbelnet 1958, 1958/1995.

2 According to van Leuven-Zwart (1989, 1990), one of three possible microstructural SHIFTS which may be observed between ST and TT TRANSEMES in the process of comparison via their corresponding ARCHITRANSEME. The relationship between the two transemes is considered to be one of modulation "if one has a synonymic relationship with the [architranseme] and the other a hyponymic relationship" (1989:159), or in other words, if a shift occurs between ST and TT transemes which either increases or decreases the degree of generality. Depending on whether the shift is towards or away from greater generality, it will be termed either GENERALIZATION or SPECIFICATION; such a shift will be either semantic or stylistic in nature. Such microstructural shifts can influence features on the macrostructural level. For example, the translation of a general, stylistically neutral word by a more specific, value-laden one may contribute to a change in the narrative standpoint by bringing the textual world closer to the reader, while a consistent change in the register of a character's speech may alter the reader's perceptions of that character (1990:72-

74). See also INTEGRAL TRANSLATION, MODIFICATION and MUTA-TION. Further reading: van Leuven-Zwart 1989, 1990.

Modulation/Generalization See GENERALIZATION.

Modulation/Specification See SPECIFICATION.

Monosemierung See SEMANTIC DISAMBIGUATION.

MT See MACHINE TRANSLATION.

Multilingual Corpora Defined by Baker (1995) as "sets of two or more monolingual corpora in different languages, built up ... on the basis of similar design criteria" (1995:232); the term is understood as referring to CORPORA of native rather than translated texts in the languages represented. Multilingual corpora have been profitably used in translator training, materials writing and the development of MA-CHINE TRANSLATION software, as they can be exploited to provide useful insights into the typical means employed by two or more languages to express similar meanings. Furthermore, a reliance on multilingual corpora is a typical feature of the methodology of con-trastive linguistics, where the aim is generally to compare the natural patterns of two or more languages through an examination of texts produced in those languages. However, since multilingual corpora can only provide information about how language is used in its "home" context, rather than in translated texts, they have only a limited theo-retical application when the object of discussion is the phenomenon of translation itself; for such study other types of corpora are more appropriate. Furthermore, since the use of corpora in Translation Studies is relatively new, it should be pointed out that a certain degree of terminological confusion exists; Aijmer et al. (1996), for example, use the term PARALLEL CORPORA to refer to corpora of this type. See also BILINGUAL CORPORA 2 and COMPARABLE CORPORA. Further read-ing: Aijmer et al. 1996; Baker 1995.

Multi-medial Texts (German *Multimediale Texte*) (formerly **Audio-medial Texts**; German *Audio-mediale Texte*) A term used by Reiss (see for example Reiss & Vermeer 1984) to refer to a sub-sidiary text-type which supplements Reiss' basic text typology (see EXPRESSIVE TEXTS, INFORMATIVE TEXTS and OPERATIVE TEXTS). The multi-medial category consists of texts in which the verbal content is supplemented by elements in other media; however, all such texts will also simultaneously belong to one of the other, main text-types. Reiss argues that this text-type forms a "superstructure" over the other three, as the "special requirements of this type take precedence over whatever basic text type a given text otherwise belongs to" (1977/1989:111). Songs, comic strips, plays, and writing for radio or television are all examples of this type (Reiss 1977/1989:111), and the translator of such texts will need to ensure that the translation is equally suited as the original for use in the relevant medium. See also SKOPOS THEORY. Further reading: Nord 1996; Reiss 1971, 1976, 1977, 1977/1989, 1990; Reiss & Vermeer 1984.

Multiple-Stage Translation Suggested by Voegelin "as a set of procedures for showing explicitly the stages of work followed when an utterance in one language is re-uttered in another" (1954:271). Although originally developed as a procedure to be followed in MA-CHINE TRANSLATION, multiple-stage translation was adapted for the purpose of demonstrating the processes involved in translating from American Indian languages. Presented as a development of the type of two-stage translation which was common in anthropological research (i.e. ST – LITERAL TT – FREE TT), multiple-stage translation can be characterized as the progressive rearrangement of SL linguistic units to produce a TT which still reflects much of the structure of SL. Voegelin identifies eight stages in the translation process, the first of which is the identification of SL words with the help of an informant, and the last the addition of TL punctuation; with each of these "translational interim stages" (Wilss 1982:106), the developing TT is brought closer and closer to its final form. However, the precision of the instructions for multiple-stage translation, some of which call for highly complex bracketing procedures and the adoption of certain typographical conventions, is redolent of the procedure's machine translation origins, implying as it does the possibility of reducing translation problems to a "sequence of standardly operative moves guaranteeing translational success" (Wilss 1994:136). For reasons such as this many commentators conclude that multiple-stage translation is impractical for most purposes. Further reading: Voegelin 1954; Wilss 1994.

Mutation A term used by van Leuven-Zwart (1989, 1990) to denote the third category of SHIFT which may occur between ST and TT

TRANSEMES. Mutation is said to have occurred if no relationship can be established between the two transemes; in this case it is not possible to establish an ARCHITRANSEME. According to van Leuven-Zwart there are three types of mutation: *"addition* of clauses or phrases, *deletion* of clauses or phrases, and *radical change of meaning"* (1989:169, emphasis original). See also GENERALIZATION, INTEGRAL TRANSLATION, MODIFICATION, MODULATION 2, and SPECIFICATION. Further reading: van Leuven-Zwart 1989, 1990.

Nairobi Declaration (or **Nairobi Recommendation**) A declaration adopted by UNESCO on 22 November 1976, the full title of which is the "Recommendation on the Legal Protection of Translators and Translations and the Practical Means to Improve the Status of Translators". The intention of the recommendation is to ensure that translators – whether salaried or unsalaried, full or part time, literary, scientific or technical – are accorded recognition commensurate with the skill required to carry out their task, and to improve the often unfavourable conditions in which they are obliged to work. One of the document's main concerns is that translators should receive rights similar to those enjoyed by authors in terms of, for example, social benefits, protection under international copyright laws, and the prominence given to their name in published translations. However, the declaration is broad in scope, covering such diverse topics as remuneration, contracts, professional organizations, training and working conditions. See also A.I.I.C., DUBROVNIK CHARTER and F.I.T. Further reading: Haeseryn 1994; Osers 1983.

Naturalness A term used to refer to the extent to which a translation is expressed in clear, unforced terms in TL. Naturalness is described by the Bible translators Beekman & Callow as "a prerequisite to ease of understanding" (1974:39). The notion of naturalness also features in a famous definition of translation formulated by Nida & Taber, who – also within the context of Bible translation – state that translating "consists in reproducing in the receptor language the closest *natural* equivalent of the source-language message, first in terms of meaning and secondly in terms of style" (1969/1982:12, emphasis added); they describe naturalness as being characterized by "the use of grammatical constructions and combinations of words which do not violate the ordinary patterns of a language" (1969/1982:203). Similarly, Beekman & Callow consider that the naturalness of TT should be comparable to the naturalness of the original in terms of the use that is made of the "inventory of linguistic forms which serve as a vehicle for any message conveyed" in a given language (1974:40). Along similar lines, Vázquez-Ayora – writing in a different tradition – states that every language has its own particular preference as regards style and manner of expression: Spanish, for example, does not have the fondness of English for explaining and describing in the most minute detail, and this must be taken into account when translating between these two languages (1977:361). See also ACCURACY, DYNAMIC FIDELITY, IDIOMATIC TRANSLATION and TRANSLATIONESE. Further reading: Beekman & Callow 1974; Vázquez-Ayora 1977.

Necessary Degree of Differentiation (or **Necessary Degree of Precision**) See DEGREE OF DIFFERENTIATION.

Negative Shift Defined by Popovič as an incorrect translational solution (or mistranslation) caused by a misunderstanding on the part of the translator ([1976]:16). Popovič states that this may be due to the fact that the translator is unfamiliar with the language, or has interpreted an ST structure superficially. See also SHIFTS. Further reading: Popovič [1976].

Nitra School A group of Slovak scholars originally based at the Nitra Pedagogical Faculty in former Czechoslovakia. The group, which included Jiří Levý, František Miko and Anton Popovič among its members, took some of the work of the Russian Formalists and the Prague linguistic circle as its starting-point in an investigation of some aspects of literary translation. Together these scholars were responsible for a number of important insights which have been taken up by later writers, in particular those associated with the MANIPULATION SCHOOL. Among these were for example an emphasis on retaining the artistic quality of a work in translation (Levý 1969), the investigation of the possibility of cataloguing the expressive features contained in a text (Miko 1970), the importance of SHIFTS as a general translational phenomenon (Popovič 1970), and the consideration of translation in the context of the wider notion of METATEXT (Popovič 1976, [1976]). As pointed out by Hermans, the group fell silent after 1980 (1995:217). Further reading: Gentzler 1993.

"No Leftover" Principle According to Toury (1995), a technique used in DESCRIPTIVE translation analysis. The purpose of the principle is to act as a guideline for establishing the precise relationships between individual ST and TT segments. A basic problem in "coupling off" pairs of replaced and replacing segments in this way is how to determine their respective boundaries, as there is no guarantee they will be identical "in rank or in scope" (1995:79), for example because of omission, addition or the results of COMPENSATION. The "no leftover" principle thus guides the researcher to identify as a replacing segment only a TT segment beyond the boundaries of which "there are no leftovers of the solution to a translation problem which is represented by one of the source text's segments, whether similar or different in rank and scope" (1995:79). Further reading: Toury 1995.

Norms A term frequently encountered in discussions of translational phenomena. A certain degree of confusion exists surrounding the use of the term (van Leuven-Zwart 1991). Traditional writing on translation and some branches of modern TRANSLATION THEORY have taken a basically normative or PRESCRIPTIVE approach, in which norms are perceived and presented as guidelines, or even rules, which a translator needs to follow in order to produce an acceptable translation. Today, for example, this approach is often associated with various areas of APPLIED TRANSLATION STUDIES (such as translator training and the writing of translation textbooks). Within other approaches, such as DESCRIPTIVE and PURE TRANSLATION STUDIES, norms are understood in more neutral terms as reflections of the translation practice which typifies the translations produced by a certain translator, school of translators or entire culture. However, the same broad definition will serve whichever approach is adopted, so that it is possible to state in general terms that: "Norms ... perform a channelling, funnelling role in that they refer problem tokens, i.e. individual utterances and occurrences, to problem types, to which a given norm can be applied" (Hermans 1991:165). Broadly speaking, the conception of norms which different writers have adopted has depended on whether they understand the rôle of translation theory as being essentially regulatory, descriptive or predictive. However, it was the contradictory nature of many of the norms laid down by normative models (see for example Savory (1957:49) for a famous list of such contradictory requirements) that led Toury (1980) to suggest his tripartite model describing translational behaviour, in which the norm was posited to occupy the middle ground between COMPETENCE and PERFORMANCE (or, in another dimension, between rules and idiosyncrasies: Toury 1995:54). In this model, norms are defined as "strategies of translation which are repeatedly opted for, in preference to other available strategies, in a given culture or textual system" (Baker 1993:240). Understood in this way, norms influence decisions in such wide-ranging areas as a TT's position between the poles of ACCEPTABILITY and ADEQUACY 2 (INITIAL NORM), whether it is acceptable in a given culture to translate a work via its translation in another language (PRELIMINARY NORMS; see also INDIRECT TRANSLATION 1), and more generally translational choices which need to be made during the course of the translation process (MATRICIAL, OPERATIONAL and TEXTUAL NORMS). Since such norms are not directly observable, they are typically reconstructed from actual texts or from extratextual sources such as corpora of TTs or various kinds of explicit statements of translation practice (Toury 1995:65), although the latter frequently reflect current *prescriptive* thinking on translation. The study of such norms is strongly associated with a TARGET TEXT-ORIENTED approach, and can provide useful insights in a number of areas. These include the preconceptions, conventions and preferences of individual translators or whole cultures, and – leading on from these – the way in which EQUIVALENCE is understood in different traditions; the identification of true UNIVERSALS OF TRANSLATION; and the position of translated literature in the literary POLYSYSTEM. It is because of such wide-ranging considerations that the notion of the norm has been deemed "an absolutely essential concept" (Hermans 1991:165). See also CONVENTIONS, EXPECTANCY NORMS and PROFESSIONAL NORMS. Further reading: Chesterman 1993; Hermans 1991; Komissarov 1993; Toury 1980, 1995.

Obligatory Equivalents A term used by Nida (1964) to describe the features of TL which the translator must of necessity employ when translating from another language. According to Nida, it is the first requirement of any translation "that it conform to the obligatory formal features of the receptor language" (1964:173). These innate features – which can include any type of grammatical category or other formal element – are what distinguish one language from another; as Nida says, citing Jakobson (1959/1966:236), "languages differ most in what they *must* convey, not in what they *may* convey" (1964:173). Translation problems thus frequently arise as a result, for example, of the presence in TL of a category which is not found, or which is only poorly defined, in SL. The existence of such features also imposes severe restrictions upon the extent to which TL expressions may be considered equivalent to the corresponding SL expressions, as the translator has no alternative but to employ obligatory equivalents in any translation, whether it is FORMALLY or DYNAMICALLY EQUIVALENT. Nida also points out that, because obligatory TL features must be introduced into the translation, there is a tendency towards gain in linguistic forms when translating from one language to another. However, this gain may be justified by the fact that there is an almost inevitable loss in total meaning between SL and TL because the two languages do not share the same cultural context (1964:174-75). See also EQUIVALENCE and OPTIONAL EQUIVALENTS. Further reading: Nida 1964.

Oblique Translation (French *Traduction Oblique*) According to Vinay & Darbelnet, a term used to refer to various types of translation procedure designed to cope with situations where, because of structural or conceptual differences between ST and TT, some stylistic effects cannot be rendered satisfactorily without disturbing the syntactic or lexical order of the text (1958:46, 1958/1995:31); as such it contrasts with DIRECT TRANSLATION 4. In such cases, the straight replacement of ST elements by parallel TL elements is not possible, as it would simply produce a translation which was unacceptable in terms of meaning, structure or style (1958:49, 1958/1995:34-35). The four types of oblique translation – ADAPTATION 2, EQUIVALENCE 2, MODULATION 1 and TRANSPOSITION – are thus stylistic devices which enable translators to produce TTs which read naturally and do not give the impression of having been translated. Further reading: Vinay & Darbelnet 1958, 1958/1995.

Observational Receiver A term used by Pym (1992b) to describe a reader (or listener) who is able to understand the message of a text, even though he or she is not specifically addressed in it; such a reader contrasts with an EXCLUDED RECEIVER and a PARTICIPATIVE RECEIVER. Pym cites the example of an English-language job advertisement appearing in a French newspaper with a literal French translation appended; even in such circumstances the non-English-speaking reader "although lingually non-excluded, by no means shares the same discursive status as the implied receiver of the English text", as he or she is still not one of those being invited to apply for the job

(1992b:176). Pym is not convinced that his categorization represents a radically new distinction, and indeed, strong parallels do exist, for example, between translation intended for an observational receiver and House's (1977) OVERT TRANSLATION. However, Fawcett argues that while other similar distinctions categorize *texts* on the basis of *function*, Pym's idea of distinguishing types of *receiver* according to their degree of *involvement* "allows the breaking of a logjam in the question of translating texts which are culture-specific either in whole or part" (1995:179). See also DOCUMENTARY TRANSLATION. Further reading: Fawcett 1995; Pym 1992b.

Offer of Information See INFORMATION OFFER.

Operational Model A model of the translation process suggested by Bathgate (1980, 1981). The operational model is designed to describe "all phases of the work done by the translator to get from a source-language text to the corresponding target-language text" (1980:113). Bathgate's model is not proposed as an alternative to the many other models of the translation process which exist, but is rather an attempt to reconcile all previous models by placing them within one overall framework. The operational model divides the process of translation into seven phases: tuning ("getting the feel of the text": Bathgate 1980:113), ANALYSIS, understanding, terminology (i.e. TRANSFER 2), RESTRUCTURING, checking and discussion (for example with a subject expert). These phases are not necessarily either distinct or sequential; for instance, the discussion phase may occur concurrently with any – or all – of the others. As can be seen from the nomenclature, Bathgate's model is to a large extent based on that proposed by Nida & Taber (1969/1982). However, according to Bathgate, other models which are also accommodated include those represented by HERMEN-EUTIC MOTION, MODULATION 1, DECISION-MAKING and MAPPING; each of these models can be allocated a place according to the phase for which it provides the greatest insights. Bathgate argues that the overview of translator activity which the operational model provides is useful in training translators. Further reading: Bathgate 1980, 1981.

Operational Norms A term used by Toury (1980, 1995) to refer to those translational NORMS which "direct actual decisions made during the translating process itself" (Toury 1980:54). There are two types of operational norm: those which affect the *matrix* of the text, or in other words the ways in which the linguistic material – especially the larger units – is distributed within the text (MATRICIAL NORMS), and those which involve the textual make-up and verbal formulation of the text (TEXTUAL NORMS). As the process of DECISION-MAKING progresses the precise operational norms which are being used will determine which options are available to the translator and which are closed off. See also INITIAL NORM and PRELIMINARY NORMS. Further reading: Toury 1980, 1995.

Operative Texts (German *Operative Texte*) (formerly **Appeal-focused Texts**; German *Appellbetonte Texte*) A term used by Reiss (1977/1989) to refer to one of three basic text-types intended both as a guide for translators and to help in the process of translation criticism (see also EXPRESSIVE TEXTS and INFORMATIVE TEXTS). As with the other categories, operative texts are distinguished by the function which they serve, and also by the language in which they are written, which reflects this function. Operative texts contain messages which are intended to persuade the receiver to undertake a certain course of action, such as buying a specific product or voting for a particular political party. In other words, in such a text "both content and form are subordinated to the extralinguistic effect which the text is designed to achieve" (Nord 1996:83). This means that a translator's main aim should be to produce a TT which has an EQUIVALENT persuasive force to that of the original. However, besides transmitting similar "impulses to action" (Reiss 1977/1989:111), the translation process will also entail preserving the basic semantic content, as well perhaps as reproducing elements of an aesthetic nature. Political manifestos, advertisements and sermons are all examples of this type of text; however, Reiss makes the point that, like the others, this category is not rigidly defined, as many texts also have further, more subsidiary aims. See also MULTI-MEDIAL TEXTS and SKOPOS THEORY. Further reading: Nord 1996; Reiss 1971, 1976, 1977, 1977/1989; Reiss & Vermeer 1984.

Optional Equivalents According to Nida (1964), the features of a language which a translator may choose to use when rendering an ST in TL. Whereas in the case of OBLIGATORY EQUIVALENTS the translator is bound by the rules which govern the formal features of TL, there is no such restriction on the use of optional equivalents, and so he or she may choose between various possible renderings, all of which reflect proximity to ST. According to Nida, the use of optional equivalents is important in maintaining the "flow" of the message, so the criteria which determine how to select them involve the principle of COMMUNICATION LOAD; Nida in addition points out that the translator must be sensitive to the style and intent of the author, and must also be empathetic to the TT receptors (1964:173-74). See also EQUIVALENCE. Further reading: Nida 1964.

Organic Form See CONTENT-DERIVATIVE FORM.

Overlapping Translation (or **Partially-overlapping Translation**)
A term used by Hervey & Higgins (1992) to describe the type of semantic near-EQUIVALENCE which combines elements of GENERAL-IZING TRANSLATION and PARTICULARIZING TRANSLATION in a single word or phrase by adding a detail not found in ST but at the same time omitting another detail which is given there. Hervey & Higgins suggest that overlapping translation may be visualized as two partially overlapping circles, as the SL and TL expressions both contain elements of shared meaning as well as features not found in the other. According to Hervey & Higgins, it is acceptable on two conditions: "first, if the TL offers no suitable alternatives; second, if the *omitted* detail is either unimportant or can be recovered from the overall TT context, and if the *added* detail is implicit in, or at least not contradictory to, the overall ST context" (1992:97). As an example of this phenomenon Hervey & Higgins discuss the English phrase *my mother-in-law's soup* and a possible French translation, *la soupe de ma belle-mère*; although the French is one of the closest possible renderings of the English, it can be termed an overlapping translation because of the fact that, on the one hand, French *soupe* is a narrower term than English *soup*, and, on the other, French *belle-mère* can refer not only to a *mother-in-law*, but also to a *step-mother* (1992:96). Further reading: Hervey & Higgins 1992.

Overt Translation A term introduced by House (1977) to refer to one of two contrasting modes of translation (see also COVERT TRANSLATION). According to her model, some STs have "independent status" in the source culture. This means that they are in some way inextricably linked to the community and culture, being specifically directed at SL addressees. In order to translate such STs appropriately, it is necessary to produce an overt translation, or one in which "the target addressees are quite 'overtly' not being directly addressed" (1986:188). Consequently, in the production of such a TT no attempt is made to produce a "second original": an overt translation "must overtly be a translation" (1986:188). Furthermore, because of the firm anchoring of ST in the source culture, it is not possible to preserve its original function (in terms of context, audience, etc.) in TT. Production of an overt translation is generally a matter of relatively straightforward linguistic recoding, usually with no necessity to carry out any subtle cultural realignment. Sermons, political speeches and much artistic literature are all examples of text-types for which such an approach would be appropriate. In this framework translations for special addressees (for example children's versions of classical works) or purposes (for example INTERLINEAR TRANSLATIONS) are defined as *overt versions* of an ST. See also DOCUMENTARY TRANSLATION, OBSERVATIONAL RECEIVER and SEMANTIC TRANSLATION. Further reading: House 1977, 1986.

Overtranslation 1 (or **Over-translation**) (French *Surtraduction*) A term used by Vinay & Darbelnet (1958, 1958/1995) to describe what occurs when two UNITS OF TRANSLATION are perceived where there is in fact only one. Vinay & Darbelnet cite as an example the translation of *aller chercher* as *to go and look for*, rather than *to fetch*; here the translator has treated the SL expression as if it were a chance combination of two words, rather than a fixed expression which has an obligatory one-word equivalent in TL (1958:31, 1958/ 1995:16). Further reading: Vinay & Darbelnet 1958, 1958/1995.

2 A term used by Newmark (1981/1988) to refer to one of two phenomena frequently found in translated texts. As is argued by Newmark, every act of translation involves some loss of ST meaning (for example because of the difficulty of finding a precise equivalent for a given word, or more generally because the writer of ST and the translator favour different modes of expression). According to Newmark, if this loss of meaning entails an increase in detail (rather than an increase in generalization) it is termed *overtranslation*. For example, the axiomatic simplicity of the English sentence *the cat sat on the mat* disappears when it is translated into French (*le chat était accroupi sur le paillasson*), partly because French lacks a generic term corresponding to English *mat*, with the result that any word chosen as an equivalent is likely to have a more specific meaning than the English word. As observed by Duff (1981), a common

symptom of overtranslation is more words being used to express an idea in TT than were used in ST. Overtranslation is typical of SEMANTIC TRANSLATION. See also DEGREE OF DIFFERENTIATION, PARTICULAR-IZING TRANSLATION and UNDERTRANSLATION. Further reading: Duff 1981; Newmark 1981/1988, 1988.

Paradigmatic Equivalence Defined by Popovič as "equivalence of the elements of a paradigmatic expressive axis upon the stylistic level as a system of expressive elements" ([1976]:6). The term *paradigmatic* is used to refer to the complete "expressive system", or in other words, the entire range of expressive possibilities from which the actual items found in a given text are drawn. This type of equivalence is not identical with "lexical synonymical equivalence" (one of several kinds of LINGUISTIC EQUIVALENCE), as it involves a "hierarchically higher stylistic category" ([1976]:6). See also EQUIVALENCE, STYLISTIC EQUIVALENCE and TEXTUAL EQUIVALENCE 2. Further reading: Popovič [1976].

Parallel Corpora (or **Bilingual Corpora**) According to Baker, a type of corpus "consists of original, source language-texts in language A and their translated versions in language B" (1995:230). Like MULTILINGUAL CORPORA, parallel corpora can be used in materials writing, translator training and the development of MACHINE TRANSLATION systems. However, their advantage over multilingual corpora is that they provide information not on the native patterns of a target *language*, but on those of specific target *texts*, and so give insight into the particular translation practices and procedures which have been used by the translator. Full exploitation of the potential of parallel corpora is possible only with the use of special software to enable the investigator to align ST sentences with their TT equivalents or to conduct bilingual concordancing operations. As is the case with terms denoting other types of CORPORA, there is still a certain lack of standardization in the way in which this term is used; Johansson & Hofland (1994), for example, extend its meaning to include the type of corpora which Baker (1995) refers to as *multilingual corpora*. See also BI-TEXT and COMPARABLE CORPORA. Further reading: Baker 1995; Granger 1996; Hartmann 1980; Johansson & Hofland 1994.

Parallel Translation A procedure described by Casagrande (1954).

Parallel translation is in effect a type of BACK-TRANSLATION in which an ST is translated simultaneously into several different TLs. According to Casagrande, such a procedure provides a researcher with useful insights: "Comparison of the translations in the several target languages may reveal significant and systematic differences in the way [SL] is handled at both the grammatical and semantic levels" (1954:340). See also SERIAL TRANSLATION. Further reading: Casagrande 1954.

Paraphrase One of three methods of translating described in the seventeenth century by Dryden (1680/1989). While IMITATION 1 and METAPHRASE are the procedures which represent the two extremes of FREE and LITERAL TRANSLATION, paraphrase is conceived as a middle way between them. Dryden defines paraphrase as "translation with latitude, where the author is kept in view by the translator, so as never to be lost, but his words are not so strictly followed as his sense" (1680/1989:8). Dryden recommends paraphrase as the preferred means of translating, and although he ascribes primacy to the author's sense, advocates exercising care in the translation of both the original's meaning and its words: when translating thoughts, it is permissible "to vary but the dress, not to alter or destroy the substance" (1680/1989:11), while if the words – "the more outward ornaments" (1680/1989:11) – can be rendered gracefully, "it were an injury to the author that they should be changed" (1680/1989:11). Dryden argues that by adopting this method of translation "the spirit of an author may be transfused, and yet not lost" (1680/1989:11); furthermore, he underlines the necessity of making a translation resemble the original by using a simile comparing the translation process with that of a painter copying from life (1680/1989:11). Finally, it should be pointed out that while Dryden's use of this term differs from the standard modern English meaning of *paraphrase*, many other writers on translation do use the term in this more common sense. Further reading: Dryden 1680/1989; Frost 1955.

Paris School See INTERPRETIVE THEORY OF TRANSLATION.

Partial Theories of Translation According to Holmes (1988e), one of the two branches of THEORETICAL TRANSLATION STUDIES. In contrast to GENERAL THEORIES OF TRANSLATION, partial theories of translation are concerned with only a limited number of the phenomena covered by the discipline of TRANSLATION STUDIES. Significant advances have been made in the area of numerous specific partial theories of translation, and considerable further development is likely to be a prerequisite of the eventual formulation of a general theory of translation. The category of partial theories of translation is further divided into six sub-types: AREA-RESTRICTED, MEDIUM-RESTRICTED, PROBLEM-RESTRICTED, RANK-RESTRICTED, TEXT-TYPE RESTRICTED and TIME-RESTRICTED THEORIES OF TRANSLATION. See also PURE TRANSLATION STUDIES and TRANSLATION THEORY. Further reading: Holmes 1988e.

Partial Translation A term used by Catford (1965) to refer to a kind of translation in which parts of the text (usually lexical items) are left "untranslated". This occurs with reasonable frequency in literary translation, either as a strategy for dealing with "untranslatable" elements, or in order to introduce an SL flavour into TT. However, to say that such elements remain "untranslated" is something of an approximation, as items will inevitably acquire new contextual meanings in TL; as illustration of this, Catford cites the examples of Finnish *sauna* and Russian *sputnik*, both of which, as foreign "borrowings", are understood in English differently from the way they are used in the languages from which they are taken. See also FULL TRANSLATION. Further reading: Catford 1965.

Partially-overlapping Translation See OVERLAPPING TRANSLATION.

Participative Receiver According to Pym (1992b), one of three types of text receiver (see also EXCLUDED RECEIVER and OBSERVATIONAL RECEIVER). As such, a participative receiver is a reader (or listener) to whom the text is explicitly addressed. Pym cites the example of a job advertisement written in English which appears in a French newspaper; even though there may be an explanation in French of the content of the advertisement, it is only those in a position to understand the English – the "participative receivers" – who are actually being invited to apply (1992b:176). Fawcett argues that such a categorization of reader involvement represents an important advance on classifications of translation function (such as House's (1977) COVERT and OVERT TRANSLATION), as it casts important light on the question of translating culture-specific texts (1995:179). See also INSTRUMENTAL TRANSLATION. Further reading: Fawcett 1995; Pym 1992b.

Particularizing Translation (or **Particularization**) Defined by Hervey & Higgins (1992) as a translation which renders an ST expression by a TL *hyponym* (or word with a less exclusive meaning). This means that the literal meaning of the TT expression is narrower and more specific than that of the corresponding ST expression. In this way a particularizing translation adds details to TT that are not explicitly expressed in ST. According to Hervey & Higgins, particularizing translation is acceptable on two conditions: "first, that the TL offers no suitable alternative; second, that the added detail is implicit in the ST and fits in with the overall context of the ST" (1992:95). However, it may not be used if there are alternatives in TL, or if the added detail creates discrepancies in TT or represents a misinterpretation of the overall context of ST (1992:95). See also GENERALIZING TRANSLATION, OVERLAPPING TRANSLATION and OVERTRANSLATION 2. Further reading: Hervey & Higgins 1992.

Patronage A term used by Lefevere (1985, 1992) in the context of a discussion of the factors which can be brought to bear on a literary SYSTEM and the individual texts of which it is composed. According to Lefevere, two types of control are exercised on a literary system. The first of these is that of professionals such as translators, critics, reviewers and teachers, whose intervention can determine the shape of a text or ensure that the way in which it is perceived fits in with the "reigning orthodoxy" (1992:15) of a culture; the second is that of what Lefevere terms *patronage*. Patronage is defined as "something like the powers (persons, institutions) that can further or hinder the reading, writing, and rewriting of literature" (1992:15). Such "powers" can take the form of individuals (such as the head of state), political or religious institutions, social classes, publishers or the media (1992:15); in each instance the influence which they exert has the purpose of ensuring that "the literary system does not fall too far out of step with the other subsystems society consists of" (1992:14). The control which the "patron" exercises consists of three elements: ideological constraints on form and subject matter, economic provision for writers, translators and other REWRITERS, and the bestowing of status on these individuals (1992:16). Patronage is termed *undifferentiated* if all three elements depend on the same persons or institutions, and it is generally the case that such patrons are concerned with maintaining the stability of society as a whole (1992:17); in systems where this is not the case the patronage is said to be *differentiated*. The influence of patronage is of course immense, as it can determine the ways in which a literary system develops, as well as shaping the canon of texts chosen for study in schools and universities (1992:20-24). See also POLYSYSTEM THEORY. Further reading: Lefevere 1985, 1992.

Performance A term used by Toury (1980). Following Chomsky's (1965) famous dichotomy, Toury uses the term *performance* to describe instances of actual translation (i.e. existing TTs) as opposed to the SYSTEM of translational possibilities which exist between any potential SL and TL (known as translation COMPETENCE). Strictly speaking, the term thus applies to instances of *interlingual* communication, and more specifically, the type of interlingual communication which is known as translation. Instances of such translational performance (i.e. individual TTs) can be studied for the information which they may reveal about translated text in general; in this connection, both the TT-ST and the TT-TL relationships which a particular TT displays are of interest. Toury suggests that the performance-competence distinction is too cut-and-dried to account for all types of translational phenomenon (whether standardly used by translators, only occasionally encountered or merely potential but basically unrealized), and consequently proposes the NORM as the third member of a tripartite model. Further reading: Toury 1980.

Phonemic Translation (or **Homophonic Translation**) One of seven strategies for translating poetic texts, which Lefevere (1975) discusses with reference to English translations of Catullus' poem sixty-four. In a phonemic translation the translator places fidelity to the sound of ST above all other considerations, to produce a TT which attempts to mimic the "phonetic image" (Kelly 1979:125) of ST while being encoded in as close an approximation to TL as possible. Thus for example Zukofsky & Zukofsky's (1969) experimental translation of the Catullus poem aims to "breathe the 'literal' meaning" with the ST author by following the sound, rhythm and syntax of ST as closely as possible (Zukofsky & Zukofsky 1969, Translators' Preface). Lefevere points out that throughout the entire TT "... an undercurrent of paraphrased sense lies hidden behind the attempted similarity of sound" (1975:21), a sense which is made up of "elaborate syntactic jigsaw puzzles" (1975:95). However, such a radically distinctive TT inevitably polarizes opinion. Lefevere is generally critical, arguing that the TT produced is awkward and frequently lacking in any kind of TL meaning; he speaks disparagingly of the way in which the translators implicitly claim to be "fusing" SL and TL in their translation (1975:96). Kelly, on the other hand, sees it as an extreme outworking of Walter Benjamin's (1923/1970) notion of a translation being an attempt to approximate PURE LANGUAGE (Kelly 1979:55). Toury cites this TT, among others, as a test-case for the claim of TARGET TEXT-ORIENTED TRANSLATION STUDIES that a wide range of different texts can be accepted as translations (1980:43-45). Venuti, who refers to this type of modernist translation as *homophonic* translation, notes the "proliferation of ambiguities" and the "dazzling range of Englishes" (1995:216) suggested by the text; he treats such eccentric TTs as examples of FOREIGNIZING TRANSLATION, a strategy which he advocates as a challenge to accepted translation practices. It should be pointed out that the category of phonemic translation is broadly analogous to Catford's (1965) PHONOLOGICAL TRANSLATION. See also BLANK VERSE TRANSLATION, IMITATION 2, INTERPRETATION, LITERAL TRANSLATION 2, METRICAL TRANSLATION, POETRY INTO PROSE, RHYMED TRANSLATION and VERSION 2. Further reading: Lefevere 1975; Venuti 1995.

Phonological Translation A term used by Catford to refer to a type of RESTRICTED TRANSLATION in which "the SL phonology of a text is replaced by equivalent TL phonology" (1965:56), the grammar and lexis remaining unchanged. While FORMAL CORRESPONDENCE may not exist between given phonological features of two different languages, it is usually possible to set up translation equivalences. The basis for such equivalences is the "relationship of SL and TL phonological units to 'the same' phonic substance [or sequence of sounds]" (1965:56). This means that sounds or groups of sounds which do not exist in the TL phonological system will not be realized when translated from the SL phonological system, or else will be realized in a way more germane to the TL phonological system. Therefore the English sequence /kats/, for example, might be rendered into a language which had no final consonant clusters as /kat/, while English /had/ would correspond to Greek /xent/, since this represents the closest Greek equivalent to the original sequence of sounds. This procedure is occasionally exploited for its potential humorous effect, as can be seen in the following phonological translation into French of the first two lines of the English nursery-rhyme "Georgie-Porgie":

> Georgie Port-régie, peu digne en paille,
> Qui se dégeule sans mais. Dame craille.
>   -de Kay (1983: no. 1)

However, besides instances of such ingenious word-play, and with the further exceptions of film DUBBING and some translations of poetry (both of which are examples of *partial* phonological translation), SL phonology is usually replaced, not translated. It should be noted that if one speaks a foreign language with the phonology of one's own language – or in other words with a foreign accent – one can be considered to be performing a phonological translation from the foreign language into one's own. See also GRAMMATICAL TRANSLATION, GRAPHOLOGICAL TRANSLATION, LEXICAL TRANSLATION and PHONEMIC TRANSLATION. Further reading: Catford 1965.

Pivot Language A term used to refer to a language which serves as an intermediate stage between SL and TL when it is for some reason not possible to transfer ST directly into TL (see INDIRECT TRANSLATION 1 and RELAY INTERPRETING). This procedure can be resorted to when for example no translator or interpreter is available who is able to work between SL and TL; it is also used as a cheap method of SUBTITLING, where it entails providing subtitles in a certain TL on the basis of a set of subtitles which has been produced for another language. Use of a pivot language is not generally encouraged since it necessitates two separate transfers – firstly from SL into the pivot language and then from the pivot language into TL – which are performed by different people and which can thus result in a TT which departs some way from the original (see Dries 1995). Further reading: Seleskovitch & Lederer 1989.

Poetry into Prose One of seven strategies of poetry translation catalogued by Lefevere (1975). Poetry into prose differs from LITERAL TRANSLATION 2 in that the translator attempts to render in TT some of the poetic qualities of the original. Opinion as to the efficacy of this strategy has always been sharply divided. Tytler, for example, designates the translation of a lyric poem into prose as "the most absurd of all undertakings" (1791/1978:207). Murry, on the other hand, considers that "no fetters of rhyme or metre should be imposed" to impede the difficult labour of translating poetry (1923:129, quoted in Holmes 1988d:31 n. 11). In the course of an analysis of English translations of a poem by Catullus, Lefevere considers the advantages and disadvantages of this technique. On the positive side, he characterizes poetry into prose translations as "accurate, closer to the source text than a verse translation could ever be", while also being "happily liberated from the deadening restraints of the doggedly word-for-word technique" (1975:42). However, he observes that the strategy also results in "an uneasy, hybrid structure, forever groping towards a precarious equilibrium between verse and prose and never really achieving it" (1975:42). In other words, the translator who chooses this translation strategy is still obliged to operate within considerable restrictions which ultimately deduct from the overall literary impact of the text. See also BLANK VERSE TRANSLATION, IMITATION 2, INTERPRETATION, METRICAL TRANSLATION, PHONEMIC TRANSLATION, RHYMED TRANSLATION and VERSION 2. Further reading: Lefevere 1975.

Polemical Translation Defined by Popovič (1976, [1976]) as a translation in which the translator's operations are intentionally "directed against another translator's operations that are representative of a different or antagonistic conception [of translation]" ([1976]:21). Alternatively, a polemical translation can also be aimed at the ST author. In such cases, a translation of this type may be devised as a parody of some aspect of the author's poetics, or may simply be intended to bring the original up to date (1976:229). Further reading: Popovič 1976, [1976].

Polysystem Theory A theory proposed by Even-Zohar (1978a, 1978b, 1990) to account for the behaviour and evolution of literary SYSTEMS. The term *polysystem* denotes a stratified conglomerate of interconnected elements, which changes and mutates as these elements interact with each other. Thus a given national literary polysystem will evolve as a result of the continuous tension between various literary models, genres and traditions; the frequently conservative, "canonized" forms (those which most closely reflect the most accepted, institutionalized aesthetic) will attempt to retain their prominent, influential position, while other, innovative, "non-canonized" genres will attempt to usurp their central position. In order to acquire a complete overview of the dynamics which shape a literary polysystem one must take account not only of so-called "high" forms (such as the established verse forms) but also of a range of "low" forms (such as works for children, popular fiction and translated literature). Translated literature usually occupies a peripheral position, but can at times assume a more influential rôle. The adoption of polysystem theory by certain groups of scholars (most notably the so-called MANIPULATION SCHOOL) has led to the development of TARGET TEXT-ORIENTED TRANSLATION STUDIES, a non-PRESCRIPTIVE approach in which the emphasis has been on describing actual translation practices (or NORMS) rather than constructing theories which propose one particular translation method as being the only correct one. See also SYSTEM. Further reading: Baker 1993; Even-Zohar 1978a, 1978b, 1990; Gentzler 1993; Hermans 1985a; Lefevere 1983.

Post-editing A term used in the context of MACHINE TRANSLATION and defined by Sager as "the adaptation and revision of output of a machine translation system either to eliminate errors which impede comprehension or to make the output read like a natural language text" (1994:327). As Sager observes, such human intervention is often necessary because output from machine translation can seem "faulty or artificial" (1994:276). The process of post-editing can be either interactive or non-interactive; however, for the use of a machine-translation system to be economically viable, the expense and effort involved in post-editing must be less than that required for a full human translation, or there would be no point in using the machine translation system. On the other hand a flexible policy towards post-editing will recognize that translations are needed for different purposes, and that the level of post-editing will vary accordingly. Thus for example one text may be translated with no post-editing at all (possibly to find out whether it merits "proper" translation), a second may require considerable post-editing in order to be presented in a highly polished state, while a third may simply need to be checked for basic intelligibility and accuracy before being submitted in a readable but less than perfect form (see Arnold et al. 1994:33-34). See also PRE-EDITING. Further reading: Arnold et al. 1994; Sager 1994.

Pragmatic Translation 1 (or **Pragmatic Approach**) A term used to refer to translation which pays attention not only to denotative meaning but also to "the way utterances are used in communicative situations and the way we interpret them in context" (Baker 1992:217). As stated by Baker, pragmatics is a branch of linguistics devoted to "the study of meaning, not as generated by the linguistic system but as conveyed and manipulated by participants in a communicative situation" (1992:217); this means that a pragmatic translation will for example attempt to convey connotative meaning, allusion, and interpersonal aspects of communication such as implicature, tone, register and so on. Many insights of pragmatics have been incorporated into various TRANSLATION THEORIES, including relevance theory (see DIRECT TRANSLATION 3 and INDIRECT TRANSLATION 2) and SKOPOS THEORY (Neubert 1994:411). See also COMMUNICATIVE TRANSLATION 1. Further reading: Baker 1992; Hatim & Mason 1990.

2 One of Casagrande's (1954) four classifications of translation, in which the chief purpose is to "translate a message as efficiently and as accurately as possible", with the emphasis on "the content of the message as such rather than on its aesthetic form, grammatical form or the cultural context" (1954:335). Examples of pragmatic translations are scientific treatises, government documents and the instructions, directions or descriptions written in several languages on packaged goods. See also AESTHETIC-POETIC TRANSLATION, ETHNOGRAPHIC TRANSLATION and LINGUISTIC TRANSLATION 2. Further reading: Casagrande 1954.

Pre-editing A term used to refer to the process of preparing an ST for translation by a MACHINE TRANSLATION system. Most such systems find it almost impossible to analyze language which is even slightly convoluted, and so it is frequently necessary to simplify, clarify and disambiguate the grammar and vocabulary of the text to be translated, in order to ensure that the output is of a reasonable quality. Such pre-editing may take the form of rewriting the text in a CONTROLLED LANGUAGE, or simply shortening sentences, reducing the number of subordinate clauses and adding explicating words such as conjunctions. However, pre-editing may also be semi-automated as some systems have a *critiquing* facility which indicates the points at which the input needs to be rewritten (Arnold et al. 1994:29). See also POST-EDITING and WRITER-ORIENTED MACHINE TRANSLATION. Further reading: Arnold et al. 1994.

Precision, Degree of See DEGREE OF DIFFERENTIATION.

Preliminary Norms According to Toury (1980, 1995), one of a number of different types of NORM which influence the translation process. Preliminary norms are defined as operating in two distinct but clearly related areas. The first of these is the question of whether or not a coherent translation "policy" can be identified in a given culture or language at a particular point in time. Such a policy is understood in terms of the individual works, authors, genres, schools or literatures which are the preferred sources for translation into a given language. Of course, different policies may apply to different subgroups of the target SYSTEM, while in some contexts no definite policy exists; one may only be said to exist if the choices made in a given area are nonrandom (Toury 1995:58). The second area in which preliminary norms are said to operate is in the attitude displayed by a given culture to translation via another TT in another language (see INDIRECT TRANSLATION 1). For example, some cultures prohibit any translation which does not use the original text as its ST, while in others such a practice may be permitted, tolerated or even preferred. Further issues would include the languages which may serve as an intermediary, and whether such a mediated translation is labelled as such or camouflaged (Toury 1980:53-54 and 1995:58). See also INI-TIAL NORM, MATRICIAL NORMS, OPERATIONAL NORMS and TEXTUAL NORMS. Further reading: Toury 1980, 1995.

Prescriptive Translation Studies A term used by Toury (1980, 1985) to refer to approaches to translation which are normative in outlook, or in other words which impose criteria stipulating the way translation should be performed in a particular culture. Two of the most significant prescriptive orientations have traditionally been the insistence on either FREE or LITERAL translation as being the only "proper" strategy to adopt; however, other prescriptions have also been made, such as for example the refusal by some cultures to accept the validity of INDIRECT TRANSLATION 1 (see Toury 1995). Toury attributes the traditional predominance of such prescriptive approaches to the "overall orientation of the discipline towards its practical applications" (1985:17), such as translation teaching and criticism (see APPLIED TRANSLATION STUDIES); such applications have represented "the main constraint on the very formulation of the theory which underlies them" (1985:17) as they have been allowed to dominate the discipline instead of serving as its "extensions ... into 'the real world'" (1985:17). In practice this has meant that the discipline of TRANSLATION STUDIES has been influenced by prescriptive pronouncements which have derived "either from sheer speculation or from theoretical and descriptive work done within the framework of *other*, more 'basic' disciplines" such as contrastive linguistics (1985:17, emphasis original). According to Toury this situation is remedied by acknowledging that Translation Studies consists not only of applied but also of DESCRIPTIVE and THEORETICAL branches; within such a framework it is possible to develop methodologies for viewing translations as target *facts* which can be studied on an empirical basis, while the applied extensions will – rightly – remain prescriptive in nature (Toury 1995; see also Holmes 1988e). See also SOURCE TEXT-ORIENTED TRANSLATION STUDIES. Further reading: Toury 1980, 1985, 1995.

Primäre Übersetzung See PRIMARY TRANSLATION.

Primary Translation (German **Primäre Übersetzung**) According to Diller & Kornelius (1978), one of two ways of translating (see also SECONDARY TRANSLATION). A TT is considered to be a primary translation if the aim is "to produce a communication between an SL sender and a TL receiver" (1978:3). In other words, the translator of a primary translation will attempt to create a text in which the target recipients seem to be addressed directly rather than being presented with a message which was originally intended for someone else. Thus primary translation is said to occur, for example, when two people converse via an interpreter, or when a bilingual secretary translates a business letter, since in both these cases the TT recipient is the intended recipient of the original communication. See also COVERT TRANSLATION. Further reading: Diller & Kornelius 1978.

Problem-restricted Theories of Translation A term used by Holmes (1988e) to refer to one of six PARTIAL THEORIES OF TRANSLATION. Problem-restricted theories of translation deal with specific translation-related problems, such as for example that concerning the nature of translation EQUIVALENCE, or the translation of metaphors or proper names. See also AREA-RESTRICTED, MEDIUM-RESTRICTED, RANK-RESTRICTED, TEXT-TYPE RESTRICTED and TIME-RESTRICTED THEORIES OF TRANSLATION. Further reading: Holmes 1988e.

Process-oriented Translation Studies (or **Process-oriented Descriptive Translation Studies**) According to Holmes (1988e), one of three varieties of DESCRIPTIVE TRANSLATION STUDIES. Process-oriented Translation Studies is concerned with an examination of the mental processes involved in the act of translating. Clearly, such processes are highly complex, yet it is hoped that the systematic application of sophisticated psychological techniques will lead to advances in this area and to the possible setting up of a new area of study which one might term *translation psychology* (1988e:72-73). See also FUNCTION-ORIENTED TRANSLATION STUDIES and PRODUCT-ORIENTED TRANSLATION STUDIES. Further reading: Holmes 1988e.

Product-oriented Translation Studies (or **Product-oriented Descriptive Translation Studies**) One of three types of DESCRIPTIVE TRANSLATION STUDIES, according to Holmes (1988e). This approach generally starts from the description of existing translations, and typically progresses to a comparative analysis of various translations of the same text into one or more TLs. A more generalized survey of a larger corpus of translations (relating to a particular period, language and/or text or discourse type) may follow on from this; such an analysis may for example focus on medieval English Bible translations. One possible eventual goal of Product-Oriented Translation Studies might be a comprehensive history of translations, although such an ambitious project is not likely to be feasible for some time (1988e:72). See also FUNCTION-ORIENTED TRANSLATION STUDIES and PROCESS-ORIENTED TRANSLATION STUDIES. Further reading: Holmes 1988e.

Professional Norms Defined by Chesterman (1993) as one of two types of translational NORM (see also EXPECTANCY NORMS). According to Chesterman, professional norms govern "the accepted methods and strategies of the translation process" (1993:8); as such they are intended to reflect the way professional translators in a given culture produce translations. Chesterman argues that the purpose of norms is not only to describe, but also to evaluate both translations and translational practice. In this way they not only reflect "the actual practice of competent professional translators" (1993:9) but are also "at least in part validated by norm authorities" (1993:9) such as editors, critics or teachers of translation. Furthermore, professional norms are also governed by the "higher-order" expectancy norms (1993:9). Chesterman identifies three main types of professional norm: the *accountability* norm, the *communication* norm and the *relation* norm. The accountability norm is an ethical norm, as it requires the translator to meet the demands of LOYALTY to the writer of ST, the commissioner of the translation and the prospective readership (1993:8). The communication norm is a social norm which specifies the ways in which the translator should act in order to "optimize communication between the original writer and/or commissioner and the prospective readership" (1993:8). The relation norm is a linguistic norm, and determines the type and level of EQUIVALENCE established between ST and TT; its nature is "determined by the translator, on the basis of his or her understanding of the intentions of the original writer and/or commissioner, the type and skopos of the text, and the nature of the prospective readership" (1993:9; see SKOPOS THEORY). See also REGULATIVE TRANSLATIONAL CONVENTIONS. Further reading: Chesterman 1993.

Prose Translation See INVERSE TRANSLATION.

Prospective Science of Translation See PROSPECTIVE TRANSLATION and SCIENCE OF TRANSLATION.

Prospective Translation A term used by Postgate to describe translation "which primarily regards the Reader" (1922:18; see also RETROSPECTIVE TRANSLATION). Prospective translation is thus a TL-oriented translation procedure in which the translator's main concern is to express the ST meaning in terms appropriate to the TL audience; in this way the translator is seen as an adapter rather than a FAITHFUL follower of the original wording. Wilss (1982:159) uses the term *prospective science of translation* to denote the subdivision of APPLIED TRANSLATION STUDIES concerned with such matters as the methodology of translation teaching and the study of translation difficulties, which are associated with translation as a process rather than a product. The term *prospective translation* is broadly synonymous with *acceptable translation* (see ACCEPTABILITY) and FREE TRANSLATION. See also SCIENCE OF TRANSLATION. Further reading: Postgate 1922; Wilss 1977, 1982.

Protest (German *Protest*) A term used by Reiss & Vermeer (1984) in the context of SKOPOS THEORY. According to Reiss & Vermeer, in any act of communication, the delivery of a message is followed by some kind of *feedback* (*Rückkoppelung*) or reaction, the purpose of which is to provide the message producer with an idea of how the message has been received. The communication is considered not to have been SUCCESSFUL if the recipient's feedback takes the form of a *protest*, or in other words if the communication is not received as it was intended; such a protest can occur because of either the content of the message or the intention of the producer. In the context of translation, a protest can in addition be directed against the translator's intention, or in other words TT's skopos. See also COHERENCE and INFORMATION OFFER. Further reading: Reiss & Vermeer 1984; Vermeer 1983.

Prototext Defined within Popovič's theory of metacommunication as a text "which serves as an object of inter-textual continuity" (1976:226). In other words, a prototext is any text which provides the starting-point for the creation of a further text (or METATEXT). Thus the concept includes STs for translation, and also the originals or inspirations for such other secondary activities as imitation, re-telling, allusion and reviewing ([1976]:31). Further reading: Popovič 1976, [1976].

Pseudotranslation 1 A term used to refer to "TL texts which are regarded in the target culture as translations though no genuine STs exist for them" (Toury 1980:31). The notion of pseudotranslation thus refers to the kind of literary forgery in which a writer attempts to present an original text as if it were a translation. Toury argues that this phenomenon has significance for Translation Studies for two main reasons. Firstly, pseudotranslation has been used on occasion "to introduce innovations into a literary system, especially when this system is resistant to deviations from canonical models and norms" (1984:83; see NORMS). Secondly, pseudotranslations provide a useful insight into prevailing notions of the features which characterize a translated text, as pseudotranslators typically utilize both linguistic and textual items common in genuine translations. Pseudotranslations have special significance in TARGET TEXT-ORIENTED approaches to translation as the fact of their existence supports the claim that "the identity of a target text as a translation is determined first and foremost by considerations pertinent to the receptor system, with no necessary connection with the source text" (1984:81). Popovič ([1976]) uses two terms – *pseudotranslation* and *fictitious translation* – to refer to the same phenomenon. A famous example of a pseudotranslation is the *Works of Ossian*, which James Macpherson published during the 1760s, claiming to have translated them from the original Gaelic, but which it seems he had in fact written himself (see Macpherson 1996). See also POLYSYSTEM THEORY and SYSTEM.

Further reading: Toury 1980, 1984, 1995.

2 A term used by Radó (1979) to refer to a TT which deviates too greatly from its ST to be considered a translation. The criterion for deciding how to categorize a work is the extent to which the ST and TT LOGEMES correspond. ADAPTATIONS 1, reworkings in a different genre (for example stage versions) and "travesties" are all according to Radó types of text which should be classified as pseudotranslations. Further reading: Radó 1979.

Public Service Interpreting See COMMUNITY INTERPRETING.

Pure Language (or **Logos**, or **True Language**, or **Universal Language**) (German *die reine Sprache*) A term used by Walter Benjamin in his writings on the nature of language and translation. Kelly describes Benjamin's approach as a "mixture of mysticism, aesthetics and philosophy" (1979:30), a statement which reflects Benjamin's view of language as something innately mysterious, sacred and even magical. In an early essay (1916/1977, 1916/1979) the term *pure language* refers to the language of Paradise which Man used in order to name everything in Creation; this act of naming is viewed by Benjamin here as "the translation of the nameless into name" and "the translation of an imperfect language into a more perfect one" (1916/1977:151, 1916/1979:117). However, it is in the sense introduced by Benjamin (1923/1963, 1923/1970) that the term *pure language* is more commonly used and understood. This latter article is concerned with the translator's task, which Benjamin sees as consisting of various elements. First of all, there is the need to release ST from its dependency on a single linguistic code by "prolonging its life" in another cultural and linguistic setting. Secondly, a good translation will increase and extend the scope and range of TL: "The translator enriches his tongue by allowing the source language to penetrate and modify it" (Steiner 1975/1992:67). Benjamin elaborates on this point in an extended quotation from Pannwitz (1917), and argues that in a good translation TL should take on some of the characteristics of SL, while a bad translation, on the other hand, merely effects a transfer of information from one language to another. Thirdly, a translation should express "the central reciprocal relationship between languages" (Benjamin 1923/1963:185, 1923/1970:72). However, Benjamin understands kinship of languages not in the usual historical sense, but rather as a similarity of *intention*: the actual words and constructions may differ, but the human experience which all languages point to is invariable. Furthermore, all languages are "fragments of a greater language" (1923/1963:191, 1923/1970:78), which is termed *the pure language*; translation from one language into another will lead to the two languages being mutually supplemented, even reconciled, or, as Steiner has it, "somehow fused" (1975/1992:67). During this process – possibly to be seen as the fitting together of fragments of a broken vessel – the pure language is approximated to more closely in a translated than in an original text: "[the translator] extends his native idiom towards the hidden absolute of meaning" (Steiner 1975/1992:67). In Benjamin's scheme of things the primary unit of translation is the *word*; consequently the essence that is the pure language is borne by the words rather than the syntax: "For if the sentence is the wall before the language of the original, literalness is the arcade" (1923/1963:192, 1923/1970:79). The syntax of a given language is portrayed as a wall because of the presence, for example, of implicit information and language-specific, ingrained metaphor, which inevitably ties the meaning of the text to a single linguistic code. It is in the light of such considerations that Benjamin comments that "The interlinear version of the Scriptures is the prototype or ideal of all translation" (1923/1963:195, 1923/1970:82); INTERLINEAR TRANSLATION, however, should not be taken to mean a simple, automatic, WORD-FOR-WORD translation, but rather an idealized version of such translation, in which the meaning is "liberated" from the syntax and norms of a single language, and is allowed to shine through the words in its purest, most unobscured form. See also BABEL (TOWER OF). Further reading: A. Benjamin 1989; W. Benjamin 1916/1977, 1916/1979, 1923/1963, 1923/1970; de Man 1986; Steiner 1975/1992.

Pure Translation Studies According to Holmes (1988e), the non-applied subdivision of TRANSLATION STUDIES. As such, Pure Translation Studies is itself split into a descriptive and a theoretical wing (see DESCRIPTIVE TRANSLATION STUDIES, THEORETICAL TRANSLATION STUDIES and TRANSLATION THEORY 2). See also APPLIED TRANSLATION STUDIES. Further reading: Holmes 1988e.

Radical Translation A term used by Quine (1959/1966, 1960) to denote the "translation of the language of a hitherto untouched people" (1960:28). For Quine, whose main concern is with the philosophy of meaning, the significance of such a situation lies in the fact that the translator has neither linguistic similarities nor common culture to rely on, and so is forced to decipher an alien language from first principles. Quine's aim is not to recommend a specific translation procedure; on the contrary, radical translation is intended as a hypothetical demonstration of the INDETERMINACY of meaning. Quine describes the imaginary, but now famous situation of a sighting of a rabbit leading to the utterance of the SL sentence "Gavagai", which the translator tentatively translates as "Rabbit". He then argues that such sentences, based on observable phenomena, provide the best point for the translator to gain a toe-hold in SL. The deciphering of the entire language would follow on from such sentences by means of inference, trial and working hypothesis, on the basis of whether the translator's attempts to "use back" sentences in various situations elicited assent or dissent from the SL informant; when the possible range of application of an SL sentence had been established with reasonable certainty, the translator would suggest a TL sentence as an equivalent. Such correspondences, or *analytical hypotheses*, Quine argues, are what provide the "parameter of translation" (1960:76), as they determine the nature of the "translation manual" which is gradually built up by the translator. However, Quine points out a number of theoretical problems which arise from the notion of radical translation. For example, the sets of circumstances which might elicit apparently equivalent SL and TL sentences may in fact be different, since the two languages will inevitably diverge in how they categorize observable phenomena. Furthermore, speakers of any language carry around with them a certain amount of cultural knowledge (or *collateral information*); such knowledge, which of course also differs from language to language, will colour the perception of even such apparently culturally neutral events as the sighting of a rabbit. Most important, however, is Quine's argument that the analytical hypotheses which a translator selects are to a large extent arbitrary. He states that

> manuals for translating one language into another can be set up in divergent ways, all compatible with the totality of speech dispositions, yet incompatible with one another. In countless places they will diverge in giving, as their respective translations of a sentence of the one language, sentences of the other language which stand to each other in no plausible sort of equivalence however loose.

(Quine 1960:27)

The purpose of radical translation is therefore to highlight the notion of indeterminacy in translation, as illustrated by these three factors. Furthermore, if taken to its logical conclusion it ultimately leads to the discovery that meaning is not absolute: "the discontinuity of radical translation tries our meanings: really sets them over against their verbal embodiments, or, more typically, finds nothing there" (Quine 1960:76). See also EQUIVALENCE. Further reading: Harrison 1979; Malmkjær 1993; Quine 1959/1966, 1960.

Rank-bound Translation Described by Catford (1965) as a type of TOTAL TRANSLATION. In accordance with the grammatical system proposed by Halliday (1961) the term *rank* is used to denote linguistic units of various sizes, ranging from a morpheme to a sentence. A rank-bound translation is therefore one in which "the selection of TL equivalents is deliberately confined to *one rank* (or a few ranks, low in the rank scale)" (Catford 1965:24; emphasis original); such a translation might thus proceed, for example, on a WORD-FOR-WORD or clause-for-clause basis. A good example of rank-bound translation is provided by the French sentence *J'ai laissé mes lunettes sur la table* and the English sentence *I've left my glasses on the table* (Catford 1965:76), which exhibit almost total correspondence on all linguistic ranks; however, such examples are uncommon, even when SL and TL have such relatively similar grammatical categories as French and English. In most contexts the TTs produced by this process "are not acceptable texts of the goal language at all" (de Beaugrande 1978:11). However, word-rank-bound translation is used in INTER-LINEAR TRANSLATION to produce a specialized text designed to fulfil a specific purpose. Another practical application for the technique has been proposed by Ure, Rodger & Ellis, who recommend providing a poet-translator unfamiliar with SL with a "crib" in the form of a rank-bound translation; such a procedure, they claim, is superior in "algorithmic rigour" (1969:14 n. 14) to such alternatives as a rough draft or word-for-word version. See also LITERAL TRANSLATION 1, RANK-RESTRICTED THEORIES OF TRANSLATION, UNBOUNDED TRANSLA-TION, UNIT SHIFT and WORD-FOR-WORD TRANSLATION. Further reading: Catford 1965; Ure, Rodger & Ellis 1969.

Rank-restricted Theories of Translation One of six types of PARTIAL THEORY OF TRANSLATION identified by Holmes (1988e). A rank-restricted theory of translation is defined as one which is only concerned with the features of translation at linguistic ranks lower than entire texts (see RANK-BOUND TRANSLATION). At the time when Holmes first wrote his now famous article (i.e. the early 1970s), most linguistically-oriented research fell within this particular category as the focus there was usually on the ranks of word, word-group or sentence (see LINGUISTIC TRANSLATION 1). However, Holmes predicted that the advent of text linguistics would eventually be likely to lead to the development of linguistic methods of translation analysis at the text rank also (1988e:75); this has to a large extent now been borne out by the arrival of approaches of the type outlined in PRAGMATIC TRANSLATION 1. See also AREA-RESTRICTED, MEDIUM-RESTRICTED, PROBLEM-RESTRICTED, TEXT-TYPE RESTRICTED and TIME-RESTRICTED THEORIES OF TRANSLATION. Further reading: Holmes 1988e.

Reader-oriented Machine Translation A term used by Sager (1994) to refer to the speedy production of a TL version of a text by means of MACHINE TRANSLATION in order simply to inform the TL reader of the content of ST. According to Sager, readers are sometimes prepared to accept machine-produced texts even if they are difficult to read, provided that they are produced quickly and inexpensively (1994:281). The result of such a procedure is "raw output", or in other words an artificial product which may require more reading effort than a human translation simply because it has not been POST-EDITED; however, it has the advantage of being available more quickly than a more "polished" version, and can now be relied on to contain a relatively small number of lexical or terminological mistakes (1994:282). Sager points out that people who frequently use such translations develop the ability to read the artificial machine-produced language which they typically contain with a high degree of fluency (1994:282). As an example of reader-oriented machine translation in action Sager cites the system SYSTRAN, which is used by the US Air Force to help survey scientific and technical literature (1994:283). See also INDUSTRIAL PROCESS (TRANSLATION AS) and WRITER-ORIENTED MACHINE TRANSLATION. Further reading: Sager 1994.

Realia (Russian *Realii*) Defined by Vlakhov & Florin (1970) as textual elements which provide local and historical colour. One of the most recalcitrantly untranslatable features of an ST, realia are generally confined to literary rather than technical translation. Vlakhov & Florin define realia as follows: "words (and collocations) of a national language which denote objects, concepts and phenomena characteristic of the geographical surroundings, culture, everyday realities or socio-historical specifics of a people, nation, country or tribe, and which thus convey national, local or historical colour; such words have no exact equivalents in other languages" (1970:438, translated). There are four categories of realia: a) geographical and ethnographical (e.g. *mistral*, *Hakka*), b) folkloric and mythological (e.g. *Baba Yaga*, *leprechaun*), c) everyday items (e.g. *hurdy-gurdy*, *rupee*) and d) socio-historical (e.g. *Bezirk*, *Infanta*). Vlakhov & Florin suggest six strategies for translating realia: TRANSCRIPTION, CALQUE, formation of a new word, assimilation, approximate translation and descriptive translation (see EXPLICITATION). When selecting the most appropriate strategy, the translator should seek to retain some local colour without encumbering the reader with an excess of new, frequently impenetrable lexical items, and should also be mindful of the influence, whether enriching or polluting, which the new coinings may exert on TL. See also CULTURAL TRANSPOSITION and VOIDS. Further reading: Florin 1993; Lehmuskallio et al. 1991; Leighton 1991; Vlakhov & Florin 1970.

Receptor Language Defined by Nida & Taber as "the language into which a message is translated from the original or source language" (1969/1982:205, emphasis removed). In other words, as regards referential meaning the term *receptor language* is basically synony-mous with the probably more widespread term TARGET LANGUAGE. However, its use tends to be associated with certain areas of TRANSLATION STUDIES, perhaps most notably Bible translation. Furthermore, some writers encourage its adoption because the overtones which it conveys are perceived as being more appropriate to a discussion of translation than those of its main rival. Thus Nida, for example, argues that its use emphasizes the fact that the message is not shot at a target, but must rather be "decoded by those who receive it" (1969:484). See also DIRECTION OF TRANSLATION and SOURCE LANGUAGE.

Reconstructions, Translation with (French *Traduction avec Reconstructions*) According to Gouadec (1990), one of seven types of translation which serve to meet the various translation needs which arise in a professional environment. In translation with reconstructions ST is translated in its entirety without regard to its form. The aim of such a translation is to communicate the content of ST in the simplest way possible; all the information is thus immediately accessible to the TL reader (1990:335). See also ABSOLUTE TRANSLATION, ABSTRACT TRANSLATION, DIAGRAMMATIC TRANSLATION, KEYWORD TRANSLATION, SELECTIVE TRANSLATION and SIGHT TRANSLATION. Further reading: Gouadec 1990; Sager 1994.

Redundancy Described by Nida (1964) as a feature of all natural languages which should be preserved through the translation process. According to Nida, the information contained in any communication needs to be diluted, and the effects of any possible interference (or "noise") overcome, by the inclusion of a certain amount of *redundancy*, the purpose of which is to "raise the predictability" (1964:127) of what is being communicated and in so doing ease the receptor's task of decoding the message. Redundancy is thus defined as "the expression more than once of the same units of information" (Nida & Taber 1969/1982:205), or in other words the inclusion of unnecessary or repeated information within a text. Nida calculates that natural languages "normally tend to produce messages of about 50 percent redundancy" (1964:129); such redundancy can be, for example, phonetic, lexical, collocational or grammatical in nature. However, in translated texts this figure can fall dramatically. This is partly because the translator can increase the unpredictability (or *information*) contained in the text by following SL patterns too literally; in such circumstances, the resulting TL awkwardness increases the target receptor's processing effort. However, another reason is that TL receptors will not share the cultural background of their SL counterparts and so will not be able to make all the inferences required for a proper understanding of the text. Because of this, texts need to be "drawn out" in the translation process by incorporating a degree of linguistic redundancy and by making implicit information more explicit. Failure to do this will lead to the receptor being "overloaded" with information. According to Nida & Taber, such a procedure is essential if DYNAMIC EQUIVALENCE is to be achieved, which leads to the conclusion that "there is a tendency for all good translations to be somewhat longer than the originals" (1969/ 1982:163). See also COMMUNICATION LOAD and EXPLICITATION. Further reading: Nida 1964; Nida & Taber 1969/1982.

Refraction A general term used by Lefevere in the early 1980s to refer to the range of literary processes to which translation can be said to belong. Lefevere defines refraction as "the adaptation of a work of literature to a different audience, with the intention of influencing the way in which that audience reads the work" (1982:4). Of the various processes which can be classified as refraction the most "obvious" is translation, while other types include criticism, commentary, historiography, teaching, anthologizing and the production of plays (1982:4). Lefevere argues that these activities are carried out against the background of the prevailing literary climate and political ideology, and that these factors act as a "spectrum" through which writers and their works are "refracted" before they reach their audience (1982:4). Lefevere remarks on the fact that refraction has not been properly studied as a phenomenon (1982:5), in spite of the fact that the works of refractors have played an immense part not only in disseminating the writings of individual authors, but also in influencing the way in which entire literary SYSTEMS have developed (1982:5). It should be noted that, as Hermans points out, the term *refraction* has more recently been replaced by REWRITING (1994:139). See also PATRONAGE. Further reading: Lefevere 1982.

Regulative Translational Conventions A term used by Nord (1991b) to denote one of two types of translational CONVENTION. Nord bases the concept on Searle's (1969) notion of *regulative rules*, or the conventions which determine how a person should behave in a given situation (an example being the rules of etiquette which provide guidelines on how to conduct interpersonal relationships). By analogy, Nord's concept refers to "the generally accepted forms of handling certain translation problems below the text rank" (1991b:100). The examples which she cites of such problems are "proper names, culture-bound realities or realia, quotations, etc." (1991b:100; see REALIA); in all of these areas, translational practice varies from culture to culture, while the specific regulative translational conventions which operate are determined by a given culture's CONSTITUTIVE TRANSLATIONAL CONVENTIONS. See also PROFESSIONAL NORMS. Further reading: Nord 1991b.

Relay Interpreting A term used to refer to the practice of interpreting between two (usually less widely spoken) languages via a third, mediating language (Seleskovitch & Lederer 1989:199). Encountered in CONFERENCE INTERPRETING, such a procedure is sometimes necessitated when no single interpreter is present who is able to work with both SL and TL. Thus for example, in a conference at which English, French, Greek and Danish delegates are present, it may only be possible to interpret speeches in Danish for the Greek delegates by first interpreting them into English or French (Seleskovitch & Lederer 1989:199). In such a situation, the second interpreter (or "relayer") does not have direct access to the communicative features of the speaker's original spontaneous delivery, and will probably also not be familiar with the source culture; in effect he or she is therefore in the same position as most of the conference delegates (Seleskovitch & Lederer 1989:200). However, Brennan & Brien (1995) actively recommend this procedure in the case of SIGNED LANGUAGE INTER-PRETING. In this context it involves a hearing interpreter communicating ST in a "sign supported" language to a Deaf interpreter who then relays the message to the TL audience in a signed language. The advantage of using the procedure here is that it enables the Deaf audience to receive the message from an interpreter who is working into his or her native language (1995:117-18). See also INTERPRET-ING and PIVOT LANGUAGE. Further reading: Seleskovitch & Lederer 1989.

Repertoreme Defined by Toury as "any sign, irrespective of rank and scope, which forms part of ... an institutionalized repertoire" (1995:268). The term *repertoire* is understood as referring to "the aggregate of rules and materials which govern both the making and use of any given product" (Even-Zohar 1990a:39); thus for example, the literary repertoire may be described as "the aggregate of rules and items with which a specific text is produced, and understood" (Even-Zohar 1990a:40). When an item belonging to such a repertoire is inserted into a particular text, it "enters into a unique network of internal relations, peculiar to that act/text" (Toury 1995:268), and consequently becomes a TEXTEME. However, in the process of translation, according to an observed translation phenomenon which Toury formulates as the *Law of growing standardization*, "textual relations obtaining in the original are often modified, sometimes to the point of being totally ignored, in favour of [more] habitual options offered by a target repertoire" (1995:268, emphasis removed); in other words, ST textemes tend to be converted into TL repertoremes (1995:268). Thus for example intentional ambiguities may be ironed out or original metaphors replaced by more standard formulations. However, it should be pointed out that while Toury posits this tendency as being almost universal, the reverse can also happen when new webs of relationships are created in TT where none existed in ST (1995:272). Further reading: Toury 1995.

Rephrasing A term used by Hervey & Higgins to refer to "the exact rendering of the message content of a given ST in a TT that is radically different in form, but neither adds nor omits details explicitly conveyed in the ST" (1992:252). In terms of the amount of information which is provided in TT this process is a theoretical midway-point between the two extremes of EXEGETIC TRANSLATION and GIST TRANS-LATION: despite the radically changed form in which TT appears, the message content is as close as possible to ST. As an example of INTRALINGUAL rephrasing Hervey & Higgins cite the sentences *I had a little drink about an hour ago* and *I consumed a small quantity of alcohol approximately 60 minutes ago* (1992:17). Hervey & Higgins observe that rephrasing never allows a precise reproduction of the message content of ST, simply because "the two forms of expression are different" (1992:18). Further reading: Hervey & Higgins 1992.

Resistancy (or **Resistance**) A term used by Venuti (1995) to refer to the strategy of translating a literary text so that it retains something of its foreignness; as such it is broadly synonymous with FOREIGNIZING TRANSLATION. According to Venuti, the approach was conceived as a way of challenging the assumption prevalent in Anglo-American culture that the only valid way of translating is to produce a TT which reads fluently in TL and is so "transparent" that it could be mistaken for a product of the target culture. Resistancy thus consists of freeing "the reader of the translation, as well as the translator, from the cultural constraints that ordinarily govern their reading and writing" and questioning the "major ... status [of English-language culture] by using it as the vehicle for ideas and discursive techniques which remain minor in it, which it excludes" (1995:305). Venuti considers the experience of being thus confronted by the cultural differences which separate TL and ST as potentially liberating for the reader (1995:306). In practice resistancy involves including unidiomatic usage and other linguistically and culturally alienating features in the translated text so as to create the impression of foreignness; in this way it requires the translator to become "a nomad in [his or her] own language, a runaway from the mother tongue" (1995:291). However, as Venuti points out, the adoption of a policy of resistancy does not necessarily lead to increased FAITHFULNESS in the translation, but rather establishes an "abusive fidelity" (1995:291; see ABUSIVE TRANS-LATION) in which some features of ST are lost but others are added (1995:300). Venuti thus sees translation as "a process that involves looking for similarities between languages and cultures" through the act of "constantly confronting dissimilarities" (1995:306). However, a translation should never seek to remove these dissimilarities completely, as through resistancy its aim should be to remind the reader "of the gains and losses in the translation process and the unbridgeable gaps between cultures" (1995:306). See also DOMESTI-CATING TRANSLATION. Further reading: Venuti 1995.

Restricted Translation A term used by Catford (1965) to refer to a mode of translation which contrasts with TOTAL TRANSLATION. Restricted translation is defined as the "replacement of SL textual material by equivalent TL textual material, at only one level" (1965:22). There are four linguistic levels, and each has its own type of restricted translation associated with it (see GRAMMATICAL TRANSLATION, GRAPHOLOGICAL TRANSLATION, LEXICAL TRANSLATION and PHONO-LOGICAL TRANSLATION). Further reading: Catford 1965.

Restructuring (or **Transformation**, or **Forward-transformation**) According to Nida & Taber (1969/1982), the third and final stage in the translation process (see also ANALYSIS and TRANSFER 2). Nida & Taber's model was designed with the problems of Bible translating specifically in mind, and is based on Chomsky's notions of deep and surface structure (see for example Chomsky 1965). The restructuring stage processes the transferred material, which exists only in the form of kernel sentences ("the basic structural elements" (Nida & Taber 1969/1982:39) which can be said to underlie the syntactically more elaborate "surface structure" of any language); its purpose is to transform the results of the transfer process into a "stylistic form appropriate to the receptor language and to the intended receptors" (1969/1982:206). Restructuring is thus defined as *forward-transformation*, or in other words the process which is the reverse of back-transformation (see ANALYSIS). Nida & Taber (1969/1982:120) argue that there are three main problem areas which are connected with the restructuring of an ST: "the varieties of language or of styles which may be desirable" (e.g. choice of oral or written forms, consideration of sociolinguistic and situational factors, selection of appropriate genre and type of discourse), "the essential components and characteristics of these various styles" (e.g. choice of formal features and lexical items, whether or not they are intended to produce a special effect), and "the techniques which may be employed in producing the type of style desired" (e.g. employing or training a stylist who is sensitive to the above factors). Throughout the restructuring process, however, it is also important to consider the impact which the emerging translation is to have on its intended receptors (Nida 1969:494-95), as only if it produces in them a response which is essentially the same as that of the original audience can the translation be held to be DYNAMICALLY EQUIVALENT to its ST. Further reading: Gentzler 1993; Nida 1969; Nida & Taber 1969/1982.

Retranslation See INDIRECT TRANSLATION 1.

Retrospective Science of Translation See RETROSPECTIVE TRANS-LATION and SCIENCE OF TRANSLATION.

Retrospective Translation A term introduced by Postgate to describe translation "which primarily regards the Author" (1922:18; see also PROSPECTIVE TRANSLATION). According to Postgate, the aim of such SL-oriented translation is "to impart a knowledge of an original to those to whom it would otherwise be unknown" (1922:22). Thus the translator is seen as a receiver whose main concern is for clear comprehension of ST rather than idiomatic expression in TL. Wilss (1982) uses the term *retrospective science of translation* to denote the study of such phenomena as error analysis and translation criticism, which belong to the subdivision of APPLIED TRANSLATION STUDIES associated with translation as a product rather than a process. As a discipline, the retrospective science of translation thus "proceeds from what it finds in the TL and compares the quality of the [TT] with that of the original; by so comparing the two, it can begin to identify the formulation processes directing the production of the [TT] and to determine how adequately they achieve what was intended" (Wilss 1982:59). The term *retrospective translation* is broadly similar in meaning to *adequate translation* (see ADEQUACY 1) and LITERAL TRANSLATION 1. See also SCIENCE OF TRANSLATION. Further reading: Postgate 1922; Wilss 1977, 1982.

Revoicing See DUBBING.

Rewording See INTRALINGUAL TRANSLATION.

Rewriting A term introduced by Lefevere (1985, 1992) to refer to a range of processes, including translation, which can be said to re-interpret, alter or manipulate an original text in some way. The term arose from the conviction that TRANSLATION STUDIES needs to deal with the socio-cultural, ideological and literary constraints which lie behind the production of texts. According to Bassnett & Lefevere, translators, critics, historians, professors and journalists are all text producers whose output can be classified as "rewriting" (1990a:10). Rewriting is thus defined as "anything that contributes to construct-ing the 'image' of a writer and/or a work of literature" (1990a:10); the term *image* is understood as the projection of an original work or author in a given culture, which frequently exerts more influence than that original (Lefevere 1992:110). It is thus one of Lefevere's main theses that "ordinary" readers of literature are exposed to rewritings much more frequently than they are to original writings (1992:7); in this way rewriting is one of the means by which the survival of a literary work is ensured (Bassnett & Lefevere 1990a:10). However, rewriting is closely connected with the political and literary power structures which operate within a given culture, as the processes of adaptation and manipulation which rewriters perform generally lead to the production of texts which reflect the dominant ideology and poetics (Lefevere 1992:8; see PATRONAGE); for this and other rea-sons, rewriting is never "innocent" (Bassnett & Lefevere 1990a:11). Seen in such a context, translation – "the most obviously recogniz-able type of rewriting" (Lefevere 1992:9) – is a process which manipulates ST by adjusting it to fit in with two important con-straints. The first of these is the translator's (conscious or unconscious) ideology. This is reflected in the way he or she treats the original's *universe of discourse*, or the "objects, concepts, customs belonging to the world that was familiar to the writer of the original" (1992:41); the translator's attitude to such items is influenced by "the status of the original, the self-image of the culture that text is translated into, the types of texts deemed acceptable in that culture, the levels of diction deemed acceptable in it, the intended audience, and the 'cul-tural scripts' that audience is used to or willing to accept" (1992:87). The translator's ideology, however, also determines his or her atti-tude to the language in which ST is written, for example in terms of the extent to which meaning is privileged over form in the translation of poetry. The second constraint which operates on translation is the poetics dominant in the target culture, a poetics being informally defined as a combination of "literary devices, genres, motifs, proto-typical characters and situations, and symbols" and the culture's notion of what the rôle of literature in the social system should be (1992:26). See also POLYSYSTEM THEORY, REFRACTION and SYSTEM. Further reading: Bassnett & Lefevere 1990; Hermans 1994; Lefevere 1985, 1992.

Rhymed Translation One of seven strategies for translating poetry described by Lefevere (1975) in the course of an examination of English translations of a poem by Catullus. Within this particular context rhymed translation is distinguished from METRICAL TRANS-LATION in that its metre is self-imposed rather than being copied from ST, which in this case was composed in non-rhyming verse. Lefevere argues that when such a strategy is being followed, or in other words when rhyme and metre have to be imposed on "pre-selected and pre-arranged" material, the search for an acceptable solution is "doomed to failure from the start" (1975:49) and runs the risk of producing a mere caricature of ST (1975:61). The reason for this is that, like most other translation strategies, rhymed translation concentrates exclu-sively on one aspect of ST rather than on the text as an integrated whole. Of course, in view of the vast complexity of the task, this is all that most translators of verse can realistically hope to achieve. See also ANALOGICAL FORM, BLANK VERSE TRANSLATION, IMITATION 2, INTERPRETATION, LITERAL TRANSLATION 2, PHONEMIC TRANSLATION, POETRY INTO PROSE and VERSION 2. Further reading: Lefevere 1975.

Science of Translation One of several overlapping terms used to denote the discipline concerned with the systematic study of translation phenomena (see also TRANSLATION THEORY 1, TRADUCTOLOGY, TRANSLATION STUDIES and TRANSLATOLOGY). However, while often broadly synonymous with these other designations, the term *science of translation* tends to contain a number of theoretical assumptions and methodological overtones which set it apart. An early use of the term can be found in Nida (1964), who suggests it as a counterbalance to the tendency to view translation exclusively as an art or a skill. Nida argues that the processes of translation "are amenable to rigorous description" (1964:3), and concludes that "the transference of a message from one language to another is ... a valid subject for scientific description" (1964:3). However, Nida does not apply the term to all types of rigorous investigation of translation, but rather reserves it for his three-stage model of the translation process (see ANALYSIS, TRANS-FER 2 and RESTRUCTURING). Thus his use of the term specifically refers to an approach influenced by Chomskyan linguistics and centred around the problems of Bible translation, and implies a preference for DYNAMIC rather than FORMAL EQUIVALENCE as well as the belief that meaning exists independently of the language, text or message in which it is encoded. Besides being employed in this way in the discussion of Bible translating, the term is also used, principally by German writers, to refer generally to any kind of academic inves-tigation of translation. In this context, the science of translation (*Übersetzungswissenschaft* or *Translationswissenschaft* in German) is typically characterized as being highly interdisciplinary in nature, as translation scholars draw on the insights and methodologies of such widely differing fields as linguistics, communication theory, cultural studies and psychology; however, scholars who use the term *science of translation* (rather than Translation Studies, for example) generally follow a broadly linguistics-based approach and concentrate on non-literary translation. As an emerging discipline in its own right the science of translation is frequently split into a number of areas not related to the other disciplines on which it draws. Thus Koller, for example, talks about process and product-oriented science of translation (1979/1992:12), while Wilss distinguishes "the model-theoretic aspect, the language-pair-oriented descriptive aspect, and the language-pair-oriented applied aspect, each of which is guided by different considerations" (Wilss 1982:79). See also LEIPZIG SCHOOL, PROSPECTIVE TRANSLATION and RETROSPECTIVE TRANSLATION. Further reading: Gentzler 1993; Koller 1979/1992; Nida 1964; Wilss 1977, 1982.

Scopos Theory See SKOPOS THEORY.

Secondary Translation (German *Sekundäre Übersetzung*) A term used by Diller & Kornelius (1978) to refer to one of two modes of translation (see also PRIMARY TRANSLATION). A secondary transla-tion is defined as a translation which has the purpose of "informing a TL receiver about a communication between an SL sender and an SL receiver" (1978:3). In other words, the recipients of a secondary translation are not the group of people for whom ST was originally composed. Instances where this type of translation is favoured in-clude the translation of literary and scientific works. See also OVERT TRANSLATION. Further reading: Diller & Kornelius 1978.

Second-hand Translation See INDIRECT TRANSLATION 1.

Sekundäre Übersetzung See SECONDARY TRANSLATION.

Selective Translation (French *Traduction Sélective* or *Traduction Documentaire*) One of seven types of translation proposed by Gouadec (1989, 1990) to fulfil the various translation needs which can occur in a professional environment. In selective translation only details relating to one specific aspect of ST are translated, thus eliminating all irrelevant information (1990:334-35). Additional information not in the original document may be added in the form of explanatory notes, tables, graphs and so on, and the TL reader will thus have rapid access to the most important information contained in ST (1989:25). See also ABSOLUTE TRANSLATION, ABSTRACT TRANSLATION, DIAGRAMMATIC TRANSLATION, KEYWORD TRANSLATION, RECONSTRUCTIONS (TRANSLATION WITH) and SIGHT TRANSLATION. Further reading: Gouadec 1989, 1990; Sager 1994.

Self Translation See AUTOTRANSLATION.

Semantic Disambiguation (German *Monosemierung*) A term used to describe a vital stage in the process of translating from a foreign language. Because of the polysemy commonly displayed by the words of any language and the strong dependence of meaning upon precise context, even the simplest text will inevitably include an element of lexical ambiguity; indeed, as asserted by Hönig (1976:54), it is likely that such ambiguity will be displayed by the majority of lexical words in any one text, at least to some extent. While such polysemic elements are automatically and effortlessly disambiguated by a native speaker on the basis of an intuitive understanding of their precise meanings in the given context, for the non-native translator they present a frequent source of difficulty: "Polysemy may be basically only potential, but for the translator it is often painfully real" (Hönig & Kussmaul 1982:91, translated). The text can thus be seen as a "chain of monosemically textualized polysemic lexemes" (Hönig 1976:53, translated), while it is the task of the translator (or reader) to determine the precise meanings of individual words on the basis of the contextual clues which are available. The concept of semantic disambiguation is particularly important in the field of translator training, as one of the jobs of the trainer is to encourage students to look at the context in which a word is used rather than relying on an automatic association of one particular SL word with one particular TL meaning or accepting without question the TL equivalents suggested by bilingual dictionaries. Further reading: Diller & Kornelius 1978; Hönig 1976; Hönig & Kussmaul 1982; Koller 1979/1992.

CONNECTED WITH THE MEANINGS of WORDS

Semantic Translation According to Newmark, one of two modes of translation (see also COMMUNICATIVE TRANSLATION 2), in which "the translator attempts, within the bare syntactic and semantic constraints of the TL, to reproduce the precise contextual meaning of the author" (1981/1988:22). A semantic translation consequently tends to strive to reproduce the form of the original as closely as TL norms will allow; furthermore, no effort is made to shift ST into a target cultural context. Greater attention is paid to rendering the author's original thought-processes in TL than to attempting to re-interpret ST in a way which the translator considers more appropriate for the target setting; a semantic translation will therefore treat the original words as sacred, even if this requires reproducing inconsistencies, ambiguities and errors. Semantic translation is usually appropriate for literary, technical and scientific texts, as well as other contexts where the language of ST is as important as the content. It should, however, be pointed out that semantic translation is not intended to be a completely watertight category; furthermore, along with communicative translation it is designed to represent the "'middle ground' of translation practice" (Hatim & Mason 1990:7) which lies between strategies such as ADAPTATION and INTERLINEAR TRANSLATION (see Newmark 1988:45). See also OVERT TRANSLATION. Further reading: Newmark 1981/1988, 1988.

Semantic Voids See VOIDS.

Sense, Theory of (French *Sens, Théorie du*) See INTERPRETIVE THEORY OF TRANSLATION.

Sense-for-sense Translation A general term used to describe the type of translation which emphasizes transfer of the meaning or "spirit" of an ST over accurate reproduction of the original wording. The purpose of such a policy is to accommodate the needs of the TL reader by producing a text which conforms to the linguistic and textual norms of the target language and culture and which does not therefore sound "foreign". Like its opposite, WORD-FOR-WORD TRANSLATION, the term was first used by the Roman writers Cicero and Horace in the first century BC. These two early commentators in effect set in motion a debate which has been raging ever since, with either sense-for-sense or word-for-word approaches gaining the upper hand as the favoured strategy in different eras, depending on contemporary fashions. For a fuller discussion of some of the issues associated with this term, see FREE TRANSLATION. Further reading: Bassnett 1980/1991.

Serial Translation Defined by Casagrande as a special type of BACK-TRANSLATION in which "a message in code A is translated successively into codes B, C, D, etc. and if desired, back into code A" (1954:339). This approach has been employed in certain areas of anthropological research, where it allows the researcher to compare the translation of an aboriginal text into more than one more familiar language. For example, according to Voegelin (1954), researchers in Mexico have had texts translated first of all into Spanish (the informant's second language) and then into English (the translator's mother tongue). However, such an approach contains obvious hazards, so that extra care needs to be taken to check the reliability of translations obtained in this way (Casagrande 1954:340). See also INDIRECT TRANSLATION 1 and PARALLEL TRANSLATION. Further reading: Casagrande 1954.

Service Translation A term used by Newmark (1988) to denote what is also known as INVERSE TRANSLATION. While service translation, or the practice of translating out of one's native language, is commonly considered to be an activity which should be discouraged, Newmark points out that such a procedure "is necessary in most countries" (1988:52). See also DIRECT TRANSLATION 2 and DIRECTION OF TRANSLATION. Further reading: Newmark 1988.

Shifts (or Shifts of Expression) Originally defined by Catford as "departures from formal correspondence in the process of going from the SL to the TL" (1965:73). Catford enumerates a number of types of shift, all of which lead to minor TT rewordings brought about by structural incompatibilities between SL and TL (see CATEGORY SHIFT, CLASS SHIFT, INTRA-SYSTEM SHIFT, LEVEL SHIFT, STRUCTURE SHIFT and UNIT SHIFT). The shifts described by Catford are therefore purely linguistic, being grammatical or lexical in nature; they are furthermore unavoidable unless the translator wishes to reproduce the ST structure extremely closely. However, in any TT there are likely to be many minor (or indeed major) deviations from ST which it may not be possible to account for within this framework. Translation critics have frequently failed to understand the motivation for such differences, and have tended to dismiss them as "errors". However, the fact that such apparent "mistakes" form a feature of almost any TT is recognized by Popovič (1970), who broadens the concept of the shift (or "shift of expression") to account for the widespread nature of their distribution. Popovič defines shifts more generally as "all that appears as new with respect to the original, or fails to appear where it might have been expected" (1970:79); he also comments that shifts represent "the relationship between the wording of the original work and that of the translation" (1970:85). In this way he includes not only linguistic phenomena, but also replacements arising from textual, literary or cultural considerations. Popovič thus recognizes not only the existence of uncircumventable linguistic differences, but also the fact that the translator is working within the constraints of NORMS which will influence the decisions made during the translation process; such differences he attributes not to lack of training, sloppiness or ignorance, but to the translator's attempt "to reproduce [the work] as faithfully as possible and to grasp it in its totality, as an organic whole" (Popovič 1970:80). The range of phenomena covered by the term is therefore wide, and includes such changes as a move from an abstract to a concrete form of expression, or a tendency, for example, towards ARCHAISM, EXPLICITATION or intensification in TT. Such phenomena variously result from the translator's personal stylistic preferences or from the translational policy or norms which are being adhered to; their precise nature and distribution have been investigated by van Leuven-Zwart (1989, 1990; see GENERALIZATION, MODIFICATION, MODULATION 2, MUTATION and SPECIFICATION). Toury (1980, 1995) further develops the notion of shifts, distinguishing two varieties, the obligatory (e.g. linguistically motivated) and the non-obligatory (e.g. motivated by literary or cultural considerations); the extent to which a TT contains non-obligatory shifts will determine whether its INITIAL NORM is one of ACCEPTABILITY or ADEQUACY 2. See also COMPENSATION, DECISION-MAKING (TRANS-LATION AS), FORMAL CORRESPONDENCE and NEGATIVE SHIFT. Further reading: Catford 1965; van Leuven-Zwart 1989, 1990; Popovič 1970; Toury 1980, 1995.

Sight Translation (French *Traduction à vue*) A term in general use which refers to the unprepared, usually oral translation of a written text. Gouadec (1990) uses it more specifically to denote one of seven types of translation which can be employed in a professional environment. According to Gouadec, in sight translation a summary of the content of ST is provided on demand; as such it contrasts with the other six types, where the information needed can be supplied at greater leisure (1990:335). See also ABSOLUTE TRANSLATION, ABSTRACT TRANSLATION, DIAGRAMMATIC TRANSLATION, KEY-WORD TRANSLATION, RECONSTRUCTIONS (TRANSLATION WITH) and SELECTIVE TRANSLATION. Further reading: Gouadec 1990.

Signed Language Interpreting A type of INTERPRETING in which the interpreter works between a spoken language and a visual-gestural language used by Deaf people. Such languages probably exist in all developed countries, and are the standard means of communication used by members of the Deaf community in each country; they are exemplified by ASL (American Sign Language) and BSL (British Sign Language). Languages of this type possess their own independent structure and are as fully developed as spoken languages; they generally function as the native language for people who have been deaf since birth, and in this way contrast with "sign supported" languages (Brennan & Brien 1995:117) such as signed English, which are used by people who have lost their hearing after they have learnt a spoken language. The term *interpreting* is strictly speaking only used in relation to languages of the former type; in the case of sign supported languages – which are essentially spoken languages conveyed visually – it is more usual to talk about *transliteration*. In many ways signed language interpreting is comparable to interpreting between two spoken languages; however, there are a number of differences. For example, since signed language interpreting involves receiving and transmitting information in different modalities (i.e. spoken and signed), the use of SIMULTANEOUS rather than CONSECU-TIVE INTERPRETING becomes less demanding, and is indeed the norm for this type of interpreting (Brennan & Brien 1995:115). This means that signed language interpreters can work simultaneously not only in conferences, but also in other, smaller-scale contexts such as doctors' surgeries, job interviews and indeed any other situation in which COMMUNITY INTERPRETING might be appropriate. Furthermore, in view of this difference in operation the interpreter frequently takes on a more visible and central rôle in the communication than would otherwise be the case (1995:116). Another important consideration is that since signed languages have no standard written form the task of *translating* from or into such a language, or indeed of preparing a piece of interpreting in advance, is highly problematic (1995:116). See also RELAY INTERPRETING. Further reading: Brennan & Brien 1995; Hayes 1992; Isham 1995; Scott-Gibson 1991.

Simultaneous Interpreting A term used to refer to one of two main modes of INTERPRETING (see also CONSECUTIVE INTERPRETING). In simultaneous interpreting the interpreter acts as a kind of invisible presence; sitting in a special booth and working with headphones and a microphone, he or she listens to an SL speech, and reformulates it in TL as it is delivered. The technique was first employed during the Nuremberg trials after the end of the Second World War, and is now typically used in settings such as conferences and televised trials (see CONFERENCE INTERPRETING and COURT INTERPRETING). Contrary to popular belief, interpreters do not generally approach the task completely "blind", as they have normally at least had the chance to peruse some documents before interpreting commences. However, in view of the intensive nature of the task interpreters tend to work in 20-30 minute shifts, and there will usually be two interpreters in the booth at any one time; ideally the "off-duty" one will be able to provide assistance as and when required (Gile 1995a:193). According to Shlesinger (1995a:194), when functioning in this mode an interpreter has to work with three major constraints. Firstly, simultaneous interpreting occurs at a pace dictated by the speaker. Secondly, at any one time the interpreter will only have recourse to a small segment of the text; he or she will therefore often "play safe" in order to avoid creating potential problems later on. Thirdly, the interpreter may not possess the general or specialized knowledge which the speaker expects in the audience. However, when difficulties arise, there are a number of strategies which can be used (Gile 1995a:192-204). For example, in certain conditions interpreters can get help from a colleague or consult a document. A passage containing complex syntax can be "segmented", or in other words reformulated so as to simplify the structure. Furthermore, when experiencing comprehension difficulties interpreters might delay their response a little, in order to gain more time to think. Indeed, experienced interpreters are able to control their "Ear-Voice-Span" (EVS) in response, on the one hand, to the limitations of short-term memory, and, on the other hand, to the need to allow themselves time to anticipate (see EFFORT MODELS). See also SIGNED LANGUAGE INTERPRETING and WHISPERED INTERPRETING. Further reading: Chernov 1978, 1987; Gile 1995a; Lambert & Moser-Mercer 1994; Moser-Mercer 1984; Pöchhacker 1994; Seleskovitch 1968, 1968/1978; Seleskovitch & Lederer 1989; Shlesinger 1995a, 1995b.

Skopos Theory (German *Skopostheorie*, from Greek *skopos* "purpose, goal") An approach to translation proposed in the late 1970s and early 1980s by Reiss & Vermeer. Skopos theory stresses the interactional, PRAGMATIC aspects of translation, arguing that the shape of TT should above all be determined by the function or "skopos" that it is intended to fulfil in the target context. Reiss & Vermeer formulate this principle into two skopos rules: "an interaction is determined by (or is a function of) its purpose", and "the skopos can be said to vary according to the recipient" (1984:101, translated). From these principles it follows that the translator should use the translation strategies which are most appropriate to achieving the purpose for which TT is intended, irrespective of whether they are considered to be the "standard" way to proceed in a particular translation context; in short, when producing a TT "the end justifies the means" (Reiss & Vermeer 1984:101, translated). An awareness of the requirements of the skopos thus "expands the possibilities of translation, increases the range of possible translation strategies, and releases the translator from the corset of an enforced – and hence often meaningless – literalness" (Vermeer 1989:186). Toury describes skopos theory as an alternative TARGET TEXT-ORIENTED paradigm (1995:25). This is certainly accurate in that a skopos-based approach represents a "dethroning" of ST (Vermeer 1986:42, translated): rather than presenting the translator with a fixed body of "facts" which he or she must pass on to the target audience, ST is seen as an INFORMATION OFFER, which the translator must interpret by selecting those features which most closely correspond to the requirements of the target situation. In this way a translation is thought of as communicating something new and original, rather than simply furnishing the TL reader with the same information in a recodified form. For example, consideration of the precise audience for which a TT was intended would determine whether translation, paraphrase or even re-editing was the most appropriate strategy to adopt in a given situation (Vermeer 1989:185). In more concrete terms, translating according to a TT's skopos might entail rendering a scientific text fairly literally, adapting Don Quixote for a children's edition, removing from the sayings of Buddha the endless repetition which would be unacceptable to most modern readers, or adding extra politeness formulae to American business letters being translated into German (examples taken from Vermeer 1982:100). The extent to which the translation had met with SUCCESS could be determined by whether it was interpreted by the target recipient in a way which was COHERENT with his or her situation, and whether or not it led to any kind of PROTEST against its meaning or form (Reiss & Vermeer 1984:112). Skopos theory was conceived independently of the clearly similar notion of TRANSLATORIAL ACTION; however, in his more recent writings (for example 1989, 1989/1992) Vermeer has suggested merging the two to form a common framework. See also COMMISSION and LOYALTY. Further reading: Nord 1997; Reiss & Vermeer 1984; Vermeer 1989, 1989/1992.

Source Language (SL) The standard term describing the language in which the text being translated (or SOURCE TEXT) is written. The source language is one of the SYSTEMS to which ST belongs (along with, for example, the source literary, textual and cultural systems); since the TARGET LANGUAGE also forms an independent system there will inevitably be a certain amount of linguistic incompatibility (and interference) between the two languages. However, for the translator a knowledge of the source language is in itself insufficient; what is also essential is a close familiarity with source culture, literary traditions, textual conventions and so forth. While the source language is on occasion the translator's native language, it is more usual for translation to take place out of a language which has been acquired. It should also be pointed out that the source language involved in a particular act of translation is not necessarily the language in which the work was originally written, as ST may itself be a translation from another source language. See also DIRECTION OF TRANSLATION, ETHNOLINGUISTIC MODEL OF TRANSLATION, INDIRECT TRANSLATION 1, SEMANTIC DISAMBIGUATION, RECEPTOR LANGUAGE and SOURCE TEXT-ORIENTED TRANSLATION STUDIES. Further reading: Kelly 1979; Sykes 1983.

Source Text (or Source-language Text) (ST) The text (written or spoken) which provides the point of departure for a translation. Except in the case of INTERSEMIOTIC and INTRALINGUAL translation, the source text will be in a different language (SOURCE LANGUAGE) from the translation (or TARGET TEXT) which the translator produces from it. The source text will typically be an original text written in SL; however, in the case of INDIRECT TRANSLATION 1, it may itself be a translation of another text in another language. Of course, the source text is not simply a linguistic entity, as it enters into networks of relationships of not only a linguistic, but also a textual and cultural nature. Furthermore, the information which it conveys to its intended recipients will be implicit as well as explicit. See also RECEPTOR LANGUAGE and SOURCE TEXT-ORIENTED TRANSLATION STUDIES.

Source Text-oriented Translation Studies A term used by Toury (1980, 1995) to refer to any approach to translation in which certain ST features are expected to be reproduced in TT – or in other words the relationship between ST and TT is expected to be of a particular kind – if TT is to "qualify" as a translation (1980:39-40). The notion of Source Text-oriented Translation Studies is thus intended to reflect the fact that the type of normative approach which is appropriate for the purposes of, for example, translator training or translation assessment (see APPLIED TRANSLATION STUDIES) has in the past been allowed to dominate other areas of the discipline too, thus stifling the possibility of certain types of inquiry into the nature of translation and the translated text (see TARGET TEXT-ORIENTED TRANSLATION STUDIES). While Toury's stance is undoubtedly polemical, there are others who share the basic insight that the discipline has been preoccupied with promoting various kinds of source-target relationship, which a TT "must" display with its ST; Nida, for example, states that "the traditional focus in discussions of translating has been the verbal comparison of the source and target ... texts", and observes that "generally arguments about the legitimacy of a translation have dealt almost exclusively with the issue of literal versus free correspondences" (1995:223; see LITERAL and FREE TRANSLATION). One result of this situation has been that many traditional approaches to translation have been centred on a normative notion of EQUIVALENCE, and have thus viewed all TTs as inadequate reflections of their STs. Some commentators on translation have even pessimistically concluded that translation (particularly the translation of poetry) is impossible, because the web of linguistic, textual and cultural relationships which ST enters into can never be fully reproduced in any TT, no matter how ingenious it may be. Associated with this perspective has been the tendency to treat any and all apparent discrepancies between ST and TT as "errors", rather than investigating the possible motivation the translator might have had for incorporating them in the translation (see SHIFTS). See also PRESCRIPTIVE TRANS- LATION STUDIES, TRANSFER-ORIENTED TRANSLATION STUDIES and TRANSLATABILITY. Further reading: Toury 1980, 1995.

Specification (or **Modulation/Specification**) A term used by van Leuven-Zwart (1989, 1990) to refer to one of two types of MODU- LATION 2. Specification is distinguished from the other type, GENERALIZATION, in that here the SHIFT which occurs between ST and TT TRANSEMES is in the direction of a higher level of explicitness. In other words, a shift towards greater specification will produce a transeme the meaning of which is made more precise, by either the addition of extra words or the use of words with a less general meaning. Van Leuven-Zwart considers the phenomenon of specification alongside that of *explanation* (see MODIFICATION), which she posits as a UNIVERSAL OF TRANSLATION; following on from work by Levý (1969) and van den Broeck & Lefevere (1979), she concludes that both these phenomena and also that of generalization are important features of translated text *per se*, although she disagrees with the earlier writers by maintaining that specification is commoner than generalization (1990:89). One possible rationalization which van Leuven-Zwart offers for the widespread occurrence of the phenomenon of specification is – in line with that offered for *explanation* by van den Broeck & Lefevere (1979) – that it is "the translator's attempt to make the text accessible to the reader by opening up and exposing as much of the foreign fictional world as possible" (1990:90); in this way she demonstrates how a consistent tendency in the shifts observed in the textual microstructure can cast significant light on the specific translational policy adopted by the translator. See also ARCHITRAN- SEME, EXPLICITATION, INTEGRAL TRANSLATION and MUTATION. Further reading: van Leuven-Zwart 1989, 1990.

Sprachschöpferische Übersetzung See LINGUISTICALLY CREATIVE TRANSLATION.

Structure Shift According to Catford (1965), a type of CATEGORY SHIFT which involves a change in grammatical structure between

ST and TT. The English sentence *I love you* with its word order subject-verb-object is translated into French as *Je t'aime* with a slightly different word order; this change from English to French structure is an example of structure shift. Like that of other types of category shift, the notion of the structure shift serves as an illustration of the microstructural incompatibility between the linguistic systems of SL and TL. See also CLASS SHIFT, INTRA-SYSTEM SHIFT, LEVEL SHIFT, SHIFTS and UNIT SHIFT. Further reading: Catford 1965.

Stylistic Equivalence (or **Translational Equivalence**) Defined by Popovič as "functional equivalence of elements in both original and translation aiming at an expressive identity with an invariant of identical meaning" ([1976]:6). Popovič also terms this type of equivalence *adequacy* ([1976]:1), *expressive correspondence* ([1976]:7) and *faithfulness to the original* ([1976]:8). Stylistic equivalence thus involves preserving the expressive character of (elements of) ST, while at the same time retaining as much as possible of its basic semantic content. However, even on the occasions when direct semantic correspondence cannot be established the translator should still choose a TL item which is stylistically equivalent with the given element of ST ([1976]:7). See also EQUIVALENCE, LINGUISTIC EQUIVALENCE, PARADIGMATIC EQUIVALENCE and TEXTUAL EQUIVALENCE 2. Further reading: Popovič [1976].

Sublanguage A term used in the context of MACHINE TRANSLATION to refer to "a language used to communicate in a specialized technical domain or for a specialized purpose" (Arnold et al. 1994:216). According to Arnold et al., sublanguages are characterized by "the high frequency of specialized terminology and often also by a restricted set of grammatical patterns" (1994:216); thus weather bulletins, medical reports and business letters can all be considered examples of this kind of language. One of the main advantages of designing a dedicated machine translation system to specifically cope with input in the form of a particular sublanguage is that the number of parameters which it will need to include will be considerably reduced, with the result that the quality of the output will be noticeably enhanced. For this reason a considerable amount of research is being carried out to improve performance in this area still further. However, a second advantage is that the use of sublanguages – as opposed to CONTROL-LED LANGUAGES – does not require the writer to simplify ST but rather exploits the linguistic restrictions which naturally occur in the type of text being translated (1994:159). Further reading: Arnold et al. 1994; Sager 1994.

Subtitling A term used to refer to one of the two main methods of language transfer used in translating types of mass audio-visual communication such as film and television (see also DUBBING). First used in 1929, subtitling can be defined as the process of providing synchronized captions for film and television dialogue (and more recently for live opera). Subtitles can be either interlingual (the type considered here) or intralingual (e.g. for the deaf), *open* (i.e. forming part of the original film or broadcast) or *closed* (i.e. broadcast separately and accessible for example by means of teletext). There are a number of reasons for choosing subtitling rather than dubbing. It is for example a faster process, and costs as little as one fifteenth as much as dubbing. However, the choice of one or other approach is to a large extent simply a matter of the preference of the country for which the new version is being produced; thus for reasons of tradition subtitles tend to be favoured, for example, in Scandinavia, The Netherlands, Belgium, Portugal, Greece, Israel, Egypt and throughout the Arab world (Gottlieb 1992:169; see also Delabastita 1990:105 n. 2 and Goris 1993:171). Up to now, subtitling has been largely ignored by TRANSLATION STUDIES as a whole, and – as pointed out by Fawcett (1996:69) – in view of the synchronization requirement some have even questioned whether it should be considered a type of translation at all. For a detailed description of the actual mechanics of subtitle production, see Luyken et al. (1991) and Dries (1995). However, it should be stated that subtitlers work under a number of constraints which are additional to those associated with other types of translation (see Luyken et al. 1991:42-48). Firstly, the addition of subtitles to a screen necessitates interfering with the visual image, at least to some extent. For this reason subtitles are usually placed at the bottom of the screen, and are generally limited to two lines of a maximum of about 35 characters each. Secondly, the time available for display depends firstly on the speed at which the material is spoken (which is generally faster than the rate at which a full transcription could be delivered), the viewers' average reading speed and the necessity of keeping a (short) interval between subtitles; all of these factors must be borne in mind if the general requirement of synchrony is to be satisfied. Thirdly, subtitles are generally inserted simultaneously with the onset of speech and removed ½ to 1½ seconds after the speech segment has finished; however, this can be ignored if for example there is a danger of the subtitle "overlapping" a scene change. Finally, it is important that the subtitles be displayed in a format which ensures their clear visibility and easy legibility, and that line-breaks be chosen in such way as to coincide with the natural breaks in sentence structure. In view of the first two constraints discussed above it is clear that there are serious limitations on the amount of information which can be conveyed by most subtitles. Consequently, subtitling a film usually entails an overall compression of the original material (although on occasion the subtitler may need to add extra information, for example to help the TL audience to understand a point which for cultural reasons might otherwise be unclear). Furthermore, only a fraction of the information contained in the original intonation or tone of voice can be conveyed, while it is not always possible to produce an effective rendition, for example, of non-standard speech or colloquial vocabulary (see Delabastita 1989:204). See also PIVOT LANGUAGE. Further reading: Delabastita 1989, 1990; Dries 1995; Fawcett 1996; Gambier 1996; Gottlieb 1992; Ivarsson 1992; Luyken et al. 1991.

Success (German *Glücken*) A term used by Reiss & Vermeer (1984). According to the model of the communication process which they use (known as *action theory*), an essential part of every interaction is the *feedback (Rückkoppelung)*, or reaction, which follows the delivery of a message. The purpose of this is so that the recipient can indicate to the message producer how the message has been received. A message is considered to have been successful (*geglückt*) if it contains no PROTEST (or leads to no subsequent protest from the originator), or in other words if both the content and the interpretation of the message have COHERENCE in the recipient's situation. The concept is particularly relevant to TRANSLATION THEORY in the context of SKOPOS THEORY, as the skopos of TT will directly determine the way in which it is received and interpreted by the recipient. See also INFORMATION OFFER. Further reading: Reiss & Vermeer 1984; Vermeer 1983.

Surtraduction See OVERTRANSLATION 1.

Syntagmatic Equivalence See TEXTUAL EQUIVALENCE 2.

System A term derived from the writings of the Russian Formalists, a group of literary theorists active in the early part of the twentieth century. For the purposes of TRANSLATION STUDIES, a system is defined as "the network of relations that can be hypothesized for a certain set of assumed observables" (Even-Zohar 1990a:27); the "assumed observables" of this definition are usually phenomena of a linguistic, textual, literary or cultural nature. In other words, a system is a "stratified entity" (Toury 1980:142) created by the dynamic interaction of all relevant factors of a linguistic, textual, literary or cultural nature. The term can denote entities of various sizes, such as for example twentieth century English literature as a whole or just works translated into English in the 1980s; however, when referring to a large system which consists of a number of smaller ones – a "system of systems" (Even-Zohar 1990b:88) – it is usual to use the term POLYSYSTEM. Toury in addition employs the term *system* more or less synonymously with COMPETENCE to refer to "the totality of possible realizations" which the rules of a certain language (or literature, etc.) could theoretically produce (Coseriu 1973:44, quoted in Toury 1980:23, translated); in this context the term *system* would, like *competence*, contrast with NORM and PERFORMANCE. Further reading: Even-Zohar 1990a, 1990b; Frank 1990b; Hermans 1991; Lefevere 1992; Toury 1980.

TAPs See THINK-ALOUD PROTOCOLS.

Target Language (TL) One of two standard terms used to denote the language which is being translated into. (The other frequently encountered term is RECEPTOR LANGUAGE, while *goal language* is also used by some writers.) The target language is usually the translator's native language, although there are exceptions to this. For example, some countries favour the practice whereby interpreters work *from* their native language, and in many contexts this practice is also used for written translation, although it is not generally considered to be an ideal arrangement. Furthermore, other more complex configurations can also occur, such as when (for example) an English-speaking Bible translator translates from an ancient language (e.g. Greek or Hebrew) into a non-Indo-European target language. Frequently, especially when TT is the product of a LITERAL translating strategy, the linguistic incompatibility between SL and the target language leads to SL patterns interfering in the TARGET TEXT; depending of the extremity of this phenomenon and the commentator's attitude to it, the result is termed either the THIRD CODE or

TRANSLATIONESE. Some writers (e.g. Toury 1980, 1995) even view the language of translated texts as a *dialect* of the target language. Sometimes such interference may be the result of deliberately following a particular translation strategy (see for example FOREIGNIZING TRANSLATION). See also DIRECTION OF TRANSLATION, ETHNOLINGUISTIC MODEL OF TRANSLATION, RECEPTOR LANGUAGE, SOURCE LANGUAGE and TARGET TEXT-ORIENTED TRANSLATION STUDIES. Further reading: Kelly 1979; Sykes 1983.

Target Text (or **Target-language Text**) **(TT)** One of the standard terms used to describe a text which has been produced by an act of translation. A target text is derived from its posited SOURCE TEXT in accordance with a particular translation strategy (or set of NORMS), which may differ widely between cultures, schools or even individual translators; consequently, what is held to be a translation in one culture may be dismissed as an IMITATION in another. This situation has led scholars working in the field of TARGET TEXT-ORIENTED TRANSLATION STUDIES to adopt a very broad view of what qualifies as a translated text, basically accepting the status of "translation" for any text upon which it is conferred by a particular culture. However, there is not always a simple, one-to-one relationship between a target text and its supposed ST, as a text marked as a translation may be based on more than one "ST", in different languages, or else, as in the case of PSEUDOTRANSLATIONS 1, there may be no ST at all. Target texts vary greatly in the extent to which they conform to the norms of the target system; furthermore, depending on the function which they are intended to fulfil, target texts are variously expected to read as a TARGET LANGUAGE original or as a FAITHFUL reproduction of the SOURCE LANGUAGE original. The investigation of the nature of target texts is one of the most important tasks facing DESCRIPTIVE TRANSLATION STUDIES; it is hoped for example that research into translated texts will provide information on a number of phenomena posited as UNIVERSALS OF TRANSLATION. Finally, for many approaches to translation it is in addition important to note that a target text also serves as a commentary on, and interpretation of, its ST (see for example Holmes 1988c, 1988d; see also METAPOEM). See also INDIRECT TRANSLATION 1 and RECEPTOR LANGUAGE. Further reading: Toury 1980, 1995.

Dutch version

Target Text-oriented Translation Studies An approach to the study of literary translation proposed by Toury (1980, 1985, 1995). Arguing

that most other approache ultimate mply in its rôle as a
reconstruction of S Tour re as ve model in which
attention is foc ssed on T and its position in the target culture; he
argues that whil a TT is typically based on another text which pre-
exists in another language, its attention is determined not so much by
ST or by translational procedures as by the constellation of the
target culture itself. Accordingly, the study of a target text-oriented
approach aims to understanding
of how the transla would be carried out; according to
Toury, "being regarded as a literary translation ... does not presuppose
any *definite* relationship ... to another text in another language and
another literary polysystem which is, as a result, regarded as its ST"
(1980:43). In other words, all texts which a given cultural or literary
system terms as translations are accepted as such, regardless of the
translational NORMS which have been followed in their production. In
this way TT is to a large extent considered to exist independently of
its original, having cut itself loose from the source SYSTEM. This kind
of approach is thus basically DESCRIPTIVE, and scholars who work
within it are chiefly interested in "the understanding and explanation
of translational phenomena within the literary [or cultural, linguistic
or other] system in their own terms" (Toury 1984:78). Because of
this reorientation, the phenomenon of PSEUDOTRANSLATION 1 also
becomes a valid object of study in its own right. In this way, TT
becomes the *point of departure* for study, while it is ST which assumes
a subordinate rôle, only being consulted to assist in the task of
reconstructing "the process of decision-making resorted to during the
act of translating, the extraction of the translational norms on the
basis of the existing translational relationships, and, ultimately, the
general concept of translation underlying the corpus in question and
responsible for those norms, relationships, decisions" (Toury 1984:78).
Ultimately, the aim of target text-oriented translation studies is to
extrapolate from particular case studies in order to reach conclusions
as to what is general or even universal in the process of translation
itself. See also POLYSYSTEM THEORY, PSEUDOTRANSLATION 1,
DECISION-MAKING (TRANSLATION AS) and UNIVERSALS OF TRANS-
LATION. Further reading: Toury 1980, 1985, 1995.

Term Banks (or **Terminological Data Banks**) A term used to refer
to automated collections of TERMINOLOGY, created to serve particular
users and stored on-line (Sager 1990:167). Traditionally, term banks

have had a very similar function to conventional glossaries and technical dictionaries; however, as Sager points out, flexibility is now becoming an increasingly important criterion in designing such machine-readable databases, as information can be stored so as to facilitate the type of searches and queries which have up to now required the user to scan the entire data-base by hand (1990: 168). Thus the type of term bank which Sager envisages should permit not only traditional, dictionary-type queries, but also for example searches for other terms which are conceptually linked with the search item, or requests for glossaries of terms related to a certain topic (1990:168-69). In the light of such considerations Sager suggests that a term bank should be defined as "a collection, stored in a computer, of special language vocabularies ... together with the information required for their identification", such a collection being exploitable "as a mono- or multilingual dictionary for direct consultation, as a basis for dictionary production, as a control instrument for consistency of usage and term creation and as an ancillary tool in information and documentation" (1990:169). See also MACHINE-AIDED TRANSLATION and MACHINE TRANSLATION. Further reading: Arnold et al. 1994; Sager 1990, 1994; Thomas 1992.

Terminology A term used to refer to the vast bodies of specialist vocabulary which is found in the discourse relating to any technical domain. A term is distinct from a general word in that it designates a single concept; terminology is thus less ambiguous than general vocabulary, and therefore also more suited to MACHINE TRANSLATION (Arnold et al. 1994:107). Although in another context the term *terminology* can also denote an entire discipline in its own right, within TRANSLATION STUDIES it generally has the more restricted meaning outlined above; furthermore, the way terminology is most likely to feature in translation is in the form of *terminology management*, or in other words the methods of creating, maintaining and utilizing TERM BANKS. Particular problems which are likely to face the translator are the sheer volume of terms which exist in any one field and the necessity to ensure consistency in the way such terms are translated (Arnold et al. 1994:108). However, careful use of resources such as term banks will help translators make correct choices about whether to use a pre-existing TL term, to create a neologism, or to paraphrase; furthermore, a general awareness of the issues connected with terminology is likely to equip them "to cope with unfamiliar subjects and the techniques of producing reliable work despite their limitations of knowledge" (Sager 1992:112). See also MACHINE-AIDED TRANSLATION. Further reading: Sager 1990, 1992.

Tertium Comparationis (Latin) (or **Interlingua**, or ***Das Gemeinte* (Intended Meaning)** (German), or **Mediating Language**, or **Lingua Universalis** (Latin)) A term used by some writers to denote a theoretical language which mediates between SL and TL. Writers who utilize this notion argue, according to Eco, that "there must ... exist a *tertium comparationis* which might allow us to shift from an expression in language A to an expression in language B by deciding that both are equivalent to an expression of a metalanguage C" (1995:346). Such a metalanguage is posited as a semantic common denominator via which the ST meaning, which is understood as an INVARIANT which exists independently of ST itself, is simply transferred from ST to TT. Koschmieder (1965a, 1965b) refers to this interlingual invariant as the *Gemeinte*, or *intended meaning*, while Popovič ([1976]:11) terms it the *mediating language*. The acceptance of such an "interlingually constant value" (Koller 1979/ 1992:97, translated) implies an inherent belief in unlimited TRANS-LATABILITY (Wilss 1982:46) and in the centrality of linguistic EQUIVALENCE; for this reason, most linguistic theories of translation implicitly rely on the concept of the tertium comparationis (see Snell-Hornby 1988/1995:15-16). Use of the notion of the tertium comparationis is particularly associated with bilingual generative models of translation inspired by Chomskyan linguistics, in which translation is conceived as the process of decoding and recoding an unchanging message; within this framework the tertium comparationis is thus viewed as an "archimedean point" from which the surface structure of both languages can be generated (Hönig 1976:49, translated). Nida & Taber's (1969/1982) model of the translation process is typical of this perspective (see for example ANALYSIS). However, as observed by Hönig, the concept of the tertium comparationis "does not represent a real basis for the translator's operations" (1976:50, translated). There are a number of reasons for this. The first of these is that the existence of the tertium comparationis cannot be verified. The second concerns what literary theorists term the "intentional fallacy" (Gentzler 1993:57), or the notion that the author's intended meaning and the meaning that a work expresses are not the same; in view of such semantic multivalency, the idea that one can reduce the meaning of a text to basic underlying forms becomes an unrealistic oversimplification. A third problem is that translation is a basically *parole*-based procedure (Koller 1979/1992:98, 223); in other words, it is not simply a matter of converting decontextualized, idealized phrases and sentences from one language to another, but rather entails recodifying an elusive, context-bound, implicature-laden ST in TL in the most appropriate way (see Gutt 1991). However, in spite of such problems, use of a kind of tertium comparationis is sometimes recommended in translation comparison (see ARCHI-TRANSEME) and translation evaluation (Sager 1994), as well as being a standard procedure in many multilingual MACHINE TRANSLATION systems (where it is termed *interlingua*; see Arnold et al. 1994 and Schubert 1992). Further reading: Eco 1995; Koller 1971, 1979/1992; Koschmieder 1965a, 1965b; Nida & Taber 1969/1982.

Text Typology See EXPRESSIVE TEXTS, INFORMATIVE TEXTS, MULTI-MEDIAL TEXTS and OPERATIVE TEXTS.

Texteme A term used by Even-Zohar (1990c) and Toury (1980, 1995) to refer to any linguistic or textual feature (ranging in size from a single sound to an entire textual segment) which takes on a special functional significance in a given literary text (or context). Toury defines textemes as "linguistic units of any type and level, participating in textual relationships and, as a result, carrying textual functions in the text in question" (1980:108). The rôle of textemes in a literary text is such that their decoding is "indispensable for a proper understanding of the text" (Even-Zohar 1990c:249). When a literary text is translated, many original textemic relations will inevitably be lost, and some will have their textemic status preserved in a modified form (Even-Zohar 1990c:249), as the translator seeks to maintain the integrity of the text as a literary entity. Key points in literary texts which consist of several simultaneous textual functions are termed by Toury (1980:115) as *junctions*. While the specific nature of textemes varies from text to text, rhyming words, key repetitions and puns are all typical examples of textemic features. See also REPERTOREME. Further reading: Even-Zohar 1990c; Toury 1980, 1995.

Text-type Restricted Theories of Translation (or **Discourse-type Restricted Theories of Translation**) A term used by Holmes

(1988e) to refer to one of six types of PARTIAL THEORY OF TRANS-
LATION. Text-type restricted theories of translation deal with the
problems of translating specific text or genre-types. Examples of this
type of theory would be discussions of the translation of scientific
texts, poetry or the Bible. However, the development of such theories
is problematic because of the lack of a formal theory of text or
discourse-types; another problem is raised by the possibility of a TT
belonging to a different text-type to that of its ST. See also AREA-
RESTRICTED, MEDIUM-RESTRICTED, PROBLEM-RESTRICTED, RANK-
RESTRICTED and TIME-RESTRICTED THEORIES OF TRANSLATION. Further
reading: Holmes 1988e.

Textual Equivalence 1 Defined by Catford as a type of EQUIVA-
LENCE which occurs when any TL text or portion of text is "observed
on a particular occasion ... to be the equivalent of a given SL text or
portion of text" (1965:27). Thus for example in the sentences *My son
is six* and *Mon fils a six ans* the English phrase *my son* and the
French expression *mon fils* would be said to be textual equivalents.
Catford suggests that textual equivalence can be identified either "on
the authority of a competent bilingual informant or translator"
(1965:27), or more formally by means of *commutation*, or changing
items in ST and observing "what changes if any occur in the TL text
as a consequence" (1965:28). Obviously, in a text of any length it is
almost certain that many items will occur more than once. In this case
textual equivalences can be computed statistically; for example, the
textual equivalences in a collection of English texts of the French
item *dans* might be observed to be *in* with a probability of 73%, *into*
with 19%, *from* with 1.5% and *about/inside* with 0.75% (1965:30).
According to Catford, probabilities of this type, if based on a large
enough corpus of texts, could be used to form "translation rules"
(1965:31). Further reading: Catford 1965.

 2 (or **Syntagmatic Equivalence**) A term used by Popovič to refer
to the "arrangement of the elements upon the syntagmatic axis of the
text" ([1976]:6). By "syntagmatic axis" Popovič means the specific
ordering of stylistic and expressive elements in a given text, so that
the term *textual equivalence* is used to denote equivalence on the
level of structure, form and shape (Bassnett 1980/1991:25). According to Popovič, textual equivalence is a function of two factors: firstly,
the "expressive feeling" of the translator, and secondly, the existence
of suitable "expressive means" in the "paradigmatic 'stock' of style"

([1976]:6). See also EQUIVALENCE, LINGUISTIC EQUIVALENCE, PARA-
DIGMATIC EQUIVALENCE and STYLISTIC EQUIVALENCE. Further reading:
Popovič [1976].

Textual Norms (or **Textual-linguistic Norms**) Defined by Toury
(1980, 1995) as one of two types of OPERATIONAL NORM (see also
MATRICIAL NORMS). The function of such NORMS is to determine the
selection of TL material to replace the textual and linguistic material
of the original. In other words, translational equivalents will be chosen
for ST items in accordance with this type of norm. Such material may
be either linguistic or literary in nature, thus including such features
as lexical items or rhyme schemes. Textual norms may be either
general (i.e. relevant to all types of translation) or *particular* (i.e.
pertaining to only one specific mode of translation or genre). It should
be pointed out that Toury (1995) uses the term *textual-linguistic
norms* to refer to this type of norm. See also INITIAL NORM and
PRELIMINARY NORMS. Further reading: Toury 1980, 1995.

Theoretical Translation Studies According to Holmes (1988e), one
of two branches making up the area of PURE TRANSLATION STUDIES
(the other being DESCRIPTIVE TRANSLATION STUDIES). The aim of
Theoretical Translation Studies is "to establish general principles by
means of which [the phenomena of translating and translation(s)] can
be explained and predicted" (1988e:71); this objective is pursued on
the basis of data provided by Descriptive Translation Studies and
insights and information from other disciplines, such as linguistics,
literary studies and psychology. Theoretical Translation Studies is
further subdivided into GENERAL and PARTIAL THEORIES OF TRANS-
LATION. For a full discussion of the content and nature of this branch
of the discipline, however, see TRANSLATION THEORY 2. See also
APPLIED TRANSLATION STUDIES and TRANSLATION STUDIES. Further
reading: Holmes 1988e.

Theory of Sense (French *Théorie du Sens*) See INTERPRETIVE
THEORY OF TRANSLATION.

Theory of Translation See THEORETICAL TRANSLATION STUDIES and
TRANSLATION THEORY 2.

Thick Translation Defined by Appiah as a translation "that seeks with its annotations and its accompanying glosses to locate the text in a rich cultural and linguistic context" (1993:817). Although Appiah is referring specifically to the problems involved in translating African proverbs it is clear that the term may be used applied to any TT which contains a large amount of explanatory material, whether in the form of footnotes, glossaries or an extended introduction. The purpose of providing such voluminous background information is to engender in the TT reader a deeper respect for the source culture and a greater appreciation for the way that people of other backgrounds have thought and expressed themselves. See also DIRECT TRANSLATION 3 and ETHNOGRAPHIC TRANSLATION. Further reading: Appiah 1993.

Think-Aloud Protocols (or **Thinking-Aloud Protocols**) **(TAPs)** A technique used to probe the cognitive processes entailed in different kinds of mental activity. TAPs constitute one of a number of empirical methods used in the investigation of the psychological aspects of the act of translating. When used in the field of TRANSLATION STUDIES, TAPs will typically involve the "subjects" verbalizing everything that comes into their minds and all the actions they perform as they work on the creation of a TT. The verbal report thus produced is recorded (or videoed) and analyzed for the insights which it reveals into what goes on inside the "black box" of the translator's mind; sometimes the translator's eye movements are also monitored for the additional information which they yield. In this way TAPs combine introspection and external observation to produce insights into such diverse features of the translation process as the subjects' understanding of translational problems, their use of reference works, their semantic analysis of ST items, the way in which they compare possible TL equivalents, and so forth (Krings 1986b:267). While research is still at an early stage, tentative models of the translation process have been produced (see for example Krings (1986b:269), who provides a flow-diagram detailing a number of different strategies which translators have recourse to while producing a TT); the ultimate goal of the approach is the establishment of a definitive psychological model of translation. Various claims have been made for the technique. Gerloff describes TAPs as "a rich source of data" (1987:152), while according to Krings "the thinking-aloud technique no doubt provides the most direct means of access to the translation process" (1986b:266). One further advantage is that TAPs are *introspective* rather than *retrospective* (Lörscher 1991:75), which means that verbalization occurs immediately rather than after some time has elapsed. However, it has been pointed out that at their present stage of development TAPs are useful only for forming rather than testing hypotheses (Lörscher 1991:75 n.). Other objections have also been raised, such as for example a) the argument that subjects' verbalizations are incomplete or are an attempt to produce commentaries on processes which are to a large extent unconscious (Krings 1987:163), b) the fact that the technique potentially confuses the spoken and written modes of translation, each of which may entail different thought processes (Toury 1995:235), and c) the question of whether the very act of thinking aloud influences what goes on in the translator's head (Lörscher 1991:71). One interesting side-effect of TAPs is that they seem to help subjects to solve translation problems more systematically and successfully than members of a control group who perform identical tasks silently (Lörscher 1991:74). See also DECISION-MAKING (TRANSLATION AS) and DESCRIPTIVE TRANSLATION STUDIES. Further reading: Fraser 1996; Gerloff 1987; Krings 1986a, 1986b, 1987; Lörscher 1991; Toury 1995.

Third Code A term coined by Frawley (1984) within the context of a discussion of literary translation. Frawley argues that TT, having what he terms dual lineage (i.e. being influenced by both ST and TL), "emerges as a code in its own right, setting its own standards and structural presuppositions and entailments, though they are necessarily derivative of [ST] and [TL]" (1984:169). In other words, within each unique set of translational circumstances, the language of TT will take over those SL and ST features that it needs in order to communicate source items in TL. The concept of the third code, which originates within a basically semiotic approach to translation, has also been taken up by writers more interested in analyzing the linguistic features which typify TTs. Thus Baker also argues that a TT is the "result of the confrontation of the source and target codes" (1993:245); on the basis of evidence from studies of phenomena such as the patterns of cohesion and the distribution of common lexical items she concludes that TTs differ in nature from both their own STs and from original texts written in TL. Although there has so far been little investigation into this phenomenon, other target features which it is believed may represent examples of the third code are EXPLICITATION and the other posited UNIVERSALS OF TRANSLATION, as well as the frequent appearance in TT of items of source culture REALIA. While none of these features constitute actual infringements of TL norms, their appearance, according to Shamaa, "leave[s] a vague impression of being culturally exotic" (1978:172, quoted in Baker 1993:245); their presence may thus account for a text being perceived as having an indefinable "translated feel". It should, however, be noted that such features are not those associated with the concept of TRANSLATIONESE; while the two notions are clearly related, the term *third code* generally denotes more subtle deviations from TL linguistic norms, and its use implies on the part of the writer not only a lack of disapproval, but also the belief that such phenomena are worthy of systematic investigation for their own sake. Toury (1980, 1995) discusses similar phenomena as part of his rationale for the discipline of TARGET TEXT-ORIENTED TRANSLATION STUDIES, claiming that TTs in a given language differ "dialectally" from original texts composed in that language (1980:42); a similar insight is provided by Rabin (1958:144-45), who argues that translation from language A to language B becomes progressively easier, as translators build up a "translation stock" of tried and tested solutions to translation problems (which would subsequently mark such TTs as translations). In this way the third code can extend and enrich the linguistic repertoire of TL, as features absorbed through translation can be adopted in the language as a whole, or at least contribute to a change which is already taking place. Useful insights into the third code can be gained from a study of PSEUDOTRANSLA-TIONS 1, and our understanding is also likely to increase as more use is made of COMPARABLE CORPORA. See also LINGUISTICALLY CREATIVE TRANSLATION and TARGET LANGUAGE. Further reading: Baker 1993, 1995; Frawley 1984; Toury 1980, 1995.

Third Language See TRANSLATIONESE.

Time-restricted Theories of Translation One of Holmes' (1988e) six types of PARTIAL THEORY OF TRANSLATION. Time-restricted theories of translation are concerned with either the translation of contemporary texts or those of an older period. In the latter case one may also speak of Cross-temporal Theories of Translation (see INTERTEMPORAL TRANSLATION); however, of the two, this is the branch which has led to fewer significant conclusions (1988e:76). See also AREA-RESTRICTED, MEDIUM-RESTRICTED, PROBLEM-RESTRICTED, RANK-RESTRICTED and TEXT-TYPE RESTRICTED THEORIES OF TRANSLATION. Further reading: Holmes 1988e.

Total Translation According to Catford's (1965) model, the mode of translation that contrasts with RESTRICTED TRANSLATION. Total translation is what is generally meant by the non-technical use of the word "translation"; however, on a formal level it may be defined as the "replacement of SL grammar and lexis by equivalent TL grammar and lexis with consequential replacement of SL phonology/graphology by (non-equivalent) TL phonology/graphology" (1965:22). Thus it is only SL grammar and lexis which is directly replaced by equivalent TL substance; the replacement on the levels of phonology and graphology, on the other hand, is concomitant on those two former levels. Consequently, phonological and graphological substance is not generally replaced by equivalent TL substance, although exceptions to this are provided by instances such as film DUBBING or the translation of poetry, where TT graphology or phonology is sometimes partially equivalent to that of ST. See also GRAMMATICAL, GRAPHOLOGICAL, LEXICAL, PHONOLOGICAL and UNBOUNDED TRANSLATION. Further reading: Catford 1965.

Tower of Babel See BABEL (TOWER OF).

Traduction Absolue See ABSOLUTE TRANSLATION.

Traduction avec Reconstructions See RECONSTRUCTIONS (TRANS-LATION WITH).

Traduction Diagrammatique See DIAGRAMMATIC TRANSLATION.

Traduction Directe See DIRECT TRANSLATION 4.

Traduction Documentaire See SELECTIVE TRANSLATION.

Traduction Sélective See SELECTIVE TRANSLATION.

Traduction Signalétique See KEYWORD TRANSLATION.

Traduction Synoptique See ABSTRACT TRANSLATION.

Traductology (French *Traductologie*; Spanish *Traductología*) A term coined in the early 1970s by Harris to refer to "the scientific study of translation" (see 1977:90-91). While enthusiastically adopted by a number of writers in various countries, the term has not acquired a very general currency as, like TRANSLATOLOGY, it is perceived by many as an unnecessary neologism (see for example Holmes 1988e:69 and Pym 1992a:181), and has – at least in English – been widely replaced by more recent, less scientistic-sounding designations such as TRANSLATION STUDIES (Holmes 1988e:70). See also SCIENCE OF TRANSLATION. Further reading: Harris 1977; Vázquez-Ayora 1977.

Transcription A general term used to refer to a type of interlingual transfer in which the forms of the original (e.g. sounds, letters or words) are preserved unchanged in TT. According to Nord, transcription represents one of the two extreme limits of TRANSLATION, the other being free text production (1991a:30); all types of "translation proper" consequently lie somewhere between these two poles. Thus like TRANSLITERATION transcription is not itself usually considered to be an example of translation as such; furthermore, because its purpose is the preservation of form rather than meaning it is not generally applied to entire texts. However, it is frequently resorted to within a translated text, for example as a technique for rendering ST names, REALIA or other items which have no precise TL equivalent (see VOIDS). It should also be pointed out that Catford (1965) uses the term *transcription* to refer to transliteration from non-alphabetical scripts such as Chinese. See also GRAPHOLOGICAL TRANSLATION and INTERLINEAR TRANSLATION. Further reading: Levý 1969.

Transeme A term used by van Leuven-Zwart (1989, 1990) to refer to a basic unit for the linguistic comparison of a literary text and its INTEGRAL TRANSLATION. Reasoning that "sentences are generally too long and words too short to be easily compared" (1989:155), van Leuven-Zwart suggests the transeme as a suitable basic unit of comparison. The transeme is ultimately derived from criteria suggested by Dik (1978), and occurs in one of two varieties: the *state of affairs transeme*, which consists of a predicate and its arguments, and the *satellite transeme*, which acts as an adverbial extension of a state of affairs transeme. In this way, a sentence will typically consist of one or more transemes. The detailed micro-structural comparison of ST and TT transemes via a hypothetical ARCHITRANSEME is the first step in a process designed to reveal the translator's translation policy and the ways in which this causes TT to differ from the original on the macrostructural level. Depending on how the ST and TT transemes each differ from the architranseme, it is possible to classify the relationship which obtains between them as being one of MODI-FICATION, MODULATION 2 or MUTATION. If consistent trends can be observed in the SHIFTS which occur between a large number of ST and TT transemes, then it may be possible to draw conclusions about the translational policies or NORMS which the translator has been adhering to in the translation process. On the basis of an investigation into an extensive corpus of Dutch translations of Spanish and Spanish-American literature, van Leuven-Zwart has observed that an average of one shift per transeme is typical. See also GENERALIZATION and SPECIFICATION. Further reading: van Leuven-Zwart 1989, 1990.

Transfer 1 A general term which has various different meanings. First of all, the term *transfer* is used by some (see for example Catford 1965) as a synonym for the process of TRANSLATION (Wilss 1982:63). Secondly, transfer is occasionally understood in the psychological sense as the interference of one language in another, whether in the process of translating or of learning another language; in translation such interference might result in the production of features associated with phenomena such as TRANSLATIONESE or the THIRD CODE. However, perhaps the term is used in TRANSLATION STUDIES most frequently to refer to the set of processes to which translation belongs and to the other members of which it may be fruitfully compared. Used in this sense the term will thus describe all processes which involve the introduction of a text (or other collection of signs) into another language (or non-linguistic system). Thus Reiss & Vermeer, for example, define translation as a "special type of transfer" (1984:108, translated) of signs from one system into another; as instances of other types, they cite the minuting of a conversation, the dramatization of a novel, the filming of a story or the constructing of a cathedral from the architect's plans (1984:89). In other words, their view of transfer broadly corresponds to Jakobson's (1959/1966) three-fold concept of translation (see INTERLINGUAL, INTERSEMIOTIC and INTRALINGUAL TRANSLATION). Similarly, Eco (1976) lists three types of semiotic transfer: copying, transcribing and translating (quoted in Frawley 1984:160). Even-Zohar (1990d) understands transfer as referring to transplantation from one cultural system to another. He talks about the advantages of viewing translation in this wider context; such a shift in perspective would, according to him, have the consequence of elucidating the nature and rôle of translation (1990d:74). An alternative view of transfer is offered by Pym, who uses the term *text trans-fer* to refer to "the simple moving of inscribed material from one place and time to another place and time" (1992a:13), or in other words, not to a more general notion than translation, but to something which is a precondition for its taking place at all (1992a:18). Pym also refers to this physical movement as *external transfer*, and con-trasts it with what he terms *internal transfer*, which denotes the "sets of rules or procedures for adapting structures to new interpretative systems" (1992b:172), and which for him is basically synonymous with translation (1992b:172-74). Thus for Pym the difference be-tween (external) transfer and translation is that the former is a material movement between cultures which entails neither adaptation nor in-terpretation (1992b:173), and which is akin to the movement of, for example, merchandise or expertise (1992a:13), while the latter is a semiotic activity which can on occasion become divorced from the physical realities of the accompanying transfer (1992a:13-14). See also TRANSFER-ORIENTED TRANSLATION STUDIES. Further reading: Even-Zohar 1990d; Pym 1992a, 1992b; Reiss & Vermeer 1984.

2 A term used to refer to the second stage of Nida & Taber's (1969/1982) three-stage model of the translation process. The model which they propose is specifically designed to reflect the process of Bible translation, and is based on elements of Chomsky's transfor-mational grammar (see for example Chomsky 1965). Nida & Taber's three stages – which do not necessarily occur strictly sequentially (1969/1982:104) – are ANALYSIS, transfer and RESTRUCTURING; trans-fer is defined as the stage "in which the analyzed material is transferred in the mind of the translator from language A to language B" (1969/1982:33). Transfer takes place near the level of the kernels – the "basic structural elements" (1969/1982:39) which are posited for a particular language – which have been derived in the analysis stage. In other words, the translator takes the kernels and, modifying them in the light of his or her knowledge of TL structure, produces forms which "will be optimal for transfer into the receptor language" (1969/1982:51). During the transfer process kernels are not treated in isolation, as the temporal, spatial and logical relations which exist between them also need to be transferred (1969/1982:104). Further-more, adjustments are made as necessary: firstly, to redistribute the semantic elements, where the need arises, through such processes as expansion (e.g. of one SL word into several TL words) and synthesis (e.g. of an SL phrase into a single TL word), and secondly, to

compensate for structural differences between SL and TL at the discourse, sentence, word and even sound level. Consequently transfer involves the reconfiguration in TL of sets of semantic and structural SL components, rather than the simple replacement of actual SL elements with their most LITERAL TL equivalents; in other words, Nida & Taber envisage the transfer being performed on the basis of CONTEXTUAL (rather than VERBAL) CONSISTENCY, thus contributing towards the establishment of DYNAMIC EQUIVALENCE. It should be pointed out that transfer is not presented as a watertight procedure which guarantees absolute "preservation of meaning", as in any transfer there is "an inevitable modification in the meaning, generally associated with some degree of loss, especially in the degree of impact of the original communication" (Nida 1969:492). Further reading: Gentzler 1993; Nida 1969; Nida & Taber 1969/1982.

Transfer-oriented Translation Studies A term used to refer to an approach to historical-descriptive translation research developed by the Göttingen Center for the Cooperative Study of Literary Translation. The transfer-oriented approach grew out of a number of practical research projects, including for example a major study of German translations of American literature. Although they share many of the concerns of POLYSYSTEM theorists and their TARGET TEXT-ORIENTED approach – such as a view of literature as being composed of SYSTEMS and an interest in the rôle played by translation in the historical development of national literatures – some of their conclusions are different from those of the latter group (Gentzler 1993:183-84). Indeed, the very name of the Göttingen group's approach implies a contrast with *target text*-oriented (and also SOURCE TEXT-ORIENTED) translation studies. The *transfer*-oriented approach focusses on a translation "as the result of an act of transfer across lingual, literary, and cultural boundaries" (Frank 1990a:12); it is thus more comprehensive than a pure TT orientation as it embraces "considerations of the source side, the target side, and of the differences between them" (1990a:12), and also significantly brings the translator into the equation. More specifically, it views literary translation as the result of a compromise on the part of the translator between the demands of four NORM areas: "the source text as understood by the translator; the source literature, language, and culture as implicated in the text; the state of translation culture (which includes concepts of translation, previous translations of the same and of other texts, etc.); and the target side (for instance in the form of publisher's policies, local theater conventions, censorship, etc.)" (1990a:12). Besides these main areas, other more minor factors also need to be taken into consideration, such as the interference of other literatures, the translator's first-hand experience of the source country, the particular dictionaries consulted by the translator, and the conditions in which the translation was produced (Frank 1992:383). In all of these areas it is of course the perceptions of the translator which are paramount (Frank 1990b:54); thus a translation will inevitably reflect an individual translator's *ethos* in that it will have been formed as a result of his or her decisions (Frank 1992:371). See also DESCRIPTIVE TRANSLATION STUDIES. Further reading: Frank 1990a, 1990b, 1992; Gentzler 1993.

Transference Defined by Catford as containing an "*implantation* of SL meanings into the TL text" (1965:48; emphasis original). In other words, the term refers to a process in which an SL item is used in a TT, but with an SL meaning. This commonly happens when for cultural, geographical or other reasons TL has no suitable equivalent for an SL item and consequently "borrows" the item. However, true transference is uncommon, as such borrowed items typically change their meaning, either because the item acquires a foreign feel or because only one of the total range of meanings which it possesses in SL is transferred. Further reading: Catford 1965.

Transformation See RESTRUCTURING.

Translat (**Translated Text**, or **Translatum**) (German) A term coined by Kade (1968) to circumvent the ambiguity of the word *Übersetzung*. While this latter word can traditionally denote either the process or the product of translation, the term *Translat* was specifically designed to refer to the translated text, as the product of the process of TRANSLATION. Further reading: Kade 1968; Reiss & Vermeer 1984.

Translatability A term used – along with its opposite, *untranslatability* – to discuss the extent to which it is possible to translate either individual words and phrases or entire texts from one language to another. Discussion of this concept has arisen from the tension between two basic arguments. The first of these is the indisputable fact that different languages do not "mesh together", in that the unique configurations of grammar, vocabulary and metaphor

which one finds in each language inevitably have some bearing on the
types of meaning that can be comfortably expressed in that language;
the second is that, in spite of this consideration, translation between
languages still occurs, often with an ostensibly high degree of success.
Considering translatability on the word level, Catford demonstrates
that grammatically encoded SL meaning (such as the inbuilt femininity
of French *elles* "they") will almost inevitably fail to find a direct
reflection in TL and will therefore be "lost"; however, he classifies
such minor linguistic discrepancies as being "functionally irrelevant"
to the question of EQUIVALENCE (1965:94). Other writers discuss
word-level lexical incompatibility, which can be caused either by
differences between source and target cultural phenomena or by the
simple non-existence of a TL word to label a given item or concept
(see REALIA and VOIDS). However, it is generally agreed that this type
of untranslatability occurs only on the level of single lexical items,
and can frequently be circumvented by means of paraphrase or
EXPLICITATION in such a way as to ensure that all the semantic features
of ST are retained; furthermore, above the word level other strategies
such as COMPENSATION can also be employed. Yet it is not enough to
consider simple retention of the same basic semantic features as the
sole criterion for translatability. The existence of further semantic
dimensions which are added by such concepts as connotation and
collocational meaning supports the conclusion that an absolute meaning
does not exist independently of any particular language and that
translatability can consequently only be a limited notion. In addition
to this, textual and contextual features such as implied meaning, as
well as formal features such as puns, wordplays and poetic devices,
which are notoriously difficult to preserve through the translation
process, indicate that meaning is to a large extent generated by a
specific text. In the light of such considerations Frawley, for example,
argues that there can be no exactness in translation in any "but rare
and trivial cases" (1984:163), and concludes that "any interlingual
translation that seeks to transfer only semantics has lost before it has
begun" (1984:168). If this is the case, then any idea of absolute
translatability must be abandoned. The notion of translatability
therefore has to be considered in relation to each instance of translation
as "a concrete act of performance" (Toury 1980:28), and must be
linked with the text-type of ST, the purpose of translation and the
translation principles being followed by the translator. Thus for
example, texts suited to House's (1977) notion of COVERT TRANS-

LATION will lend themselves to different kinds of translation strategies from those for which OVERT TRANSLATION would be more appropriate, with the result that different types of equivalence will be established in each of these two types of translation. Similarly, a text which would be considered highly untranslatable using, for example, a strategy based on FORMAL EQUIVALENCE might be held to be more translatable if the opposite approach, that of DYNAMIC EQUIVALENCE, were to be employed. Because of such considerations Wilss concludes that the translatability of a text can "be measured in terms of the degree to which it can be recontextualized in the TL, taking into account all linguistic and extralinguistic factors" (1982:49). See also INDETERMINACY and TERTIUM COMPARATIONIS. Further reading: Catford 1965; Koller 1979/1992; Toury 1980; Wilss 1977, 1982.

· hon specifico
· amplio

Translation An incredibly broad notion which can be understood in many different ways. For example, one may talk of translation as a process or a product, and identify such sub-types as literary translation, technical translation, SUBTITLING and MACHINE TRANSLATION; moreover, while more typically it just refers to the transfer of written texts, the term sometimes also includes INTERPRETING. A number of scholars have also suggested further distinctions between different types of translation (see for example COVERT vs. OVERT TRANSLATION, or DOMESTICATING vs. FOREIGNIZING TRANSLATION). Furthermore, many writers also extend its reference to take in related activities which most would not recognize as translation as such (see for example DIAGRAMMATIC TRANSLATION, INTER-SEMIOTIC TRANSLATION, PARAPHRASE and PSEUDOTRANSLATION 1). Translation is frequently characterized metaphorically, and has – amongst many other things – been compared to playing a GAME or making a MAP. Each of these analogies, however, is only intended to capture one particular facet of translation. Not surprisingly, many formal definitions have also been offered, each of which reflects a particular underlying theoretical model. The linguistic aspects of the translation process have been encapsulated in a large number of definitions, mostly dating from the 1960s or earlier. Thus Catford, for example, defines translation as "the replacement of textual material in one language (SL) by equivalent textual material in another language (TL)" (1965:20). However, as Sager points out, most older definitions of this type tend to centre around the importance of maintaining some kind of EQUIVALENCE between ST and TT (1994:121). Thus for Sager Jakobson's definition is in this sense innovative. Jakobson sees translation in semiotic terms as "an interpretation of verbal signs by means of some other language" (1959/1966:233; see INTERLINGUAL TRANSLATION), understanding the translation process as a substitution of "messages in one language not for separate code-units *but for entire messages in some other language*" (1959/1966:233, emphasis added). Working along similar lines, Lawendowski defines translation as "the transfer of 'meaning' from one set of language signs to another set of language signs" (1978:267). An approach based on the importance of preserving the effect of the original is reflected in Nida & Taber's definition: "translating consists in reproducing in the receptor language the closest natural equivalent of the source-language message, first in terms of meaning and secondly in terms of style" (1969/1982:12). However, as stated by Koller, many definitions tend to be normative rather than DESCRIPTIVE, as they frequently state not only what translation is, but also what it is *supposed* to be (1979/1992:94; see also PRESCRIPTIVE TRANSLATION STUDIES). An exception to this is Toury's TARGET TEXT-ORIENTED definition, which states that a translation is "taken to be any target-language utterance which is presented or regarded as such within the target culture, on whatever grounds" (1985:20). Vermeer, rejecting notions of translation as a two-stage process of decoding and recoding, offers a similarly non-normative definition of translation as "'information' about a source text in another language" (1982:97, translated; see INFORMATION OFFER). This approach engenders a view of translation in which the way a TT functions in a specific cultural context is paramount: "translation is the production of a functional target text maintaining a relationship with a given source text that is specified according to the intended or demanded function of the target text (translation skopos)" (Nord 1991a:28; see SKOPOS THEORY). Finally, to reflect the environment in which much professional translation activity takes place Sager suggests widening previous definitions by specifying that "translation is an externally motivated industrial activity, supported by information technology, which is diversified in response to the particular needs of this form of communication" (1994:293; see INDUSTRIAL PROCESS (TRANSLATION AS)). See also *TRANSLATION*. Further reading: Bathgate 1981; Kelly 1979; Koller 1979/1992; Neubert 1991a; Neubert & Shreve 1992; Sager 1994; Wilss 1977, 1982.

● *Translation* **(Process of Translation)** (German) A term introduced by Kade (1968) as a general designation for the two distinct concepts *ÜBERSETZEN* (i.e. written TRANSLATION) and *DOLMETSCHEN* (i.e. IN-TERPRETING). Previously German had had no satisfactory word which could be used to refer generically to both of these terms. However, unlike the English word 'translation', *Translation* refers exclusively to the translation process, rather than to the translated text, which is known by the term *TRANSLAT*. Further reading: Kade 1968; Reiss & Vermeer 1984.

Translation and the Theory of Games See GAMES (TRANSLATION AND THE THEORY OF).

Translation as Decision-making See DECISION-MAKING (TRANSLA-TION AS).

Translation as Industrial Process See INDUSTRIAL PROCESS (TRANS-LATION AS).

Translation Equivalence See EQUIVALENCE.

✗**Translation Studies** A term used to describe the "discipline which concerns itself with problems raised by the production and description of translations" (Lefevere 1978:234). The term was originally suggested by Holmes (see for example 1988e) to address a perceived problem with the use of the term TRANSLATION THEORY 1 as a title for the discipline; Holmes argued that much research was being carried out into translation which did not, strictly speaking, "fall within the scope of theory formation" (1988e:69). Thus Holmes proposed using the designation *Translation Studies* to give a "more tentative and open range to scholarly activities than 'science', 'theory', etc." (Lambert 1991:26-27). However, the fact that the term was originally suggested by Holmes and enthusiastically adopted by the scholars associated with the so-called MANIPULATION SCHOOL, who tend to approach translation from a background in comparative literature, has led to the mistaken perception that Translation Studies refers exclusively to the study of *literary* translation and translations. It is true that some writers both inside and outside the "manipulation school" (e.g. Gentzler 1993; see also Lambert 1991:27) use the term to distinguish this school from other approaches found within the discipline; yet it is clear that Holmes' original intention was that

"Translation Studies" should contain no such limitation (1988e:71ff.). Indeed, Holmes' (1988e) division of the discipline (sometimes illustrated by means of a "map"; see for example Toury 1995:10) into APPLIED, DESCRIPTIVE and THEORETICAL TRANSLATION STUDIES, along with a multitude of further smaller categories, indicates the breadth of his vision for the discipline. (Working along similar lines, Bassnett (1980/1991:7-8) divides Translation Studies into four categories: history of translation, translation in the TL culture, translation and linguistics, and translation and poetics.) The tendency to use the term as the overall designation for the discipline has been strengthened in recent years by Snell-Hornby's (1988/1995) choice of Translation Studies as the expression under which to unite the separate interests and emphases of the "manipulation" approach and that associated with the SCIENCE OF TRANSLATION. Snell-Hornby stresses that "a discipline of translation studies must embrace a spectrum including all kinds of translation, from literary to technical, and should also extend to the neglected field of interpreting" (1991:19). She envisages the discipline – or *interdiscipline*, to use her preferred term (which she (1991:19) attributes to Toury; see also Snell-Hornby et al. 1994) – as consisting of "special language studies, terminology and lexicography, machine translation and machine-aided translation; relevant areas of linguistics such as semantics, contrastive grammar, text linguistics, socio- and psycholinguistics; literary translation (including all forms of stage translation, film dialogue and dubbing, sub-titles and so forth) and neighbouring fields of interest from literary history to psychology" (Snell-Hornby 1991:19; see also DUBBING, MACHINE-AIDED TRANSLATION, MACHINE TRANSLATION, SUBTITLES and TERMINOLOGY). However, not even such an extended list manages to do justice to the staggeringly interdisciplinary nature of Translation Studies, which also overlaps with such further areas as anthropology, comparative literature, economics, ethnology, history, philosophy, politics and semiotics. See also TRADUCTOLOGY and TRANSLATOLOGY. Further reading: Bassnett 1980/1991; Gentzler 1993; Holmes 1988e; Leuven-Zwart & Naaijkens 1991; Neubert 1991a; Neubert & Shreve 1992; Snell-Hornby 1988/1995; Snell-Hornby et al. 1994; Toury 1995.

Translation Theory 1 A term used to refer to the entire discipline of TRANSLATION STUDIES. Thus Popovič, for example, defines translation theory as a "discipline engaged in the systematic study of translation", whose task consists of "modeling the translational process and text" ([1976]:23). However, this use of the term is probably most closely associated with Newmark, who describes translation theory as "the body of knowledge that we have and have still to have about the process of translating" (1981/1988:19). Such views, however, increasingly represent the minority, as the term is now more widely used in the sense discussed under TRANSLATION THEORY 2; thus Lambert, for example, states that at the time of writing "few theoreticians define the entire field of scholarly work linked to translation as 'Translation Theory'" (1991:30). The reason for this, as argued by Holmes, is that "there is much valuable study and research being done in the discipline, and a need for much more to be done, that does not, strictly speaking, fall within the scope of theory formation" (1988e:69). See also MANIPULATION SCHOOL, SCIENCE OF TRANSLATION, TRADUCTOLOGY and TRANSLATOLOGY. Further reading: Holmes 1988e.

2 (or **Theory of Translation**) A term used to refer to a specific attempt to explain in a systematic way some or all of the phenomena related to translation. However, the use of the term is surrounded with some confusion. The reason for this is that in an area which lacks unanimity over any universal principles of translation, the term has often been used to refer to statements which lay down guidelines about *how* translation should be done, and which often exist in rivalry with other such statements. Thus for example Reiss & Vermeer define a theory as containing "1) the statement of its basis, 2) the description of its object, and 3) an inventory of rules" (1984:3, translated). Similarly, Newmark – who also uses the term in the sense described under TRANSLATION THEORY 1 – argues that translation theory's chief concern is to determine "appropriate translation methods" and to provide "a framework of principles, restricted rules and hints for translating texts and criticizing translations" (1981/1988:19). However, there is a broad consensus within at least part of the discipline of TRANSLATION STUDIES that "Theory attempts to account for what happens, not tell you how it should happen" (Baker, quoted in Gamal 1994:16). Thus Holmes, for example, defines a *theory* in general terms as a "series of statements, each of which is derived logically from a previous statement or from an axiom and which together have a strong power of explanation and prediction regarding a certain phenomenon" (1988f:93-94); elsewhere he describes a theory of translation as "a full, inclusive theory accommodating so many

elements that it can serve to explain and predict all phenomena falling within the terrain of translating and translation, to the exclusion of all phenomena falling outside it" (1988e:73). Yet the fact is that the formulation of such a theory is a matter of extreme difficulty. The reasons for this are basically twofold, and are related to the multi-faceted nature not only of translation itself, but also of the discipline as a whole. As regards the first of these, Graham sees translation as comprising "an indefinite or fuzzy set of somewhat similar smaller problems" (1981:29) which differ from each other sufficiently to make it difficult to view them all within a single theoretical frame-work. It is thus no easy matter to derive useful, non-banal generalizations about such an unpromisingly varied phenomenon; indeed, the only form in which it is likely to prove possible is as a complex, abstract, "highly formalized" (Holmes 1988e:73) body of statements, which taken together are capable of providing a broad enough view of all the phenomena which translation involves. Regarding the second reason – which comes about largely as a result of the first – it should be stated that the production of a theory of translation is made harder not only because of the wide-ranging inter-disciplinary nature of Translation Studies, but also because of the fact that theorists inevitably approach the matter with their own, frequently mutually exclusive assumptions, preconceptions and agen-das (see for example Pym 1992a:188). The result of this has been that theories have often been produced which only address a particu-lar set of problems associated with translation, or else which specifically concern themselves only with certain types of transla-tion. Thus Holmes, for example, considers that many translation theories to date are not general but specific in scope, and deal with only some of the various aspects of translation theory (1988e:73; see PARTIAL THEORIES OF TRANSLATION). Furthermore, Pym talks about the lack of a sufficiently high vantage point from which to view all possible facets of translation (1992a:186), and also about the mutual exclusivity of the various "external assumptions" brought to bear on translation, concerning such matters as "the nature of God's Word, the supposed equality of different cultures or the ethical duty to con-vey information" (1992a:188). It is considerations like these that lead Holmes to conclude that "most of the theories that have been produced to date are in reality little more than prolegomena to ... a general translation theory" (1988e:73; see GENERAL THEORIES OF TRANSLATION). Holmes posits that such a comprehensive theory would need to consist of at least four sub-theories, concerned with the translation *process*, the translation *product*, the *function* of translation and translation *didactics* (1988f:95); furthermore, he argues that the fourth – the only element which should be normative – can only be constructed on the basis of the other three (1988f:95-96), which would in turn be developed using the insights gained by DESCRIPTIVE TRANSLATION STUDIES (1988e:73). Thus translation theory will, according to Toury, become a "series of truly interconnected hypotheses" (1995:267); these will be probabilistic in nature and stated largely in the form of *if ... then* laws (1995:264-65). See also THEORETICAL TRANSLATION STUDIES. Further reading: Holmes 1988e, 1988f; Pym 1992a; Toury 1995.

Translation Unit See UNIT OF TRANSLATION.

Translation Universals See UNIVERSALS OF TRANSLATION.

Translation with Reconstructions See RECONSTRUCTIONS (TRANSLATION WITH).

Translational Equivalence See STYLISTIC EQUIVALENCE.

Translationese (or **Third Language**) A generally pejorative term used to refer to TL usage which because of its obvious reliance on features of SL is perceived as unnatural, impenetrable or even comical. Translationese is typically caused by an excessively LITERAL approach to the translation process or an imperfect knowledge of TL (as for example in INVERSE TRANSLATION when used in inappropriate contexts), and is reflected in the perception that "the source language of a translation seems reluctant to make its exit; it prefers to seek reincarnation in the target language" (Tsai 1995:242). Inappropriate SL metaphors and syntax, unnatural word order and a high concentration of unnatural-sounding terminology are the sort of features which are typical of translationese. Duff uses the term *the third language* to refer to the same phenomenon, claiming that a text can be preserved as a coherent entity only if the translation does not represent a mixture of styles and languages, or a "patchwork" made up of SL and TL elements (1981:12); so strong does he consider the potential influence of SL interference to be that he talks of SL wielding a "tyranny" over TT (1981:113). In this way, examples of translationese are not simply "anecdotal instances of bad translations" (Gellerstam 1986:88), but rather reveal a "systematic influence on [TL] from [SL]" (1986:88). Some theorists, such as Robinson (e.g. 1991:60) and Venuti (e.g. 1995:3-4, 117-18), however, question the inevitable association of translationese with "bad" translation, arguing that there is simply a cultural taboo against allowing a translation to sound like a translation. Translationese generally differs from the related notion of the THIRD CODE in that it represents a more extreme deviation from target norms, although some writers (for example Granger 1996) use the term to refer to language reflecting the more elusive features usually associated with this latter concept. In applied linguistics the phenomena linked with translationese are also known as *inter-language*. The potential of translationese is frequently tapped for its comic effect, as can be seen in Malcolm Bradbury's spoof guide-book, *Why Come To Slaka?*, the whole of which is written in a kind of mock translationese, and which for example contains the advice that "the waters of our cities are potable usually, but in the country always fry your waters before tippling" (Bradbury 1987:63). See also OVERTRANSLATION 2 and UNDERTRANSLATION. Further reading: Duff 1981; Gellerstam 1986.

Translatology (German *Translatologie*) A term suggested as a pos-sible title for the discipline now generally known as TRANSLATION STUDIES. The term *translatology* has been used since the early 1970s by some authors, most notably in Canada, Germany and Denmark. Where it is used by English-language writers it tends to refer to linguistically oriented approaches to translation (Snell-Hornby 1988/1995:14), while the term in German has the advantage of explicitly including both written TRANSLATION and spoken INTERPRETING (Reiss & Vermeer 1984:1; see also *TRANSLATION*). However, there seems to be a high level of resistance to this term amongst many English-speaking writers on translation (see for example Holmes 1988e:69 and Pym 1992a:181) as, like TRADUCTOLOGY, it is widely perceived as an ungainly neologism. Thus Goffin's (1971:59) prediction that it would soon come to be the standard name for the discipline has so far failed to come true. See also SCIENCE OF TRANSLATION. Further read-ing: Harris 1977; Radó 1979.

Translatorial Action (or **Translational Action**, or **Intercultural Cooperation**) (German *Translatorisches Handeln*) A term introduced by Holz-Mänttäri (1984) to describe the collaborative process which leads up to the production of a TT. Holz-Mänttäri's concept is in many ways similar to that of SKOPOS THEORY, although it is arguably more radical than that approach. The radicalness of Holz-Mänttäri's translatorial action is reflected in the term itself, in which the word *translation* is avoided, being replaced by the neologism *translatorial* (German *translatorisch*); indeed, her entire description of the concept is typified by such terminological innovation. However, the reason for this is only partly terminological, since the term *translatorial action* represents a more general concept than does *translation*, as it includes other types of text production such as paraphrase and re-editing. The concept of translatorial action places the act of (technical) translation in its broader professional context, in which not only the translator, but also the ST author, the client or commissioner and the TT reader play a role in the process of TT-production. The translator is viewed as an *expert* who cooperates with other experts in the production of a TT which is in line with the *product specification* which has been agreed on in advance by the parties concerned. The rôle of translatorial action is then to produce a target *message transmitter* (or text) which will overcome all cultural barriers in order to fulfil its function in the target situation. The extent to which such a *message transmitter* will reflect ST depends on the respective functions of ST and TT, as ST is viewed as only "part of the source material" (1986:362) which might contribute to the final shape of TT. In other words, for Holz-Mänttäri, ST exists solely in order to "meet the requirements of the situation" (Nord 1991a:28); should the function of TT which has been agreed in the product specification differ from that of ST then the translator is expected to make the necessary changes to ST, or to supplement it with additional material by way of explanation. Consequently, although translatorial action is a more literal English translation of the term, Nord's (1991a) rendering *intercultural cooperation* more effectively conveys the essence of the type of professional interaction which Holz-Mänttäri is visualizing. See also COMMISSION and LOYALTY. Further reading: Holz-Mänttäri 1984, 1986; Vermeer 1989.

Translatum See *TRANSLAT*.

Transliteration 1 According to Catford, a process in which "SL graphological units are replaced by TL graphological units" (1965:66).

However, Catford distinguishes between transliteration and the related concept of GRAPHOLOGICAL TRANSLATION. This can be seen by the fact that the transliterated version of the Russian word СПУТНИК is not CHYTHNK (the graphological translation equivalent) but SPUTNIK. Transliteration is seen as a three-stage process, which can be summarized as follows: SL letters → SL phonological units → TL phonological units → TL letters (1965:66). However, the process is complicated by the presence of three theoretical problems (1965:67-68). Firstly, an SL letter can have more than one phonological equivalent. Secondly, there may not be one-to-one equivalence between SL and TL phonological units. Thirdly, it is possible that arbitrary choices may have to be made between more than one TL letter which can represent a TL phonological unit. According to Catford, when languages such as Chinese are involved the conversion of SL into TL forms is known as *transcription*. Transliteration as a process is distinct from TRANSLATION because of its conventionalized, predictable nature; consequently, most commentators do not include it in their consideration of translation. See also TRANSCRIPTION. Further reading: Catford 1965.

2 See SIGNED LANGUAGE INTERPRETING.

Transmutation See INTERSEMIOTIC TRANSLATION.

Transposition (French *Transposition*) According to Vinay & Darbelnet (1958, 1958/1995), one of seven translation procedures. Transposition is defined as the process of "replacing one word class with another without changing the meaning of the message" (1958/ 1995:36). For example, we might translate French *il a annoncé qu'il reviendrait* as *he announced that he would return* or as *he announced his return*; here the former translation would be literal, and the latter *transposed*. Transposition may be obligatory or optional. For example, *dès son lever* must be translated into English as *as soon as he gets/got up* since English lacks a noun which corresponds to French *lever*; on the other hand, *après son retour* may be translated as either *after he comes back* or *after his return* (1958:50, 1958/ 1995:36). Vinay & Darbelnet refer to a particularly frequent type of transposition as *interchange* (French *chassé-croisé*); this occurs when SL and TL emphasize different elements of a phrase, with the result that the components of the phrase change grammatical category when translated from SL to TL, as for example in *blown away* and *emporté* *par le vent* (1958:105, 1958/1995:103). Transposition is classified as one of four types of OBLIQUE translation, in that it does not involve a direct transfer between parallel SL and TL categories or concepts (1958:46, 1958/1995:31). See also ADAPTATION 2, BORROWING, CALQUE, EQUIVALENCE 2, LITERAL TRANSLATION and MODULATION 1. Further reading: Vinay & Darbelnet 1958, 1958/1995.

***Übersetzen* (Written Translation)** (German) The usual German word for written TRANSLATION, redefined by Kade (1968) to include any act of interlingual transfer in which ST is fixed, or can be repeated at will, and which may consequently be checked or corrected by the translator on a subsequent occasion. This means, for example, that the translation of a recording of a speech belongs to the activity of *Übersetzen*. See also CORRECTABILITY, *DOLMETSCHEN* and VERIFI- ABILITY. Further reading: Kade 1968; Reiss & Vermeer 1984.

Unbounded Translation A term used by Catford to denote a type of TOTAL TRANSLATION in which "equivalences shift freely up and down the rank scale" (1965:25; the "rank scale" is a kind of hierarchy of linguistic units which is used in Halliday's (1961) grammatical system). In other words, what unbounded translation describes is a "normal" translation in which the translator is free to translate an SL grammatical unit of a certain size by a TL equivalent of a dif- ferent size (for example, a word by a clause or a morpheme by a word). The opposite of unbounded translation is RANK-BOUND TRANSLATION, a somewhat artificial procedure which nevertheless has some limited practical application; however, the inevitable linguistic discrepancies which occur even between two "closely related" languages make unbounded translation in most contexts a necessity. See also FREE TRANSLATION. Further reading: Catford 1965.

Undertranslation A term used by Newmark (1981/1988) to refer to one of two phenomena frequently found in translated texts (see also OVERTRANSLATION 2). According to Newmark, the inevitable loss of ST meaning entailed by every act of translation can, depending on the precise circumstances, lead to an increase in either detail or gen- eralization in TT; if it leads to the latter, it is termed *undertranslation*. An example of undertranslation would be if, translating for a general audience, a translator decided to render the Russian *bely grib* ("white mushroom") in general terms as *wild mushroom*, rather than using

the more precise, but relatively unknown, equivalent *cep*. COMMUNI-
CATIVE TRANSLATION 2, with its tendency of conforming to TL conventions,
frequently favours undertranslation. See also DEGREE OF DIFFEREN-
TIATION and GENERALIZING TRANSLATION. Further reading: Duff 1981;
Newmark 1981/1988, 1988.

Unit of Translation (or **Translation Unit**) A term used to refer to
the linguistic level at which ST is recodified in TL. Barkhudarov
defines a unit of translation as "the smallest unit of SL which has an
equivalent in TL"; he comments that a unit of translation can itself
"have a complex structure", although "its parts taken individually are
'untranslatable', in that no equivalents can be established for them in
TT" (1969:3, translated). Thus for example not only the word *generally*, but also the expression *by and large*, although it is made up of
three words, would be treated as a single unit. For Barkhudarov the
possible units of translation are phonemes (e.g. in TRANSCRIPTION),
morphemes (e.g. in CALQUES), words, phrases, sentences and entire
texts. The wording at a given point in ST would determine the most
appropriate unit of translation, which could be expected to vary in the
course of a text or even a single sentence. Furthermore, it frequently
happens that an ST unit is translated by a TL unit of a different size;
for example, a word may be translated by a phrase or *vice versa*. If a
translator uses larger translation units than is necessary to convey the
basic meaning of ST this will lead to a FREE TRANSLATION being
produced; similarly, translating at a lower level than necessary will
result in a LITERAL TRANSLATION. However, as argued by Koller, it
seems likely that a translation between unrelated languages will usually involve larger units than if SL and TL are closely related (1979/
1992:100). Barkhudarov (1993) raises the problem of whether units
of translation should be elements of linguistic form or content; Vinay
& Darbelnet (1958, 1958/1995), however, consider that units of
thought, lexicological units and units of translation are synonymous.
Barkhudarov (1969) argues that the entire text can sometimes serve
as the unit of translation, although in practice limits this to the case of
poetry; in a similar way Koller (1979/1992) restricts this possibility
to poetry and advertising. However, Bassnett, writing about literary
translation, widens the applicability of this perception to include prose
texts (and by implication other genres too); she argues that in such
translation the text is the prime unit, as every text is "made up of a
series of interlocking systems, each of which has a determinable

function in relation to the whole" (1980/1991:118). Thus a translator who translated such a text sentence by sentence might lose certain important structural features, which a more non-linear approach (which might, for example, include use of COMPENSATION strategies) would permit to be preserved. See also LOGEME, UNBOUNDED TRANSLATION and UNIT SHIFT. Further reading: Barkhudarov 1993; Koller 1979/1992; Vinay & Darbelnet 1958, 1958/1995.

Unit Shift According to Catford (1965), a type of CATEGORY SHIFT in which strict rank-rank CORRESPONDENCE (that is, EQUIVALENCE between SL and TL sentences, clauses, groups, words and morphemes) is not observed; as such, unit shifts clearly constitute a major feature of virtually any "normal" translation. A situation in which unit shift frequently occurs is when an SL lexical item for which no one convenient TL equivalent exists is translated by a phrase (such as French *vieillard* "old man" or Russian *belet'* "to appear white"). Like other types of category shift, unit shifts as envisaged by Catford represent an obligatory rewording forced on the translator through minor linguistic incompatibilities between SL and TL. See also CLASS SHIFT, INTRA-SYSTEM SHIFT, LEVEL SHIFT, SHIFTS and STRUCTURE SHIFT. Further reading: Catford 1965.

Universals of Translation A term used to refer to a number of features of TTs which are posited by some as being the almost inevitable by-products of the process of translation, irrespective of the specific language pair involved. Baker defines universals of translation as "features which typically occur in translated text rather than original utterances and which are not the result of interference from specific linguistic systems" (1993:243). She suggests six features which might be viewed as belonging to this category; these are as follows. 1) A tendency towards EXPLICITATION is a common characteristic of translated texts. 2) Many TTs tend to simplify and disambiguate passages which are unclear in ST. 3) A TT will frequently "normalize" wayward SL grammar as well as standardizing other unconventional features of ST. 4) Instances of repetition will either be rephrased using synonyms, or else some of the occurrences will be simply omitted (Toury 1980:130). 5) In an attempt to "naturalize" TT, a translator may exaggerate or overuse typical TL features. 6) The process of translation might give rise to "a specific type of distribution of certain features in translated texts vis-à-vis source texts and original texts in the target language" (Baker 1993:245); such features might include, for example, cohesive devices or certain lexical items. The presence of unusual distributions of features of this type is one of the factors contributing to the phenomenon which is sometimes known as the THIRD CODE. The existence of universals of translation is still only being tentatively and intuitively suggested, and it is generally agreed that much more investigation of specific texts will be needed before any more detailed statements can be made on the subject. Further reading: Baker 1993, 1997; Laviosa-Braithwaite 1997.

Untranslatability See TRANSLATABILITY.

Verbal Consistency (or Concordance, or Verbal Concordance) Defined by Nida & Taber within the context of Bible translation as the "quality resulting from the effort to translate a given word from the original consistently by a single word in the receptor language" regardless of the variety of contexts in which it appears (1969/ 1982:208); as such it contrasts with the quality of CONTEXTUAL CON-SISTENCY. However, as Nida & Taber observe, words are not simply "points of meaning" (1969/1982:15), and because the semantic areas covered by corresponding words in different languages are not identi-cal, the choice of the word in TL which will translate an SL item depends upon the context, rather than upon a fixed system of equivalences (1969/1982:15). An approach based on verbal consist-ency thus tends to result in FORMAL EQUIVALENCE, and frequently produces renderings which are "both unnatural and misleading" (1969/ 1982:16). Beekman & Callow (1974) also discuss the concept of verbal consistency, although use the term *concordance*. Further read-ing: Beekman & Callow 1974; Nida & Taber 1969/1982.

Verbal Translation See METAPHRASE.

Verifiability (German *Kontrollierbarkeit*) Suggested by Reiss & Vermeer (1984), on the basis of Kade (1968), as one of two features which distinguish the process of *ÜBERSETZEN* (i.e. TRANSLATION) from that of *DOLMETSCHEN* (i.e. INTERPRETING). For a TT to be considered *verifiable* it is necessary for the translator to be able to revise his or her translation while it is still being produced, for example by cross-referencing with sections which have already been completed. This means that oral translation without the aid of a recording tends in most situations to be considered an example of *Dolmetschen* rather than *Übersetzen*. See also CORRECTABILITY. Further reading: Kade 1968; Reiss & Vermeer 1984.

Version 1 A term commonly used to describe a TT which in the view of the commentator departs too far from the original to be termed a translation. Typical reasons for using this term include the fact that the translator has ADAPTED the text for a particular target audience, has imposed a definite interpretation on it or foregrounded one of several possible interpretations contained in ST, or has simply used a FREE rather than LITERAL translation strategy. Use of this term can frequently be PRESCRIPTIVELY motivated and even pejorative; however, some writers prefer to see versions as constituting a separate text-type and serving a different but equally valid purpose to that of "translations proper". This view is represented by Hollander, who argues that when we use the term *version* rather than *translation* "we tend to emphasize the unique properties of the particular rendering in question" (1959/1966:220). Further reading: Hollander 1959/1966.

2 A term used by Lefevere (1975) to refer to one of two sub-types of the translation strategy which he terms INTERPRETATION. In all, Lefevere's typology consists of seven categories, which he identifies in his study of English translations of a poem by Catullus. However, as with the other sub-type, IMITATION 2, Lefevere considers the procedure of version-writing to be distinct from translation proper. He characterizes versions as ADAPTATIONS 1 of ST made in accordance with the taste of both version-writer and TL audience (1975:102) in order to heighten the communicative impact of the text in the target context (1975:76). Thus use of paraphrase, colloquialisms, additional similes and metaphors, asides and modernization are all typical features of versions. However, unlike the producer of imitations, the version-writer basically shares the ST author's interpretation of the work, although makes substantial changes to the form in which it is presented (1975:76, 84). In this way the production of a version can be seen as an exercise in REWRITING (1975:103). See also BLANK VERSE TRANSLATION, LITERAL TRANSLATION 2, METAPOEM, METRICAL TRANSLATION, PHONEMIC TRANSLATION, POETRY INTO PROSE and RHYMED TRANSLATION. Further reading: Lefevere 1975.

Vertical Translation According to Folena (1973/1991), one of two modes of translation used in the Middle Ages (see also HORIZONTAL

TRANSLATION). Folena, whose main concern is with the "role played by translation in the Middle Ages in the development of vernacular languages" (Bassnett 1994:153), coins the term to refer to the type of translation where "the source language, usually Latin, has prestige and value which transcend that of the target language" (1973/1991:13, translated). According to Bassnett, there are two ways in which this process of "vulgarization" can be performed: either WORD-FOR-WORD or SENSE-FOR-SENSE (1980/1991:53). See also INTERTEMPORAL TRANSLATION. Further reading: Bassnett 1980/ 1991; Folena 1973/1991.

Voids (or **Semantic Voids**, or *Lacunes* (French), or **Blank Spaces**, or **Gaps**) Defined by Dagut as the "non-existence in one language of a one-word equivalent for a designatory term found in another" (1978:45). Voids are found only at word level, as larger SL units may always be expressed in TL, if necessary through the use of rewording. Similarly, SL words which lack a TL equivalent may also be periphrastically glossed in TL. However, as Dagut points out, "the absence of any one-word [TL] equivalent clearly reflects the unconcern of [TL]-speakers as a whole with this aspect of 'reality'" (1978:46); a void thus tends to be revealed only when speakers of a language are made "uncomfortably aware" of it (1978:84) through contact with other languages. Dagut identifies four types of void. Firstly, *environmental* voids are those voids which arise from the untranslatability of natural phenomena (e.g. Arabic *wadi* or Russian *tundra*). The most effective way to deal with such voids is through TRANSCRIPTION; as can be seen from the examples, such transcribed forms are frequently accepted into TL as new words. The second type consists of *cultural* voids, divided by Dagut into the religious and the secular. Hebrew *bar mitzvah*, English *cream tea* and Russian *samovar* all frequently give rise to voids of this type as they all point to cultural phenomena which would almost certainly have no direct TL equivalent. Generally more translation-resistant than type one, such voids can once again generally be most effectively filled in TL by means of transcription, if necessary with a footnote added. These first two types both "stand beyond the limit of full translatability" (1978:83); however, in the case of the third type, the *lexical* void, while no single TL word exists, the "referents are present in the experience of the speech community" (Rabin 1958:127, quoted in Dagut 1978:65). For example, German *gemütlich* or Russian *toska* both denote concepts for which there is no one-word equivalent in English. With this type of void the problem is that a particular set of semantic features denoted by a single word in one language may only be expressible by a phrase in another. However, in contrast with the first two types, it is sometimes possible to find an adequate and intelligible formulation to fill a lexical void. Three translation tactics are commonly encountered: selecting a one-word equivalent which covers part of the meaning of the SL original, paraphrasing selected features of the SL item (a technique which is sometimes unacceptable for stylistic reasons), or omitting it altogether. The last type of voids are termed *syntactical* voids. These are caused by "structural asymmetries between SL and TL" (1978:89); in other words, TL has a suitable equivalent, but it may only be used if some syntactical rearrangement is made. For example, translating Russian *podruga* as "girl-friend" involves adding a separate gender-marker, while German *der wievielte* ("*the how many-th*") cannot be directly translated into English, even though the semantic information it contains is conveyed by English *how many*, a different part of speech. See also REALIA. Further reading: Dagut 1978; Ivir 1977; Rabin 1958; Vinay & Darbelnet 1958, 1958/1995.

Whispered Interpreting (French *Chuchotage*) A form of INTER-PRETING in which the interpreter sits next to the client or delegate for whom he or she is interpreting and whispers the interpreted version of what is being said. It is used in various settings, such as business meetings, conferences and trials; perhaps most famously it was one of the interpreting modes employed in the Demjanjuk trial (The State of Israel vs. Ivan John Demjanjuk, Criminal Case 373/86, Jerusalem 1987-8). It is usually carried out simultaneously, but occasionally consecutively; however, it does not strictly speaking classify as SIMULTANEOUS INTERPRETING proper because the interpreter does not work from a booth; as a reflection of this, Mackintosh classifies it as a third interpreting mode, alongside CONSECUTIVE and simultaneous interpreting (1995:125). See also CONFERENCE INTERPRETING and COURT INTERPRETING.

Word-for-word Translation (or **Word-by-word Translation**) A method of translating which entails precise fidelity to the wording of ST. Like its opposite, SENSE-FOR-SENSE TRANSLATION, the term was originally coined in the first century BC by the Roman writers Cicero

and Horace. Although it is held by some to be synonymous with
LITERAL TRANSLATION 1 (see for example Vinay & Darbelnet 1958,
1958/1995), most writers now consider it an extreme form of literal
translation in which a TL word is substituted for each ST word without reference to syntactical factors such as word order. Thus for
example *Ich habe gelesen das Buch* would be a (grammatically incorrect) word-for-word translation of *I have read the book*, while the
more standard *Ich habe das Buch gelesen* would be merely literal
(see Wilss 1982:88). In linguistic terms word-for-word translation
is defined by Catford as RANK-BOUND TRANSLATION performed at
the word-rank, although possibly also including some morpheme-
morpheme equivalences (1965:25). Word-for-word translation can
be a useful technique for illustrating how the syntax of a foreign
language works, or as a reading aid for people with only a limited
knowledge of a language, although in such contexts it is often termed
BACK-TRANSLATION or INTERLINEAR TRANSLATION. See also FREE
TRANSLATION and UNIT OF TRANSLATION. Further reading: Catford
1965.

Writer-oriented Machine Translation According to Sager (1994),
the method of producing a MACHINE-TRANSLATED text on the basis of
interaction with the writer of the original. Such a procedure involves
a writer in a PRE-EDITING process in which the machine asks questions about elements which it cannot analyze (for example because
they are not included in its grammar or dictionaries); the machine's
editing device is TL-sensitive, and so will anticipate translation difficulties. The main advantage of this procedure is that the writer's
original intention will be translated by the machine, rather than a
translator's interpretation of what the writer wished to communicate
(1994:283); furthermore, where interaction with the writer has resolved any points of uncertainty the approach can produce TTs which
are fully usable without the need for POST-EDITING. See also INDUS-
TRIAL PROCESS (TRANSLATION AS) and READER-ORIENTED MACHINE
TRANSLATION. Further reading: Sager 1994.

Bibliography

Where later editions of a work have been consulted both the date of the first edition and that of the later one are given, separated by a slash (e.g. Snell-Hornby 1988/1995); where appropriate, a slash is also used with translations to separate the date of the original from that of the translation (e.g. Vinay & Darbelnet 1958/1995). Square brackets are used with undated publications to indicate that the date given is only approximate (e.g. Popovič [1976]). For some important articles alternative locations are also suggested. For ease of reference, works about translation, actual translations and other works are all listed together.

Aijmer, Karin, Bengt Altenberg, & Mats Johansson (1996) "Text-based Contrastive Studies in English. Presentation of a Project", in Karin Aijmer, Bengt Altenberg, & Mats Johansson (eds) *Languages in Contrast: Papers from a Symposium on Text-based Cross-linguistic Studies, Lund 4-5 March 1994* [Lund Studies in English No. 88], Lund: Lund University Press, 73-85.

Appiah, Kwame Anthony (1993) "Thick Translation", in *Callaloo* 16:4, 808-19.

Arnold, D., L. Balkan, R. Lee Humphreys, S. Meijer & L. Sadler (1994) *Machine Translation: An Introductory Guide*, Manchester & Oxford: NCC Blackwell.

Baker, Mona (1992) *In Other Words: A Coursebook on Translation*, London: Routledge.

Baker, Mona (1993) "Corpus Linguistics and Translation Studies: Implications and Applications", in Mona Baker, Gill Francis & Elena Tognini-Bonelli (eds) *Text and Technology: In Honour of John Sinclair*, Amsterdam & Philadelphia: John Benjamins Publishing Company, 233-50.

Baker, Mona (1995) "Corpora in Translation Studies: An Overview and Some Suggestions for Future Research", in *Target* 7:2, 223-43.

Baker, Mona (1997) "Corpus-based Translation Studies: The Challenges that Lie Ahead", in Harold Somers (ed.) *Technology, LSP and Translation: Studies in Language Engineering, in Honour of Juan C. Sager*, Amsterdam & Philadelphia: John Benjamins Publishing Company, 175-86.

Ballester, Ana (1995) "The Politics of Dubbing. Spain: A Case Study", in Peter Jansen (ed.) *Translation and the Manipulation of Discourse: Selected Papers of the CERA Research Seminars in Translation Studies 1992-1993*, Leuven: CETRA, The Leuven Research Center for Translation, Communication and Cultures [Preprint collection], 159-81.

Barkhudarov, Leonid (1969) "Urovni yazykovoy iyerarkhii i perevod" ["Levels of language hierarchy and translation"], in *Tetradi perevodchika* [*The Translator's Notebooks*] 6, 3-12.

Barkhudarov, Leonid (1993) "The Problem of the Unit of Translation", in Palma Zlateva (ed. & trans.), 39-46.

Barnstone, Willis (1993) *The Poetics of Translation: History, Theory, Practice*, New Haven & London: Yale University Press.

Barsky, Robert F. (1996) "The Interpreter as Intercultural Agent in Convention Refugee Hearings", in *The Translator* 2:1, 45-63.

Barthes, Roland (1964) "Criticism as Language", in *The Critical Moment: Essays on the Nature of Literature*, London: Faber & Faber, 123-29.

Bassnett, Susan (1980/1991) *Translation Studies*, London: Routledge.

Bassnett, Susan (1994) Review of Gianfranco Folena (1973/1991) *Volgarizzare e tradurre*, in *Translation and Literature* 3, 153-54.

Bassnett, Susan & André Lefevere (eds) (1990) *Translation, History and Culture*, London: Pinter Publishers.

Bassnett, Susan, & André Lefevere (1990a) "Introduction: Proust's Grandmother and the Thousand and One Nights: The 'Cultural

Turn' in Translation Studies", in Susan Bassnett & André Lefevere (eds), 1-13.

Bathgate, Ronald H. (1980) "Studies of Translation Models 1: An Operational Model of the Translation Process", in *The Incorporated Linguist* 19:4, 113-14.

Bathgate, Ronald H. (1981) "Studies of Translation Models 2: A Theoretical Framework", in *The Incorporated Linguist* 20:1, 10-16.

de Beaugrande, Robert (1978) *Factors in a Theory of Poetic Translating*, Assen: Van Gorcum.

Beeby Lonsdale, Allison (1996) *Teaching Translation from Spanish to English: Worlds beyond Words*, Ottawa: University of Ottawa Press.

Beekman, John & John Callow (1974) *Translating the Word of God*, Grand Rapids, Michigan: Zondervan.

Benjamin, Andrew (1989) *Translation and the Nature of Philosophy: A New Theory of Words*, London: Routledge.

Benjamin, Walter (1916/1977) "Über die Sprache überhaupt und über die Sprache des Menschen", 140-57 in *Gesammelte Schriften* II.1, Frankfurt am Main: Suhrkamp Verlag.

Benjamin, Walter (1916/1979) "On Language as such and on the Languages of Man", in *One Way Street* (translated by Edmund Jephcott & Kingsley Shorter), London: NLB, 107-23. [Translation of W. Benjamin 1916/1977.]

Benjamin, Walter (1923/1963) "Die Aufgabe des Übersetzers", in Hans Joachim Störig (ed.) (1963) *Das Problem des Übersetzens*, Darmstadt: Wissenschaftliche Buchgesellschaft [Wege der Forschung Band VIII], 182-95.

Benjamin, Walter (1923/1970) "The Task of the Translator: An Introduction to the Translation of Baudelaire's *Tableaux parisiens*", in *Illuminations* (edited and introduced by Hannah Arendt; translated by Harry Zohn), London: Jonathan Cape, 69-82. [Translation of W. Benjamin 1922/1963.]

Berk-Seligson, Susan (1990) *The Bilingual Courtroom: Interpreters in the Judicial Process*, Chicago: Chicago University Press.

Blum-Kulka, Shoshana (1986) "Shifts of Cohesion and Coherence in Translation", in Juliane House & Shoshana Blum-Kulka (eds), 17-35.

Bradbury, Malcolm (1987) *Why Come To Slaka?*, London: Arena.

Brennan, Mary & David Brien (1995) "MA/Advanced Diploma in British Sign Language/English Interpreting, Deaf Studies Research Unit, University of Durham", course profile in *The Translator* 1:1, 111-28.

Brislin, Richard W. (ed.) (1976) *Translation: Applications and Research*, New York: Gardner Press.

Broeck, Raymond van den (1978) "The Concept of Equivalence in Translation Theory: Some Critical Reflections", in James S. Holmes, José Lambert & Raymond van den Broeck (eds), 29-47.

Broeck, Raymond van den & André Lefevere (1979) *Uitnotiging tot de vertaalwetenschap* [*Invitation to Translation Studies*], Muiderberg: Coutinho.

Brower, Reuben A. (ed.) (1959/1966) *On Translation*, New York: OUP.

Burgess, Anthony (1962/1972) *A Clockwork Orange*, Harmondsworth: Penguin.

Casagrande, Joseph B. (1954) "The Ends of Translation", in *International Journal of American Linguistics* 20:4, 335-40.

Catford, J. C. (1965) *A Linguistic Theory of Translation*, London: OUP.

Chan, Sin-Wai & David E. Pollard (eds) (1995) *An Encyclopaedia of Translation: Chinese-English - English-Chinese*, Hong Kong: The Chinese University Press.

Chernov, G. V. (1978) *Teoriya i praktika sinkhronnogo perevoda* [*Theory and Practice of Simultaneous Interpreting*], Moscow: Mezhdunarodnye otnosheniya.

Chernov, G. V. (1987) *Osnovy sinkhronnogo perevoda* [*Fundamentals of Simultaneous Interpreting*], Moscow: Vysshaya shkola.

Chesterman, Andrew (ed.) (1989) *Readings in Translation Theory*, Finland: Oy Finn Lectura Ab.

Chesterman, Andrew (1993) "From 'Is' to 'Ought': Laws, Norms and Strategies in Translation Studies", in *Target* 5:1, 1-20.

Chomsky, Noam (1965) *Aspects of the Theory of Syntax*, Cambridge, Massachusetts: MIT Press.

Chukovsky, Kornei Ivanovich (1966) *Vysokoe iskusstvo* [*A High Art*] [Collected Works, Vol. 3, 237-627], Moscow: Khudozhestvennaya literatura.

Chukovsky, Kornei Ivanovich (1984) *The Art of Translation: Kornei Chukovsky's "A High Art"* (edited & translated by Lauren G. Leighton), Knoxville, Tenn.: University of Tennessee Press. [Translation of Chukovsky 1966.]

Clark, Robert (1994) "Computer-assisted Translation: the State of the Art", in Cay Dollerup & Annette Lindegaard (eds) *Teaching Translation and Interpreting 2: Insights, Aims and Visions. Papers from the Second Language International Conference, Elsinore, 4-6 June 1993*, Amsterdam & Philadelphia: John Benjamins Publishing Company, 301-308.

Colin, Joan & Ruth Morris (1996) *Interpreters and the Legal Process*, Winchester: Waterside Press.

Coseriu, Eugenio (1973) *Probleme der strukturellen Semantik*, Tübingen: Gunter Narr Verlag. [Tübinger Beiträge zur Linguistik Band 40].

Cowley, Abraham (1656/1905) *Works. The English Writings of Abraham Cowley. Volume 1: Poems. Miscellanies, The Mistress, Pindarique Odes, Davideis, Verses Written on Several Occasions, etc.* (ed. A. R. Waller), Cambridge: University Press.

Dagut, Menachem (1978) *Hebrew-English Translation: A Linguistic Analysis of Some Semantic Problems*, Haifa: University of Haifa.

Danan, Martine (1991) "Dubbing as an Expression of Nationalism", in *Meta* 36:4, 606-14.

Davidson, Donald (1984) *Inquiries into Truth and Interpretation*, Oxford: OUP.

Delabastita, Dirk (1989) "Translation and Mass-Communication: Film and TV Translation as Evidence of Cultural Dynamics", in *Babel* 35:4, 193-218.

Delabastita, Dirk (1990) "Translation and the Mass Media", in Susan Bassnett & André Lefevere (eds), 97-109.

Delisle, Jean (1980) *L'analyse du discours comme méthode de traduction*, Ottawa: Presses de l'Université d'Ottawa.

Delisle, Jean (1988) *Translation. An Interpretive Approach*, translation of Part I of *L'Analyse du discours comme méthode de traduction* (translated by Patricia Logan & Monica Creery), Ottawa: University of Ottawa Press.

Delisle, Jean (1993) *La traduction raisonnée*, Ottawa: Presses de l'Université d'Ottawa.

Derrida, Jacques (1978) "The *Retrait* of Metaphor" (translated by Frieda Gasdner, Biodun Iginla, Richard Madden & William West), in *Enclitic* 2:2, 5-33. [Translation of "Le retrait de la métaphore", *Poésie* 7 (1978), 103-26.]

Derrida, Jacques (1980) "Des Tours de Babel", in *Psyché. Inventions de l'autre*, Paris: Galilée, 203-36. [Also in Joseph F. Graham (ed.) (1985), 209-48.]

Derrida, Jacques (1985) "Des Tours de Babel" (translated by Joseph F. Graham), in Joseph F. Graham (ed.), 165-207. [Translation of Derrida 1980.]

Dik, Simon C. (1978) *Functional Grammar*, Amsterdam, New York & Oxford: North-Holland.

Diller, Hans-Jürgen (1992) "Old Stories in Other Words: The Historicity of Linguistic Systems as a Problem in Translating *Beowulf* into Modern German", in Harald Kittel (ed.) *Geschichte, System, Literarische Übersetzung/Histories, Systems, Literary Translations*, Berlin: Erich Schmidt Verlag, 281-306.

Diller, Hans-Jürgen & Joachim Kornelius (1978) *Linguistische Probleme der Übersetzung*, Tübingen: Niemeyer.

Downing, Bruce T. & Kate Helms Tillery (1992) *Professional Training for Community Interpreters: A Report on Models of Interpreter Training and the Value of Training*, Minneapolis: Center for Urban and Regional Affairs.

Dries, Josephine (1995) *Dubbing and Subtitling: Guidelines for Production and Distribution*, Manchester: The European Institute for the Media.

Dryden, John (1680/1989) "Metaphrase, Paraphrase and Imitation", in Andrew Chesterman (ed.) (1989), 7-12. [Originally appeared as the *Preface to Ovid's Epistles, Translated by Several Hands*; also in T. R. Steiner (1975), 68-72.]

Duff, Alan (1981) *The Third Language: Recurrent Problems of Translation into English*, Oxford: Pergamon Press.

Eco, Umberto (1976) *A Theory of Semiotics*, Bloomington: Indiana University Press.

Eco, Umberto (1995) *The Search for the Perfect Language* (translated by James Fentress), Oxford: Basil Blackwell.

Edwards, Alicia Betsy (1995) *The Practice of Court Interpreting*, Amsterdam & Philadelphia: John Benjamins Publishing Company.

Even-Zohar, Itamar (1978a) *Papers in Historical Poetics*, Tel Aviv: Porter Institute for Poetics and Semiotics. [Papers on Poetics and Semiotics 8.]

Even-Zohar, Itamar (1978b) "The Position of Translated Literature within the Literary Polysystem", in James S. Holmes, José Lambert & Raymond van den Broeck (eds), 117-27.

Even-Zohar, Itamar (1990) *Polysystem Studies* [special issue of *Poetics Today* 11:1].

Even-Zohar, Itamar (1990a) "The 'Literary System'", in Even-Zohar (1990), 27-44.

Even-Zohar, Itamar (1990b) "System, Dynamics, and Interference in Culture: A Synoptic View", in Even-Zohar (1990), 85-94.

Even-Zohar, Itamar (1990c) "The Textemic Status of Signs in Translation", in Even-Zohar (1990), 247-51.

Even-Zohar, Itamar (1990d) "Translation and Transfer", in Even-Zohar (1990), 73-78.

Fawcett, Peter (1995) "Translation and Power Play", in *The Translator* 1:2, 177-92.

Fawcett, Peter (1996) "Translating Film", in Geoffrey T. Harris (ed.) *On Translating French Literature and Film*, Amsterdam: Rodopi, 65-88.

Fitch, Brian T. (1983) "L'intra-intertextualité interlinguistique de Beckett: la problématique de la traduction de soi", in *Texte* 2, 85-100.

Fitch, Brian T. (1985) "The Status of Self-translation", in *Texte* 4, 111-25.

Fitch, Brian T. (1988) *Beckett and Babel: An Investigation into the Status of the Bilingual Work*, Toronto, Buffalo & London: University of Toronto Press.

Florin, Sider (1993) "Realia in Translation", in Palma Zlateva (ed. & trans.), 122-28.

Fodor, István (1976) *Film Dubbing: Phonetic, Semiotic, Esthetic and Psychological Aspects*, Hamburg: Helmut Buske.

Folena, Gianfranco (1973/1991) *Volgarizzare e tradurre*, Turin: Einaudi. [Originally published in 1973 as "'Volgarizzare' e 'tradurre': idea e terminologia della traduzione dal Medio Evo italiano e romanzo all'umanesimo europeo", in *La Traduzione. Saggi e studi*, Trieste: Edizioni LINT, 57-120.]

Frank, Armin Paul (1990a) "Forty Years of Studying the American/ German Translational Transfer: A Retrospect and Some Perspectives", in *Amerikastudien/American Studies*, 35:1, 7-20.

Frank, Armin Paul (1990b) "Systems and Histories in the Study of Literary Translations: A Few Distinctions", in Roger Bauer & Douwe Fokkema (eds) *Proceedings of the XIIth Congress of the International Comparative Literature Association (Munich 1988)*, München: Iudicium, 1, 41-63.

Frank, Armin Paul (1991) "Translating and Translated Poetry: The Producer's and the Historian's Perspectives", in Kitty M. van Leuven-Zwart & Ton Naaijkens (eds), 115-40.

Frank, Armin Paul (1992) "Towards a Cultural History of Literary Translation: 'Histories,' 'Systems,' and Other Forms of Synthesizing Research", in Harald Kittel (ed.) *Geschichte, System, Literarische Übersetzung/Histories, Systems, Literary Translations*, Berlin: Erich Schmidt Verlag, 369-87.

Fraser, Janet (1996) "The Translator Investigated: Learning from Translation Process Analysis", in *The Translator* 2:1, 65-79.

Frawley, William (1984) "Prolegomenon to a Theory of Translation", in William Frawley (ed.) *Translation: Literary, Linguistic, and Philosophical Perspectives*, London & Toronto: Associated University Presses, 159-75.

Frost, William (1955) *Dryden and the Art of Translation*, New Haven, Connecticut: Yale University Press. [Yale Studies in English, Vol. 128.]

Gamal, Muhammad Y. (1994) "The Second International Conference on Linguistics, Literature and Translation" (Report on Conference which took place on 4-8 April 1994, Yarmouk University, Irbid, Jordan), in *Language International* 6:4, 16.

Gambier, Yves (ed.) (1996) *Les transferts linguistiques dans les médias audiovisuels*, Villeneuve d'Ascq: Presses Universitaires du Septentrion.

Gellerstam, Martin (1986) "Translationese in Swedish Novels Translated from English", in Wollin, Lars and Hans Lindquist (eds) *Translation Studies in Scandinavia: Proceedings from The Scandinavian Symposium on Translation Theory (SSOTT) II Lund 14-15 June, 1985* [Lund Studies in English 75], Lund: CWK Gleerup, 88-95.

Gentile, Adolfo, Uldis Ozolins & Mary Vasilakakos (eds) (1996) *Liaison Interpreting: A Handbook*, Melbourne: Melbourne University Press.

Gentzler, Edwin (1993) *Contemporary Translation Theories*, London: Routledge.

Gerloff, Pamela (1987) "Identifying the Unit of Analysis in Translation: Some Uses of Think-Aloud Protocol Data", in Claus Færch & Gabriele Kasper (eds) *Introspection in Second Language Research*, Clevedon & Philadelphia: Multilingual Matters Ltd., 135-58.

Gerver, David & H. Wallace Sinaiko (eds) (1977) *Language Interpretation and Communication*, NATO Conference Series, New York & London: Plenum Press.

Gile, Daniel (1985) "Le modèle d'efforts et l'équilibre d'interprétation en interprétation simultanée", in *Meta* 30:1, 44-48.

Gile, Daniel (1988) "Le partage de l'attention et le modèle d'effort en interprétation simultanée", in *The Interpreters' Newsletter* 1, 4-22.

Gile, Daniel (1995a) *Basic Concepts and Models for Interpreter and Translator Training*, Amsterdam & Philadelphia: John Benjamins Publishing Company.

Gile, Daniel (1995b) *Regards sur la recherche en interprétation de conférence*, Lille: Presses universitaires de Lille.

Gile, Daniel (1995c) "Fidelity Assessment in Consecutive Interpretation: An Experiment", in *Target* 7:1, 151-64.

Goffin, Roger (1971) "Pour une Formation Universitaire 'sui generis' du Traducteur: Réflexions sur Certains Aspects Méthodologiques et sur la Recherche Scientifique dans le Domaine de la Traduction", in *Meta* 16:1-2, 57-68.

González, Dueñas Roseann, Victoria F. Vásques & Holly Mikkelson (1991) *Fundamentals of Court Interpretation: Theory, Policy and Practice* (University of Arizona Summer Institute for Court Interpretation Series), Durham, North Carolina: Carolina Academic Press.

Goris, Olivier (1993) "The Question of French Dubbing: Towards a Frame for Systematic Investigation", in *Target* 5:2, 169-90.

Gorlée, Dinda L. (1986) "Translation Theory and the Semiotics of Games and Decisions", in Wollin, Lars and Hans Lindquist (eds) *Translation Studies in Scandinavia: Proceedings from The Scandinavian Symposium on Translation Theory (SSOTT) II Lund 14-15 June, 1985* [Lund Studies in English 75], Lund: CWK Gleerup, 96-104.

Gorlée, Dinda L. (1994) *Semiotics and the Problem of Translation: With Special Reference to the Semiotics of Charles S. Peirce*, Amsterdam: Rodopi.

Gottlieb, Henrik (1992) "Subtitling - A New University Discipline", in Cay Dollerup & Anne Loddegaard (eds) *Teaching Translation and Interpreting: Training, Talent and Experience*, Amsterdam & Philadelphia: John Benjamins Publishing Company, 161-70.

Gouadec, Daniel (1989) *Le traducteur, la traduction et l'entreprise*, Paris: AFNOR gestion.

Gouadec, Daniel (1990) "Traduction Signalétique", in *Meta* 35:2, 332-41.

Graham, Joseph F. (1981) "Theory for Translation", in Marilyn Gaddis Rose (ed.) *Translation Spectrum: Essays in Theory and Practice*, Albany: State University of New York Press, 23-30.

Graham, Joseph F. (ed.) (1985) *Difference in Translation*, Ithaca: Cornell University Press.

Gran, Laura & Christopher Taylor (eds) (1990) *Aspects of Applied and Experimental Research on Conference Interpretation*, Udine: Campanotto Editore.

Granger, Sylviane (1996) "From CA to CIA and back: An Integrated Contrastive Approach to Bilingual and Learner Computerised Corpora", in Karin Aijmer, Bengt Altenberg, & Mats Johansson (eds) *Languages in Contrast: Papers from a Symposium on Text-based Cross-linguistic Studies, Lund 4-5 March 1994* [Lund Studies in English No. 88], Lund: Lund University Press, 37-51.

Grutman, Rainier (1994) "Honoré Beaugrand traducteur de lui-même", in *Ellipse* 51, 45-53.

Guide to Good Practice (1989) Cambridge: British Association of Community Interpreters.

Gutt, Ernst-August (1991) *Translation and Relevance*, Oxford: Basil Blackwell.

Güttinger, Fritz (1963) *Zielsprache. Theorie und Technik des Übersetzens*, Zürich: Manesse Verlag.

Haeseryn, René (1994) "International Federation of Translators and its Role in the Arab World", in Robert de Beaugrande, Abdulla Shunnaq & Mohamed H. Heliel (eds) *Language Discourse and Translation in the West and Middle East*, Amsterdam & Philadelphia: John Benjamins Publishing Company, 209-19.

Halliday, M. A. K. (1961) "Categories of the Theory of Grammar", in *Word*, 17:3, 241-92.

Halliday, M. A. K., A. McIntosh & P. D. Strevens (eds) (1964) *The Linguistic Sciences and Language Teaching*, London & New York: Longman.

Harris, Brian (1977) "Toward a Science of Translation", in *Meta* 22:1, 90-2.

Harris, Brian (1988) "Bi-text, a New Concept in Translation Theory", in *Language Monthly*, 54, 8-10.

Harrison, Bernard (1979) *An Introduction to the Philosophy of Language*, London: Macmillan.

Hartmann, R. R. K. (1980) *Contrastive Textology*, Heidelberg: Julius Groos.

Harvey, Keith (1995) "A Descriptive Framework for Compensation", in *The Translator* 1:1, 65-86.

Hatim, Basil, & Ian Mason (1990) *Discourse and the Translator*, London & New York: Longman.

Hayes, P. L. (1992) "Educational Interpreters for Deaf Students: their Responsibilities, Problems and Concerns", in *Journal of Interpretation* 5:1, 5-24.

Herbst, Thomas (1994) *Linguistische Aspekte der Synchronisation von Fernsehserien*, Tübingen: Niemeyer.

Hermans, Theo (ed.) (1985) *The Manipulation of Literature: Studies in Literary Translation*, London: Croom Helm.

Hermans, Theo (1985a) "Introduction: Translation Studies and a New Paradigm", in Theo Hermans (ed.), 7-15.

Hermans, Theo (1991) "Translational Norms and Correct Translations", in Kitty M. van Leuven-Zwart & Ton Naaijkens (eds), 155-69.

Hermans, Theo (1994) "Translation between Poetics and Ideology", in *Translation and Literature* 3, 138-45. [Article reviewing various works, including André Lefevere (1992) *Translation, Rewriting, and the Manipulation of Literary Fame.*]

Hermans, Theo (1995) "Toury's Empiricism Version One: Review of Gideon Toury's *In Search of a Theory of Translation*", in *The Translator* 1:2, 215-23.

Hervey, Sándor & Ian Higgins (1992) *Thinking Translation: A Course in Translation Method: French to English*, London: Routledge.

Hockett, Charles F. (1954) "Translation via Immediate Constituents", in *International Journal of American Linguistics* 20:4, 313-15.

Hollander, John (1959/1966) "Versions, Interpretations, and Performances", in Reuben A. Brower (ed.), 205-231.

Holmes, James S. (1988) *Translated! Papers on Literary Translation and Translation Studies*, Amsterdam: Rodopi.

Holmes, James S. (1988a) "On Matching and Making Maps: From a Translator's Notebook", in Holmes (1988), 53-64.

Holmes, James S. (1988b) "Describing Literary Translations: Models and Methods", in Holmes (1988), 81-91.

Holmes, James S. (1988c) "Poem and Metapoem: Poetry from Dutch to English", in Holmes (1988), 9-22.

Holmes, James S. (1988d) "Forms of Verse Translation and the Translation of Verse Form", in Holmes (1988), 23-33.

Holmes, James S. (1988e) "The Name and Nature of Translation

Studies", in Holmes (1988), 67-80. [Also in Gideon Toury (ed.) (1987), 9-24.]

Holmes, James S. (1988f) "Translation Theory, Translation Theories, Translation Studies, and the Translator", in Holmes (1988), 93-98.

Holmes, James S. (1988g) "The Future of Translation Theory: A Handful of Theses", in Holmes (1988), 99-102.

Holmes, James S. (1988h) "The Cross-Temporal Factor in Verse Translation", in Holmes (1988), 35-44.

Holmes, James S., José Lambert & Raymond van den Broeck (eds) (1978) *Literature and Translation: New Perspectives in Literary Studies with a Basic Bibliography of Books on Translation Studies*, Leuven: Acco.

Holz-Mänttäri, Justa (1984) *Translatorisches Handeln. Theorie und Methode*, Helsinki: Suomalainen Tiedeakatemia.

Holz-Mänttäri, Justa (1986) *Translatorisches Handeln – theoretisch fundierte Berufsprofile*, in Snell-Hornby (ed.) *Übersetzungswissenschaft – eine Neuorientierung: Zur Integrierung von Theorie und Praxis*, Tübingen: Franke Verlag, 348-74.

Hönig, Hans G. (1976) "Zur Analysephase beim Übersetzen aus der Fremdsprache", in Drescher, Horst W. & Signe Scheffzek (eds) *Theorie und Praxis des Übersetzens und Dolmetschens: Referate und Diskussionsbeiträge des internationalen Kolloquiums am Fachbereich Angewandte Sprachwissenschaft der Johannes Gutenberg-Universität Mainz in Germersheim (2.-4. Mai 1975)*, Frankfurt am Main: Peter Lang, 48-58.

Hönig, Hans G. & Paul Kussmaul (1982) *Strategie der Übersetzung: Ein Lehr- und Arbeitsbuch*, Tübingen: Gunter Narr Verlag. [Tübinger Beiträge zur Linguistik Band 205.]

House, Juliane (1977) *A Model for Translation Quality Assessment*, Tübingen: TBL Verlag Gunter Narr.

House, Juliane (1986) "Acquiring Translational Competence in Interaction", in Juliane House & Shoshana Blum-Kulka (eds), 179-91.

House, Juliane & Shoshana Blum-Kulka (eds) (1986) *Interlingual and Intercultural Communication*, Tübingen: Gunter Narr Verlag.

Hutchins, W. J. & H. L. Somers (1992) *An Introduction to Machine Translation*, London: Academic Press.

Isham, William P. (1995) "On The Relevance of Signed Languages to Research in Interpretation", in *Target* 7:1, 135-49.

Ivarsson, Jan (1992) *Subtitling for the Media: A Handbook of an Art*, Stockholm: Transedit.

Ivir, Vladimir (1969) "Contrasting via Translation: Formal Correspondence vs. Translation Equivalence", in *The Yugoslav Serbo-Croatian - English Contrastive Project, Studies* 1, 13-25.

Ivir, Vladimir (1977) "Lexical Gaps: A Contrastive View", *Studia Romanica et Anglica Zagrabiensia* 43, 167-76.

Ivir, Vladimir (1981) "Formal Correspondence vs. Translation Equivalence Revisited", in *Poetics Today* 2:4, 51-59.

Jakobson, Roman (1959/1966) "On Linguistic Aspects of Translation", in Reuben A. Brower (ed.), 232-39.

Jakobson, Roman (1960) "Closing Statement: Linguistics and Poetics", in Thomas A. Sebeok (ed.) *Style in Language*, Cambridge, Massachusetts: MIT Press, 350-77.

Johansson, Stig & Knut Hofland (1994) "Towards an English-Norwegian Parallel Corpus", in Udo Fries, Gunnel Tottie & Peter Schneider (eds) *Creating and Using English Language Corpora: Papers from the Fourteenth International Conference on English Language Research on Computerized Corpora*, Amsterdam: Rodopi, 25-37.

Kade, Otto (1968) *Zufall und Gesetzmässigkeit in der Übersetzung*,

Leipzig: VEB Enzyklopädie. [Beiheft zur Zeitschrift Fremd-sprachen I.]

de Kay, Ormonde (1983) *N'Heures Souris Rames: The Coucy Castle Manuscript*, London: Angus & Robertson Publishers.

Keith, H. A. (1985) "Liaison Interpreting as a Communicative Language-learning Exercise", in Noel Thomas & Richard Towell (eds) *Interpreting as a Language Teaching Technique: Proceedings of a Conference Convened by and Held at the University of Salford, 2-5 January 1985*, London: Centre for Information on Language Teaching and Research, 1-12.

Kelly, Louis G. (1979) *The True Interpreter: A History of Translation Theory and Practice in the West*, Oxford: Basil Blackwell.

Koller, Werner (1971) "Übersetzungswissenschaft", in *Folia Linguistica: Acta Societatis Linguisticae Europaeae* V, 194-221.

Koller, Werner (1979/1992) *Einführung in die Übersetzungswissenschaft*, Heidelberg: Quelle & Meyer.

Koller, Werner (1989) "Equivalence in Translation Theory" (translated by Andrew Chesterman), in Andrew Chesterman (ed.), 99-104. [Translation of Koller 1979 (i.e. first edition of 1979/1992), 186-91.]

Komissarov, Vilen (1993) "Norms in Translation", in Palma Zlateva (ed. & trans.), 63-75.

Koschmieder, Erwin (1965a) "Das Gemeinte", in *Beiträge zur allgemeinen Syntax*, Heidelberg: Carl Winter, 101-106.

Koschmieder, Erwin (1965b) "Das Problem der Übersetzung", in *Beiträge zur allgemeinen Syntax*, Heidelberg: Carl Winter, 107-115.

Krings, Hans P. (1986a) *Was in den Köpfen von Übersetzern vorgeht. Eine empirische Untersuchung zur Struktur des Übersetzungsprozesses an fortgeschrittenen Französischlernern*, Tübingen: Gunter Narr Verlag.

Krings, Hans P. (1986b) "Translation Problems and Translation Strategies of Advanced German Learners of French (L2)", in Juliane House & Shoshana Blum-Kulka (eds) (1986), 263-76.

Krings, Hans P. (1987) "The Use of Introspective Data in Translation", in Claus Færch & Gabriele Kasper (eds) *Introspection in Second Language Research*, Clevedon & Philadelphia: Multilingual Matters Ltd., 159-76.

Lambert, José (1991) "Shifts, Oppositions and Goals in Translation Studies: Towards A Genealogy of Concepts", in Kitty M. van Leuven-Zwart & Ton Naaijkens (eds), 25-37.

Lambert, Sylvie & Barbara Moser-Mercer (1994) *Bridging the Gap: Empirical Research in Simultaneous Interpretation*, Amsterdam & Philadelphia: John Benjamins Publishing Company.

Larson, Mildred L. (1984) *Meaning-Based Translation: A Guide to Cross-language Equivalence*, Lanham: University Press of America.

Lavault, Elisabeth (1996) Review of Marianne Lederer's *La traduction aujourd'hui*, in *The Translator* 2:1, 96-100.

Laviosa-Braithwaite, Sara (1997) *The English Comparable Corpus (ECC): A Resource and a Methodology for the Empirical Study of Translation*, Ph.D. Thesis, Manchester: UMIST.

Lawendowski, Bogusław P. (1978) "On Semiotic Aspects of Translation", in Thomas A. Sebeok (ed.) *Sight, Sound and Sense*, Bloomington: Indiana University Press, 264-82.

Lederer, Marianne (1994) *La traduction aujourd'hui*, Paris: Hachette.

Leech, Geoffrey N. (1969) *A Linguistic Guide to English Poetry*, London: Longmans.

Lefevere, André (1975) *Translating Poetry: Seven Strategies and a Blueprint*, Assen & Amsterdam: Van Gorcum.

Lefevere, André (1978) "Translation Studies: The Goal of the Discipline", in James S. Holmes, José Lambert & Raymond van den Broeck (eds), 234-5.

Lefevere, André (1982) "Mother Courage's Cucumbers: Text, System and Refraction in a Theory of Literature", in *Modern Language Studies* 12:4, 3-20.

Lefevere, André (1983) "Poetics (Today) and Translation (Studies)", in Daniel Weissbort (ed.) *Modern Poetry in Translation: 1983*, London & Manchester: MPT/Carcanet, 190-95.

Lefevere, André (1985) "Why Waste Our Time on Rewrites? The Trouble with Interpretation and the Role of Rewriting in an Alternative Paradigm", in Theo Hermans (ed.), 215-43.

Lefevere, André (1992) *Translation, Rewriting, and the Manipulation of Literary Fame*, London: Routledge.

Lehmuskallio, Arto, Viktor Podbereznyj & Hannu Tommola (1991) "Towards a Finnish-Russian Dictionary of Finnish Culture-Bound Words", in Sonja Tirkkonen-Condit (ed.), 157-64.

Leighton, Lauren G. (1991) *Two Worlds, One Art: Literary Translation in Russia and America*, DeKalb: Northern Illinois University Press.

Leuven-Zwart, Kitty M. van (1989) "Translation and Original: Similarities and Dissimilarities, I", in *Target* 1:2, 151-81.

Leuven-Zwart, Kitty M. van (1990) "Translation and Original: Similarities and Dissimilarities, II", in *Target* 2:1, 69-95.

Leuven-Zwart, Kitty M. van (1991) "Translation and Translation Studies: Discord or Unity?", in Sonja Tirkkonen-Condit (ed.), 35-44.

Leuven-Zwart, Kitty M. van & Ton Naaijkens (eds) (1991) *Translation Studies: The State of the Art. Proceedings of the First James S. Holmes Symposium on Translation Studies*, Amsterdam: Rodopi.

Levý, Jiří (1965) "Will Translation Theory be of Use to Translators?", in Rolf Italiaander (ed.) *Übersetzen: Vorträge und Beiträge vom Internationalen Kongress literarischer Übersetzer in Hamburg 1965*, Frankfurt am Main: Athenäum Verlag, 77-82.

⚓ Levý, Jiří (1967) "Translation as a Decision Process", in *To Honor Roman Jakobson*, The Hague: Mouton, Vol. 2, 1171-82. [Also in Andrew Chesterman (ed.) (1989), 37-52.]

Levý, Jiří (1969) *Die literarische Übersetzung: Theorie einer Kunstgattung*, Frankfurt am Main: Athenäum.

Lewis, Philip E. (1985) "The Measure of Translation Effects", in Joseph F. Graham (ed.), 31-62.

Lörscher, Wolfgang (1991) "Thinking-Aloud as a Method for Collecting Data on Translation Processes", in Sonja Tirkkonen-Condit (ed.), 67-77.

Luce, R. D. & H. Raiffa (1957) *Games and Decisions in Conflict Resolution*, New York: Wiley.

Luyken, Georg-Michael, with Thomas Herbst, Jo Langham-Brown, Helen Reid & Herman Spinhof (1991) *Overcoming Language Barriers in Television: Dubbing and Subtitling for the European Audience*, Manchester: The European Institute for the Media.

Mackintosh, Jennifer (1995) "A Review of Conference Interpretation: Practice and Training", in *Target* 7:1, 119-33.

Macpherson, James (1996) *The Poems of Ossian and Related Works* (ed. Howard Gaskill), Edinburgh: Edinburgh University Press. [A collection of writings first published in the 1760s.]

Malmkjær, Kirsten (1993) "Underpinning Translation Theory", in *Target* 5:2, 133-48.

de Man, Paul (1986) "'Conclusions': Walter Benjamin's 'The Task of the Translator'", in *The Resistance to Theory* [Theory and History of Literature, Volume 33], Minneapolis: University of Minnesota Press, 73-105.

Melby, Alan (1992) "The Translator Workstation", in John Newton (ed.), 147-65.

Miko, František (1970), "La théorie de l'expression et la traduction", in James S. Holmes, Frans de Haan and Anton Popovič (eds) *The Nature of Translation*, The Hague: Mouton, 61-77.

Morris, Ruth (1995) "The Moral Dilemmas of Court Interpreting", in *The Translator* 1:1, 25-46.

Moser-Mercer, Barbara (1984) "Testing Interpreting Aptitude", in Wolfram Wilss & Gisela Thome (eds) *Translation Theory and Its Implementation in the Teaching of Translation and Interpreting*, Tübingen: Gunter Narr Verlag, 318-25.

Murry, John Middleton (1923) *Pencillings: Little Essays on Literature*, London: Collins.

Nabokov, Vladimir (1964/1975) "Foreword", in A. S. Pushkin *Eugene Onegin*, (edited & translated by Vladimir Nabokov, 4 Vols.), London: Routledge & Kegan Paul, vii-xii.

Neubert, Albrecht (1970) "Elemente einer allgemeinen Theorie der Translation", in A. Graur (editor-in-chief) *Actes du Xe Congrès International des Linguistes. Bucarest 28 août - 2 septembre 1967*, Editions de l'Académie de la République Socialiste de Roumanie, Bucarest, Vol. 2, 451-56.

Neubert, Albrecht (1973) "Invarianz und Pragmatik: Ein zentrales Problem der Übersetzungswissenschaft", in Walter Graul, Otto Kade, Karl Kokoschko & Hans Zikmund (eds) *Neue Beiträge zu Grundfragen der Übersetzungswissenschaft*, Leipzig: VEB Verlag Enzyklopädie [Beihefte zur Zeitschrift Fremdsprachen, V-VI], 13-26.

Neubert, Albrecht (1985) *Text and Translation*, Leipzig: VEB Verlag Enzyklopädie.

Neubert, Albrecht (1991a) "Models of Translation", in Sonja Tirkkonen-Condit (ed.), 17-26.

Neubert, Albrecht (1991b) "Computer-Aided Translation: Where Are the Problems?", in *Target* 3:1, 55-64.

Neubert, Albrecht (1994) "Competence in translation: a complex skill, how to study and how to teach it", in Mary Snell-Hornby, Franz Pöchhacker & Klaus Kaindl (eds), 411-20.

Neubert, Albrecht & Gregory M. Shreve (1992) *Translation as Text*, Kent, Ohio: The Kent State University Press. [Translation Studies 1.]

Newman, A. (1980) *Mapping Translation Equivalence*, Leuven: Acco.

Newmark, Peter (1981/1988) *Approaches to Translation*, Hemel Hempstead: Prentice Hall.

Newmark, Peter (1988) *A Textbook of Translation*, Hemel Hempstead: Prentice Hall.

Newton, John (ed.) (1992) *Computers in Translation: A Practical Appraisal*, London: Routledge.

Newton, John (1992a) "Introduction and Overview", in John Newton (ed.) (1992), 1-13.

Nida, Eugene A. (1964) *Toward a Science of Translating: With Special Reference to Principles and Procedures Involved in Bible Translating*, Leiden: E. J. Brill.

Nida, Eugene A. (1969) "Science of Translation", in *Language* 45:3, 483-98. [Also in E. Nida (1975) *Language Structure and Translation: Essays by Eugene A. Nida* (selected and introduced by Anwar S. Dil), Stanford University Press, 79-101, and in Andrew Chesterman (ed.) (1989), 80-98.]

Nida, Eugene A. (1995) "Dynamic Equivalence in Translating", in Sin-Wai Chan & David E. Pollard (eds), 223-30.

Nida, Eugene A. & Charles R. Taber (1969/1982) *The Theory and Practice of Translation*, Leiden: E. J. Brill.

Nord, Christiane (1988) *Textanalyse und Übersetzen: Theoretische Grundlagen, Methode und didaktische Anwendung einer übersetzungsrelevanten Textanalyse*, Heidelberg: Groos.

Nord, Christiane (1991a) *Text Analysis in Translation*, Amsterdam: Rodopi. [English version of Nord 1988.]

Nord, Christiane (1991b) "Scopos, Loyalty, and Translational Conventions", in *Target* 3:1, 91-109.

Nord, Christiane (1996) "Text Type and Translation Method, An Objective Approach to Translation Criticism: Review of Katharina Reiss' *Möglichkeiten und Grenzen der Übersetzungskritik*", in *The Translator* 2:1, 81-88.

Nord, Christiane (1997) *Translating as a Purposeful Activity: Functionalist Approaches Explained*, Manchester: St. Jerome Publishing.

Oettinger, Anthony G. (1960) *Automatic Language Translation: Lexical and Technical Aspects, with Particular Reference to Russian*, Cambridge, Massachusetts: Harvard University Press. [Harvard Monographs in Applied Science 8.]

Osers, Ewald (1983) "International Organizations", in Catriona Picken (ed.), 171-82.

Ozolins, Uldis (1995) "Liaison Interpreting: Theoretical Challenges and Practical Problems around the World", in *Perspectives* 1995:2, 153-60.

Pannwitz, Rudolf (1917) *krisis der europäischen kultur*, Nürnberg: H. Carl.

Pergnier, M. (1980) *Les fondements sociolinguistiques de la traduction*, Paris: Librairie Honoré Champion.

Picken, Catriona (ed.) (1983) *The Translator's Handbook*, London: Aslib.

Pöchhacker, Franz (1994) *Simultandolmetschen als komplexes Handeln*, Tübingen: Gunter Narr Verlag.

Pol, Balth van der (1956) "An Iterative Translation Test", in Colin Cherry (ed.) *Information Theory: Papers read at a Symposium on 'Information Theory' held at the Royal Institution, London, September 12th to 16th 1955*, London: Butterworths Scientific Publications, 397-98.

Popovič, Anton (1970) "The Concept 'Shift of Expression' in Translation Analysis", in James S. Holmes, Frans de Haan and Anton Popovič (eds) *The Nature of Translation*, The Hague: Mouton, 78-87.

Popovič, Anton (1976) "Aspects of Metatext", in *Canadian Review of Comparative Literature* 3, 225-35.

Popovič, Anton ([1976]) *Dictionary for the Analysis of Literary Translation*, Edmonton: Department of Comparative Literature, The University of Alberta.

Postgate, J. P. (1922) *Translation and Translations: Theory and Practice*, London: G. Bell & Sons, Ltd..

Pound, Ezra (1954) *Literary Essays*, London: Faber.

Puurtinen, Tiina (1989) "Assessing Acceptability in Translated Children's Books", in *Target* 1:2, 201-13.

Pym, Anthony (1992a) *Translation and Text Transfer: An Essay on the Principles of Intercultural Communication*, Frankfurt am Main: Peter Lang.

Pym, Anthony (1992b) "The Relation between Translation and Material Text Transfer", in *Target* 4:2, 171-89.

Quine, W. V. (1959/1966) "Meaning and Translation", in Reuben A.

Brower (ed.), 148-72.

Quine, W. V. (1960) *Word and Object*, Cambridge, Massachusetts: MIT Press.

Rabin, C. (1958) "The Linguistics of Translation", in A. H. Smith (ed.) *Aspects of Translation* (The Communication Research Centre, University College, London: Studies in Communication, Vol.5), London: Secker & Warburg, 123-45.

Radó, György (1979) "Outline of a Systematic Translatology", in *Babel* 25:4, 187-96.

Reiss, Katharina (1971) *Möglichkeiten und Grenzen der Übersetzungskritik. Kategorien und Kriterien für eine sachgerechte Beurteilung von Übersetzungen*, München: Max Hueber Verlag. [Hueber Hochschulreihe 12.]

Reiss, Katharina (1976) *Texttype und Übersetzungsmethode. Der operative Text*, Kronberg: Scriptor.

Reiss, Katharina (1977) "Texttypen, Übersetzungstypen und die Beurteilung von Übersetzungen", in *Lebende Sprachen* 22:3, 97-100.

Reiss, Katharina (1977/1989) "Text-types, Translation Types and Translation Assessment" (translated by Andrew Chesterman), in Andrew Chesterman (ed.) (1989), 105-15.

Reiss, Katharina (1990) "Brief an den Herausgeber", in *Lebende Sprachen* 35:4, 185.

Reiss, Katharina & Hans J. Vermeer (1984) *Grundlegung einer allgemeinen Translationstheorie*, Tübingen: Niemeyer.

Roberts, Roda (1985) "Translation and Communication", in *Nucleo* 1, 139-76.

Robinson, Douglas (1991) *The Translator's Turn*, Baltimore: Johns Hopkins.

Rose, Marilyn Gaddis (1981) "Translation Types and Conventions", in Marilyn Gaddis Rose (ed.) *Translation Spectrum: Essays in Theory and Practice*, Albany: State University of New York Press, 31-40.

Sager, Juan C. (1990) *A Practical Course in Terminology Processing*, Amsterdam & Philadelphia: John Benjamins Publishing Company.

Sager, Juan C. (1992) "The Translator as Terminologist", in Cay Dollerup & Anne Loddegaard (eds) *Teaching Translation and Interpreting: Training, Talent and Experience*, Amsterdam & Philadelphia: John Benjamins Publishing Company, 107-22.

Sager, Juan C. (1994) *Language Engineering and Translation: Consequences of Automation*, Amsterdam & Philadelphia: John Benjamins Publishing Company.

Sager, Juan C., D. Dungworth & P. F. McDonald (1980) *English Special Languages: Principles and Practice in Science and Technology*, Wiesbaden: Brandstetter.

Savory, Theodore (1957) *The Art of Translation*, London: Cape.

Schleiermacher, Friedrich (1838/1963) "Ueber die verschiedenen Methoden des Uebersezens", in Hans Joachim Störig (1963) *Das Problem des Übersetzens*, Darmstadt: Wissenschaftliche Buchgesellschaft [Wege der Forschung Band VIII], 38-70.

Schleiermacher, Friedrich (1838/1977) "On the Different Methods of Translating", in André Lefevere (ed. & trans.) (1977) *Translating Literature: The German Tradition from Luther to Rosenzweig*, Assen & Amsterdam: Van Gorcum, 66-89. [Translation of Schleiermacher 1838/1963].

Schubert, Klaus (1992) "Esperanto as an Intermediate Language for Machine Translation", in John Newton (ed.), 78-95.

Scott-Gibson, Liz (1991) "Sign Language Interpreting: An Emerging

Profession", in Susan Gregory & Gillian M. Hartley (eds) *Constructing Deafness*, London: Pinter Publishers, Ltd., 253-58.

Searle, John (1969) *Speech Acts: An Essay in the Philosophy of Language*, London: Cambridge University Press.

Seleskovitch, Danica (1968) *L'interprète dans les conférences internationales*, Paris: Minard Lettres Modernes.

Seleskovitch, Danica (1968/1978) *Interpreting for International Conferences: Problems of Language and Communication* (translated by Stephanie Dailey & E. Norman McMillan), Washington, D.C.: Pen & Booth. [Translation of Seleskovitch 1968.]

Seleskovitch, Danica (1976) "Interpretation, A Psychological Approach to Translating", in Richard W. Brislin (ed.), 92-116.

Seleskovitch, Danica (1977) "Take care of the sense and the sounds will take care of themselves or why interpreting is not tantamount to translating languages", in *The Incorporated Linguist* 16, 27-33.

Seleskovitch, Danica & Marianne Lederer (1984) *Interpréter pour traduire*, Paris: Didier Erudition.

Seleskovitch, Danica & Marianne Lederer (1989) *Pédagogie raisonnée de l'interprétation*, Bruxelles & Luxembourg: Office des Publications des Communautés Européennes, and Paris: Didier Erudition.

Sengupta, Mahasweta (1990) "Translation, Colonialism and Poetics: Rabindranath Tagore in Two Worlds", in Susan Bassnett & André Lefevere (eds), 56-63.

Shackman, Jane (1984) *The Right to be Understood, a Handbook on Working with, Employing and Training Community Interpreters*, Cambridge: National Extension College.

Shamaa, N. (1978) *A Linguistic Analysis of Some Problems of Arabic to English Translation*, D. Phil. Thesis, Oxford University.

Shen, Dan (1989) "Literalism: NON 'formal-equivalence'", in *Babel* 35:4, 219-35.

Shen, Dan (1995) "Literalism", in Sin-Wai Chan & David E. Pollard (eds), 568-79.

Shlesinger, Miriam (1991) "Interpreter Latitude vs. Due Process. Simultaneous and Consecutive Interpretation in Multilingual Trials", in Sonja Tirkkonen-Condit (ed.), 147-55.

Shlesinger, Miriam (1995a) "Shifts in Cohesion in Simultaneous Interpreting", in *The Translator* 1:2, 193-214.

Shlesinger, Miriam (1995b) "Stranger in Paradigms: What Lies Ahead for Simultaneous Interpreting Research?", in *Target* 7:1, 7-28.

Shveitser, A. D. (1988) *Teoriya perevoda: status, problemy, aspekty* [*Translation Theory: Status, Problems, Aspects*], Moscow: Nauka.

Shveitser, A. D. (1993) "Equivalence and Adequacy", in Palma Zlateva (ed. & trans.), 47-56.

Snell, Barbara & Patricia Crampton (1983) "Types of Translations", in Catriona Picken (ed.), 109-20.

Snell-Hornby, Mary (1987) "Translation as a Cross-cultural Event: *Midnight's Children - Mitternachtskinder*", in Gideon Toury (ed.), 91-105.

Snell-Hornby, Mary (1988/1995) *Translation Studies: An Integrated Approach*, Amsterdam & Philadelphia: John Benjamins Publishing Company.

Snell-Hornby, Mary (1991) "Translation Studies – Art, Science or Utopia?", in Kitty M. van Leuven-Zwart & Ton Naaijkens (eds), 13-23.

Snell-Hornby, Mary, Franz Pöchhacker & Klaus Kaindl (eds) (1994) *Translation Studies: An Interdiscipline*, Amsterdam & Philadelphia: John Benamins Publishing Company.

Spalatin, L. (1967) "Contrastive Methods", in *Studia Romanica et Anglica Zagrabiensia* 23, 29-48.

Sperber, Dan & Deirdre Wilson (1986) *Relevance: Communication and Cognition*, Oxford: Blackwell.

Spilka, I. (1978) "Translation in a Bilingual Situation", in *McGill Journal of Education* 13:2, 211-18.

Stein, Dieter (1979) "Texttheorie - Instruktionslinguistik -Übersetzen", in *Mitteilungsblatt für Dolmetscher und Übersetzer* 25:2, 6-15.

Stein, Dieter (1980) *Theoretische Grundlagen der Übersetzungswissenschaft*, Tübingen: Gunter Narr Verlag. [Tübinger Beiträge zur Linguistik 140.]

Steiner, George (1972) "Extraterritorial", in *Extraterritorial: Papers on Literature and the Language Revolution*, London: Faber & Faber, 3-11.

Steiner, George (1975/1992) *After Babel: Aspects of Language and Translation*, Second Edition, Oxford: OUP.

Steiner, T. R. (1975) *English Translation Theory 1650-1800*, Assen: van Gorcum.

Sturrock, John (1991) "On Jakobson on Translation", in Thomas A. Sebeok & Jean Umiker-Sebeok (eds) *Recent Developments in Theory and History: The Semiotic Web 1990*, Berlin & New York: Mouton de Gruyter, 307-21.

Sykes, John B. (1983) "The Intellectual Tools Employed", in Catriona Picken (ed.), 41-45.

Thomas, Patricia (1992) "Computerized Term Banks and Translation", in John Newton (ed.), 131-46.

Tirkkonen-Condit, Sonja (ed.) (1991) *Empirical Research in Translation and Intercultural Studies: Selected Papers of the TRANSIF Seminar, Savonlinna 1988*, Tübingen: Gunter Narr Verlag. [Language in Performance 5.]

Tommola, Jorma (ed.) (1995) *Topics in Interpreting Research*, Turku: University of Turku.

● Toury, Gideon (1980) *In Search of a Theory of Translation*, Tel Aviv: The Porter Institute for Poetics and Semiotics.

Toury, Gideon (1984) "Translation, Literary Translation and Pseudotranslation", in E. S. Shaffer (ed.) *Comparative Criticism* 6, Cambridge: Cambridge University Press, 73-85.

Toury, Gideon (1985) "A Rationale for Descriptive Translation Studies", in Theo Hermans (ed.), 16-41.

Toury, Gideon (1986) "Translation: A Cultural-Semiotic Perspective", in Thomas A. Sebeok (ed.) *Encyclopaedic Dictionary of Semiotics*, Berlin: Mouton de Gruyter, Vol. 2, 1111-24.

Toury, Gideon (1991) "What are Descriptive Studies into Translation Likely to Yield apart from Isolated Descriptions?", in Kitty M. van Leuven-Zwart & Ton Naaijkens (eds), 179-92.

Toury, Gideon (1995) *Descriptive Translation Studies and Beyond*, Amsterdam & Philadelphia: John Benjamins Publishing Company.

Toury, Gideon (ed.) (1987) *Translation Across Cultures*, New Delhi: Bahri.

Tsai, Frederick (1995) "Europeanized Structure in English-Chinese Translation", in Sin-Wai Chan & David E. Pollard (eds), 242-48.

Turk, Horst (1990) "Probleme der Übersetzungsanalyse und der Übersetzungstheorie", in *Jahrbuch für Internationale Germanistik* 21:2, 8-82.

Tymoczko, Maria (1985) "How Distinct are Formal and Dynamic Equivalence?", in Theo Hermans (ed.), 63-86.

● Tytler, Alexander Fraser (1791/1978) *Essay on the Principles of Translation* (new edition with an introductory article by Jeffrey F. Huntsman), Amsterdam & Philadelphia: John Benjamins Publishing Company. [Amsterdam Studies in the Theory and History of Linguistic Science 13.]

Ure, Jean, Alexander Rodger & Jeffrey Ellis (1969) "Somn: Sleep – An Exercise in the Use of Descriptive Linguistic Techniques in Literary Translation", in *Babel* 15:1, 4-14 & 15:2, 73-82.

Vázquez-Ayora, Gerardo (1977) *Introducción a la Traductología*, Washington D. C.: Georgetown University Press.

Venuti, Lawrence (1995) *The Translator's Invisibility*, London: Routledge.

Vermeer, Hans J. (1982) "Translation als ‚Informationsangebot'", in *Lebende Sprachen* 27:3, 97-101.

Vermeer, Hans J. (1983) *Aufsätze zur Translationstheorie*, Heidelberg: Groos.

Vermeer, Hans J. (1986) "Übersetzen als kultureller Transfer", in Mary Snell-Hornby (ed.) *Übersetzungswissenschaft – eine Neuorientierung: Zur Integrierung von Theorie und Praxis*, Tübingen: Franke Verlag, 30-53.

Vermeer, Hans J. (1989) "Skopos and Commission in Translational Action" (translated by Andrew Chesterman), in Andrew Chesterman (ed.), 173-87.

Vermeer, Hans J. (1989/1992) *Skopos und Translationsauftrag – Aufsätze*, Frankfurt am Main: IKO.

Vinay, Jean-Paul & Jean Darbelnet (1958) *Stylistique comparée du français et de l'anglais: Méthode de Traduction*, Paris: Didier.

Vinay, Jean-Paul & Jean Darbelnet (1958/1995) *Comparative Stylistics of French and English: A Methodology for Translation* (translated and edited by Juan C. Sager & M.-J. Hamel), Amsterdam & Philadelphia: John Benjamins Publishing Company. [Translation of Vinay & Darbelnet 1958.]

Vladova, Iliana (1993) "Essential features and specific manifestations of historical distance in original texts and their translations", in Palma Zlateva (ed. & trans.), 11-17.

Vlakhov, Sergei & Sider Florin (1970) "Neperevodimoye v perevode: realii" ["The Untranslatable in Translation: Realia"], in *Masterstvo perevoda 1969* [*The Craft of Translation 1969*], Moscow: Sovetskii pisatel', 432-56.

Voegelin, C. F. (1954) "Multiple Stage Translation", in *International Journal of American Linguistics* 20:4, 271-80.

de Waard, Jan & Eugene A. Nida (1986) *From One Language to Another: Functional Equivalence in Bible Translating*, Nashville: Thomas Nelson Publishers.

Wadensjö, C. (1992) *Interpreting as Interaction – On Dialogue Interpreting in Immigration Hearings and Medical Encounters*, Linköping University: Department of Communication Studies.

Wadensjö, C. (1995) "Dialogue Interpreting and the Distribution of Responsibility", in *Hermes, Journal of Linguistics* 14, 111-29.

Wandruszka, Mario (1978) "Die falschen Freunde des Übersetzers", in Lillebill Grähs, Gustav Korlén & Bertil Malmberg (eds) *Theory and Practice of Translation (Nobel Symposium 39, Stockholm, September 6-10, 1976)*, Bern: Peter Lang, 213-34.

Whitman-Linsen, Candace (1992) *Through the Dubbing Glass: The Synchronization of American Motion Pictures into German, French, and Spanish*, Frankfurt am Main & New York: Peter Lang.

Wilss, Wolfram (1977) *Übersetzungswissenschaft. Probleme und Methoden*, Stuttgart: Klett.

Wilss, Wolfram (1982) *The Science of Translation: Problems and Methods*, Tübingen: Gunter Narr Verlag. [English version of Wilss 1977.]

Wilss, Wolfram (1988) *Kognition und Übersetzen: Zu Theorie und Praxis der menschlichen und der maschinellen Übersetzung*, Tübingen: Niemeyer.

Wilss, Wolfram (1994) "A Framework for Decision-Making in Translation", in *Target* 6:2, 131-50.

Wittgenstein, Ludwig (1953) *Philosophical Investigations* (translated by G.E.M. Anscombe), Oxford: Basil Blackwell. [References are to parts and paragraphs.]

Zimmer, Rudolf (1981) *Probleme der Übersetzung formbetonter Sprache: Ein Beitrag zur Übersetzungskritik*, Tübingen: Niemeyer.

Zimman, Leonor (1994) "Intervention as a pedagogical problem in community interpreting", in Cay Dollerup & Annette Lindegaard (eds) *Teaching Translation and Interpreting 2: Insights, Aims and Visions. Papers from the Second Language International Conference, Elsinore, 4-6 June 1993*, Amsterdam & Philadelphia: John Benjamins Publishing Company, 217-24.

Zlateva, Palma (ed. & trans.) (1993) *Translation as Social Action: Russian and Bulgarian Perspectives*, London: Routledge.

Zukofsky, Celia & Louis Zukofsky (translators) (1969) *Catullus (Gai Valeri Catulli Veronensis Liber)*, London: Cape Goliard. [Translation of poems by Catullus.]